D1707977

Junge deutsche Architekten und Architektinnen / Young German Architects 1

Klaus-Dieter Weiss

JUNGE DEUTSCHE ARCHITEKTEN UND ARCHITEKTINNEN YOUNG GERMAN ARCHITECTS 1

Birkhäuser Verlag
Basel · Boston · Berlin

Gestaltung: / Graphic Design:
Studio Archea featuring *Fausto Bergamaschi & Riccardo Bianchi*

Translation from German into English: Bruce Almberg, Katja Steiner, Ehingen

A CIP catalogue record for this book is available from the Library of Congress, Washington D.C., USA

Deutsche Bibliothek Cataloging-in-Publication Data

Junge deutsche Architekten und Architektinnen = Young German architects / Klaus-Dieter Weiss. – Basel ; Boston ; Berlin : Birkhäuser
1. / [Transl. from German into English: Bruce Almberg ; Katja Steiner] 1998
ISBN 3-7643-5782-7 (Basel...)
ISBN 0-8176-5782-7 (Boston)

© 1998 Birkhäuser – Verlag für Architektur, P.O.Box 133, CH-4010 Basel, Switzerland
Printed on acid-free paper produced from chlorine-free pulp. TCF ∞
Printed in Germany
ISBN 3-7643-5782-7
ISBN 0-8176-5782-7

9 8 7 6 5 4 3 2 1

Inhalt / Contents

Verführung zum Experiment

«Merkwürdig genug, daß Deutschland zwar den Architekten der Welt Tür und Tor öffnet, daß es aber den deutschen Architekten selbst in den seltensten Fällen gelungen ist, außerhalb der eigenen Landesgrenzen zu bauen.»[1] Mißlingen ist mit Unvermögen verknüpft. Scheitern deutsche Architekten also im europäischen Wettbewerb? Oder können sie – feine, aber bedeutsame Nuance – an diesem aus bürokratischen Gründen, von seltenen Wettbewerbs-Zuladungen abgesehen, erst gar nicht teilnehmen? Wer den Schaden hat, braucht für den Spott nicht zu sorgen. Nirgendwo dürfte es leichter sein, sich unabhängig von der eigenen Nationalität als Architekt niederzulassen, als in Deutschland. Darin liegt neben der härteren Konkurrenz für deutsche Architekten unbestritten eine große Chance. Nur sollten die hervorragenden Arbeitsbedingungen ausländischer Architekten in Deutschland nicht dazu führen, aus der einzigartigen architektonischen Weltoffenheit Deutschlands den Umkehrschluß zu ziehen und die Bedeutung deutscher Architektur an diesem ungeeigneten Maßstab zu messen. Dazu müßte der Austausch architektonischer Ideen im Maßstab 1:1 auch außerhalb Deutschlands international angelegt sein. Das aber ist nicht der Fall. Dem einleitenden österreichischen Standpunkt des Jahres 1997 ist darum die zehn Jahre ältere, nach wie vor nicht eingelöste Utopie von Günther Feuerstein für die Stadt Wien anzufügen: «In Zukunft wird es mehr und mehr notwendig sein, den Landburschen und den Tirolern und sogar – Gott bewahre! – den Angelsachsen und den Deutschen zu erlauben, in die Stadt zu kommen und zu bauen. Berlin hat es so gemacht, und dort hat die Diskussion unzweifelhaft einen Aufschwung erfahren.»[2]

Junge deutsche Architektinnen und Architekten befinden sich – eine wenig beachtete Tatsache – in einer erdrückenden Konkurrenz. Aus zwei Gründen. In der Tradition der großen Internationalen Bauausstellungen – Stuttgarter Weißenhofsiedlung 1927, Berliner Interbau 1957, Berliner IBA 1987, IBA Emscher Park – ist Deutschland, so Wilfried Wang, zur internationalen Architekturbühne geworden. «Es dürfte inzwischen kaum mehr einen bedeutenden Entwerfer in der Welt geben, der hier nicht einige seiner Ideen umsetzen durfte. [...] Wohl in keinem anderen Land gibt es eine derartige Dichte von Bauwerken, die von europäischen und nordamerikanischen Architekten stammen.»[3] Dabei geht es längst nicht mehr nur um die großen Städte, die prominenten Aufgaben, die international agierenden Bauherren. Der Kalifornier Frank O. Gehry zum Beispiel macht nach dem Erfolg bei Vitra auch in der norddeutschen Provinz von sich reden, in Orten zwischen 40.000 und 60.000 Einwohnern, die niemand wirklich kennen muß. Auch dieser Hinweis darf wie das zufällige Beispiel Österreichs jedoch nicht mißverstanden werden. Es geht nicht darum, diesen fruchtbaren architektonischen Austausch einzuschränken oder gar zu stoppen. Zu wünschen ist vielmehr, daß das Beispiel Schule macht. Von Bedeutung ist dieser Aspekt hier darum, weil er die Arbeitssituation junger Absolventen mitbestimmt, die sich aus dem Stand einem internationalen Wettbewerb stellen müssen. Im übrigen sind, vor dem geschilderten internationalen Hintergrund nicht anders zu erwarten, auch die jungen deutschen Architekten nicht unbedingt Deutsche im Sinne des Gesetzes oder auch nur in Deutschland geboren. Vielmehr finden sich in der hier präsentierten Auswahl als Herkunftsländer auch die Schweiz, die Niederlande, Polen und das ehemalige Jugoslawien.

Die zweite Hürde liegt im mangelhaften Instrumentarium des Wettbewerbswesens, das bisher die besten Profilierungschancen für Absolventen bot. Nach europäischem Recht ist selbst bei kleinen Bauaufgaben eine regionale Begrenzung offener Wettbewerbe nicht möglich. Ab einer Auftragssumme von 200.000 ECU wird europaweit ausgeschrieben oder – der bei weitem häufigere Fall – die Teilnehmerflut wird schon aus Kostengründen durch begrenzte und geladene Wettbewerbe rigoros eingedämmt. Nicht das Innovationspotential eines Büros zählt, sondern im besten Fall die fachliche Erfahrung der Teilnehmer. Ohne zum letzten Hilfsmittel ausgleichender Gerechtigkeit zu greifen, dem Gottesurteil der Auslosung, bleiben erprobte große Büros im Vorteil. Wer eine ähnliche Aufgabe schon gelöst hat, darf sich in Wiederholung und Konvention üben. Kein Wunder also, daß sich viele junge Architekten an derartigen Wettbewerbsverfahren bzw. Vorauswahl-Verfahren nicht mehr beteiligen können und wollen. Der Versuch, europaweit Chancengleichheit herzustellen, hat in der Praxis gerade das Gegenteil bewirkt. Junge Architektinnen und Architekten werden nicht gefördert, sondern diskriminiert.

Die Folge ist geistiger Stillstand, der nur deswegen nicht eklatant wird, weil genügend internationale Beiträge für Bewegung sorgen. Fehlt auch dieser frische Wind, wird der Mangel offensichtlich. So in der Stadt München, die laut Süddeutscher Zeitung «augenscheinlich nur von jenen gestaltet werden darf, die mindestens noch die persönliche Bekanntschaft mit Ludwig I vorweisen können».[4] Das Hamburger Szeneblatt Szene Hamburg feiert dagegen schon den Durchbruch einer neuen Generation, die mit der Kreativität einer wachen Zeit gegen den altväterlichen Biedersinn der Backsteinbarone freche Siege erringt. «Diese seit einigen Jahren mit zunehmendem Erfolg überall in Deutschland arbeitende Generation junger Architekten ist gerade dabei, die Zunft der sechzigjährigen Architekturmaurer abzulösen, die mit biederer Genügsamkeit und künstlerischem Rheuma den miserablen Ruf deutscher Architekten im Ausland begründet haben und die Städte zu Orten der Langeweile werden ließen.»[5]

Das jüngste Architekten-Ranking der Bauwelt, das zweite seiner Art[6], dokumentiert zwar keinen Durchbruch junger Architektinnen und Architekten, aber immerhin eine starke Unterwanderung. In den Top 50 findet sich ein gutes Dutzend junger Architekten. Auf Günter Behnisch, Jahrgang 1922, und Josef Paul Kleihues, Jahrgang 1933, folgt nach steilem Aufstieg von Rang 21 Christoph Ingenhoven, Jahrgang 1960, auf Platz 3. Großaufträge wie das RWE-Hochhaus in Essen, der Hauptbahnhof in Stuttgart oder das 250 m hohe Wan Xiang International Plaza in Shanghai unterstreichen den Anspruch und die Durchsetzungskraft dieses Büros. Beim Wettbewerb um die Frankfurter Commerzbank scheiterte Christoph Ingenhoven mit 31 Jahren nicht am erstplazierten Norman Foster, sondern am Bauherrn, den das Renommee des Architekten lockte, nicht die Jury-Entscheidung, beide Preisträger überarbeiten zu lassen. 1991 wirbelte dieser unrühmliche Ausgang des Verfahrens viel Staub auf. Ob die Bank bei ihrer Investition dem richtigen Instinkt folgte, bleibt sehr zweifelhaft. Gemeinhin gilt der Bau nicht als ein herausragendes Werk Fosters. Wie könnte er das auch, in einer derartigen weltweit herrschenden Auftragsflut?

Dieses Paradebeispiel dafür, welche Ängste und Hürden prominente Bauherren jungen Architekten in Deutschland in den Weg stellen können, zeigt, wie schwierig es noch zu Beginn des Jahrzehnts war sich durchzusetzen. Angesichts der doppelten Entscheidung für Florian Nagler im Fall des deutschen Expo-Pavillons in Hannover scheint die notwendige Aufgeschlossenheit für Architektur als Neuerung und Wagnis (be)greifbarer geworden zu sein. So ist zu hoffen. Im vor kurzem entschiedenen Wettbewerbsverfahren für den Hauptsitz der Bayerischen Rückversicherung in München waren die Jungen bereits unter sich. Einen ähnlichen Richtungswechsel zeigt der Deutsche Architekturpreis. Bisher waren die Preisträger in aller Regel weit jenseits der 50: Günter Behnisch 55 bzw. 71, Fritz Auer und Carlo Weber 56 und 55, Joachim Schürmann 55 bzw. 65, Uwe Kiessler 58. Nur Doris und Ralph Thut (34/36) fielen 1979 als ausländische Beiträge in dieser Runde ebenso aus dem Rahmen wie 1983 Hans Hollein (49). Den Generationswechsel unter den deutschen Preisträgern markierten die Münchner Architekten Markus Allmann, Amandus Sattler und Ludwig Wappner erst 1997.

Dennoch sind wir von niederländischen Verhältnissen noch weit entfernt. Die Newcomer, die in Holland zur Zeit für das größte Aufsehen sorgen: MVRDV, konnten ihr erstes großes Projekt, das Bürohaus Villa VPRO, mit 28 bzw. 34 Jahren in Angriff nehmen – nach dem Motto «Let's give them a chance and see what comes from it». In Holland wird jungen Architekten schon dann die Chance zur Realisierung eingeräumt, wenn sie ihr Können noch nicht unter Beweis gestellt haben. Nur so werden Experimente und Erfahrungen möglich. Außerdem ist die gesellschaftliche und ökonomische Situation in den Niederlanden eine andere. MVRDV: «In Holland herrscht eine besondere Situation – das Land ist enorm dicht besiedelt, es verfügt über eine ziemlich gesunde Wirtschaft und die Nachfrage nach Wohnraum ist groß, was wiederum eine hohe Bauproduktion zu relativ niedrigen Kosten verursacht. Letztendlich ist die Chance, interessante Projekte zu finden, bei diesem ansteigenden Bedarf wesentlich größer. Außerdem sehen die Menschen allmählich ein, daß es sich durchaus lohnt, in Architektur zu investieren...»[7]

Das Spektrum der hier vorgestellten aktuellen Bauten und Projekte reicht typologisch dennoch erstaunlich weit: von der Fachhochschule über Universitätsbibliothek, Sporthalle und Einkaufszentrum bis zu Bahnhof und Therapiezentrum, von der Villa über Hochhaus und Expo-Pavillon bis zu Kindergarten, Schule, Rathaus, Museum, Kirche und Friedhof, vom Gewerbebetrieb über die Hauptverwaltung bis zum sozialen Wohnungsbau. Neben Neubauten finden sich Erweiterungen, Aufstockungen, Revitalisierungen, Nachverdichtungen und Stadtergänzungen. Trotz aller Durchsetzungsschwierigkeiten junger Architekten gegenüber etablierten Büros zeigt sich darin ein großes Entwicklungspotential – von der ausländischen Fachpresse vielfach ernster genommen als von der deutschen (vgl. Architektur Aktuell/Wien) –, mit dem in Zukunft zu rechnen sein wird. Dabei dominiert die architektonische Entwicklung in den westlichen alten Bundesländern nach wie vor die Entwicklung in den östlichen neuen Bundesländern. Hier konnte sich bislang, gemessen allein an der architektonischen Qualität, (noch) kein Gegengewicht etablieren. Vielleicht wird jedoch schon der Folgeband von Rudolf Stegers in einem Jahr in dieser Frage zu einer anderen Gewichtung kommen können. Bislang ist dem Urteil von Gerd Zimmermann in dieser Frage nichts hinzuzufügen: «Der eigentliche psychopolitische Defekt war die weitgehende Unterdrückung der Subjektivität, die Abschaffung gewissermaßen des Architekten, welche die grassierende Gesichtslosigkeit und Ausdrucksschwäche des Gebauten nach sich zog.»[8]

Der Titel dieses Buches benennt eher zwei Fragen, als daß er eine Behauptung aufstellte: Wann sind Architekten «jung» und wann «deutsch»? Es macht wenig Sinn, sich auf internationaler Bühne an Nationalitäten zu klammern. Den «deutschen» Architekten gibt es darum im Grunde nur noch rein geographisch. Ebenso ergeht es zwangsläufig der «deutschen» Architektur, eine Spätfolge deutscher Vergangenheit mit deutlich positivem Vorzeichen. Selbst Norman Foster wundert sich, daß er den Berliner Reichstag umbaut. Insofern war Auswahlkriterium hier nur der Umstand, daß die Architekten in Deutschland leben und arbeiten – und schon mehrfach gebaut haben. Was das Alter betrifft, hat sich eingebürgert, die Jugend der Architektin/des Architekten bis zur magischen Zahl 40 auszudehnen, was hier im Durchschnitt – aus purem Zufall – knapp gelingt. Mit einer Streuung zwischen 35 und 47 Jahren, die sich bei mehreren Partnern in einem Büro ohnehin nicht vermeiden läßt. Das Jungsein war bei dieser breit angelegten Recherche nicht an ein Alterslimit gebunden. Entscheidend war allein, verschiedene anspruchsvolle und möglichst eigenständige Ansätze anhand aktueller Realisierungen zu dokumentieren. Der geographische Proporz – Berlin, Hamburg, Stuttgart und München jeweils doppelt besetzt, Hannover, Köln, Frankfurt, Darmstadt einfach – ergab sich dabei wie schon die Altersstruktur auf Basis des nachgefragten architektonischen Anspruchs. Das Suchfeld war bei weitem größer angelegt. In der engeren Wahl standen ca. 50 Büros. Eine Reihe prominenter Namen fiel aus, weil bereits ausführliche Monographien vorliegen oder in Arbeit sind bzw. aktuelle Bauten fehlten. In anderen vielfach deutlich jüngeren Büros reichte aus den geschilderten Gründen die Zahl der Projekte nicht aus, um eine Entwicklungslinie zu dokumentieren .

Dennoch ist die Frage, nach den menschlichen Bedingungen junger, «revolutionärer» Architektur nicht ohne Witz. Im Jahr Eins nach dem ersten Architekten-Ranking der Bauwelt sehen sich die Kandidaten vergleichend um, auch was das Alters-/Leistungsverhältnis betrifft. Adolf Loos begann nach diesem Maßstab als junger Architekt – von ca. 40 Jahren – das Haus am Michaelerplatz, Le Corbusier baute die Häuser der Weißenhofsiedlung, die Villa Stein und zeichnete den Völkerbundpalast, Aldo Rossi nahm den Friedhof San Cataldo in Modena in Angriff, Norman Foster das Verwaltungsgebäude in Ipswich. Sehr selten sind heutzutage die theoretischen Vorstöße junger Architekten geworden. Mit 36 gab Le Corbusier seine gesammelten Artikel aus «L'Esprit Nouveau» unter dem Titel «Vers une architecture» heraus, mit 38 schrieb Adolf Loos «Ornament und Verbrechen», mit 41 Robert Venturi «Learning from Las Vegas». Als die erste Nummer von *Archigramm* erschien, war Peter Cook 25 Jahre alt.

Das dynamische Adjektiv «jung» steht jedoch grundsätzlich nicht nur für «frisch» und «neu», sondern auch für «unreif», «unausgegoren» und «unerfahren». Darin liegt vielleicht ein grundsätzliches Mißverständnis nicht der deutschen Sprache, sondern der deutschen Architektur bzw. ihres Publikums heute. Im Vergleich zu anderen Nationalitäten, insbesondere den Niederländern, ist den jungen deutschen Architekten mehr Vertrauen in ihr Engagement und neben den nachweisbaren architektonischen Erfolgen wie dem Deutschen Architekturpreis 1997 mehr Publizität zu wünschen. Ohne die Ideen und Bauten junger Architekten wäre manches wichtige Kapitel der deutschen Baugeschichte nicht geschrieben worden. Fritz Höger eröffnete sein Büro mit 20 Jahren und baute das Chilehaus im Alter von 35 Jahren. Walter Gropius machte sich mit 27 Jahren selbständig – drei Jahre älter als Oswald Mathias Ungers, zwei Jahre älter als Alvar Aalto beim Start – und baute im gleichen Jahr zusammen mit Adolf Meyer die Faguswerke. Erich Mendelsohn begann den Einsteinturm im Alter von 30 Jahren, Rudolf Schwarz die Fronleichnamskirche in Aachen mit 31, Ungers sein eigenes Wohnhaus mit 33 Jahren. Mies van der Rohe zeichnete seine spektakulären gläsernen Hochhäuser mit 34 Jahren, in einem Alter, in dem sich Hans Scharoun an der Stuttgarter Weißenhofsiedlung beteiligte, Bruno Taut sein Glashaus baute und Hans Kollhoff den Wohnblock am Berlin Museum in Angriff nahm. Den Barcelona-Pavillon realisierte Mies van der Rohe mit 42 Jahren – wie Hugo Häring das Gut Garkau und Le Corbusier die Villa Savoye. Josef Paul Kleihues begann die Berliner Stadtreinigung mit 36 Jahren, die Gebrüder Luckhardt ihre Villen am Rupenhorn mit 38 Jahren, Ernst May die Frankfurter Römerstadt mit 41 Jahren, Gottfried Böhm die Wallfahrtskirche in Neviges mit 43 Jahren, Egon Eiermann die Taschentuchweberei Blumberg unmittelbar nach Kriegsende mit 45 Jahren. Günter Behnisch nahm in diesem Alter die Münchner Olympiabauten in Angriff, Frei Otto war drei Jahre jünger. Mit dieser Umorganisation der Baugeschichte nach Karriere-Kriterien wären auch gleich die wichtigsten zeitgenössischen und historischen Anknüpfungsmöglichkeiten der deutschen Architektur umrissen. Um es vorwegzunehmen, nationale Bezugspunkte spielen für die hier vorgestellten Architekten eine relativ geringe Rolle.

Was ist also ein junger Architekt? Der Revolutionär des Wandels? Guiseppe Terragni baute sein Meisterwerk – die Casa del Fascio – mit 28, den Wohnblock Novocomum bereits mit 23 Jahren. Es gibt auch die Gegenbeispiele. Frank O. Gehry realisierte sein eigenes Haus, Inkunabel des Dekonstruktivismus, erst mit 49, Emil Steffann war jenseits der 50, als er sich als freier Architekt selbständig machte, Karljosef Schattner nach seiner Tätigkeit als Diözesanbaumeister 65. Warum müssen Architekten in Deutschland immer älter werden, um bauen zu können bzw. bauen zu dürfen? Ist die Ausbildung zu wenig praxisgerecht? Lassen die etablierten Architekten einschließlich der ausländischen Beiträge in angespannter ökonomischer Lage zuwenig Entfaltungsraum? Oder setzen die Bauherren zu sehr auf Sicherheit? Manch Jüngerem gilt ein 40 Jahre junger Architekt schon als «Grufti». «Aber wie geht es den wirklich jungen Architekten? Denen unter 30? Sie werden in Hülle und Fülle ausgebildet, haben aber auf einem «Markt», der fest in Händen etablierter Kreise liegt und nur jene hereinläßt, die einen Zuwachs an Renommee versprechen, kaum eine Chance.»[9] Tatsache ist, daß den Architektenkammern in ihrer föderalen Gliederung nicht einmal die Anzahl dieser Architekten bekannt ist. Zwar weist das statistische Bundesamt aus, daß es in Deutschland etwa 105.000 zugelassene Architekten gibt (und doppelt so viele nicht registrierte), mithin hat jeder Architekt weit weniger als 1.000 Einwohner zu betreuen. Aber eine Altersschichtung ist nicht abzufragen, weil von den Kammern die allein aussagekräftige Gesamtstatistik gar nicht geführt wird. Unabhängig davon ist ein Architekturparadies aber erst dann zu erwarten, wenn junge Architekten nicht nur Statistiken füllen, sondern auch bauen dürfen.

Die in Europa einzigartige Aufgeschlossenheit in architektonischen Fragen führt in Deutschland zu vielfältigen persönlichen Kontakten (Studium und Bürotätigkeit im Ausland) und besonders intensivem Austausch von unterschiedlichen, zum Teil völlig konträren Auffassungen und Standpunkten. Insofern reichen die Bezugspunkte dieses auf den ersten Blick undurchschaubaren Architektur-Labors Deutschland bis in die USA. Das Resultat dieser architektonischen Weltoffenheit kann zwangsläufig keine einheitliche Formensprache sein. Diesem Nachteil der Vielsprachigkeit steht jedoch der immense Vorteil des ungehinderten Experimentierens gegenüber. In keinem Fall lassen sich eindeutige Abhängigkeiten der «Schüler» von einem beherrschenden «Lehrer» diagnostizieren. überraschenderweise gibt es kaum Verbindungslinien zu Günter Behnisch, aber auch wenig Anlehnung an die sicheren Fundamente Oswald Mathias Ungers, Gottfried Böhm, Karljosef Schattner oder Frei Otto. Dennoch gehören diese wie andere Vor-Bilder zum unabdingbaren Erfahrungsschatz.

Die Biographien der hier dokumentierten zwanzig Architekten weisen u.a. wesentliche Verbindungen zu folgenden Architekten aus: Hinrich und Inken Baller, Bangert-Jansen-Scholz-Schultes, Werner Düttmann, Johann Eisele und Nicolas Fritz, Hardt-Waltherr Hämer, Hans Kollhoff, Peter C. von Seidlein, Joachim Schürmann, Rudolf Wienands... Diesen stehen jedoch ebenso viele ausländische Architekturgrößen gegenüber: Raimund Abraham, Carlo Aymonino, Norman Foster, Johannes Gsteu, Haus-Rucker-Co, Friedrich Kurrent, Richard Meier, Gustav Peichl, Boris Podrecca, Fabio Reinhart, Dolf Schnebli, Peter Wilson... Drei Viertel der zwölf Büros sind in der Hochschularbeit engagiert. Zwei Drittel der Büros weisen im Werdegang eines Gründers starke Auslandsbezüge auf, was jeweils sehr signifikant mit ihrem Engagement als Hochschullehrer korreliert.

Unter den bevorzugten deutschen Architekturfakultäten dominieren TU München, TU Berlin, TU Braunschweig und Universität Stuttgart. Den weiteren Nennungen (TH Karlsruhe, TH Darmstadt, GH Kassel, FH Hamburg, Städelschule Frankfurt...) stehen Hochschulen in der Schweiz, den USA, Österreich, England, den Niederlanden und Italien bereits gleichgewichtig gegenüber. Kein Wunder ist die nach wie vor starke Präsenz der ETH Zürich. Überraschend sind jedoch neben der Architectural Association in London die übrigen Hochschulerfahrungen im Ausland: Akademie der bildenden Künste Wien, Gerrit Rietveld Akademie Amsterdam, Universität Rom, Harvard University Cambridge/USA, Virginia Polytechnic Insitute Blacksburg/USA, Illinois Institute of Technology Chicago.

Auf der Suche nach einer komplexen und innovativen Raumsprache, die nach den Erfahrungen Postmoderne, Dekonstruktivismus und Berliner Rekonstruktion nicht nur Bildersprache bleibt, wird das Suchfeld räumlich wie zeitlich ganz bewußt ausgedehnt. Eine international orientierte offene Szene, die selbst utopischen Perspektiven der Vergangenheit mit neuem Instrumentarium zu neuem Leben verhilft. Konstruktive, ökologische, technische und künstlerische Schwerpunkte lassen sich nicht leugnen, eine Architektur, die Komplexität ernst nimmt, wandelt sich jedoch mit jeder ihrer Bedingungen und Vorgaben. Eine 1983 geäußerte Befürchtung von Heinrich Klotz hat sich nicht bewahrheitet: «So erfreulich ideenreich die junge Architektengeneration auch erscheint, so sehr muß man aber auch fürchten, daß sich ein neuer Einheitsstil etabliert, der bereits zu dominieren beginnt und die Erfindungskraft hemmt, weil schon ein neues Kleid vorhanden ist, noch bevor die neue Gestalt existiert.»[10] Der Pluralismus, der sich auf den folgenden Seiten mit jedem konkreten Einzelfall neu aufbaut, ist nicht Folge einer Suche nach dem neuen Dogma, sondern macht vorhandene Vielfalt ablesbar, ist nicht aufgesetzt, sondern tief verankert. Neben urbaner Tektonik steht die Tektonik der Bilder, Images und Identitäten. Konrad Paul Liessmann, der – Jahrgang 1953 – an der Universität Wien Philosophie lehrt, hat dieses Phänomen sehr anschaulich beschrieben. «Möglich, daß es dort, wo wirklich die Kraft des Ästhetischen auf dem Spiel steht, nach der Postmoderne, nach den Umbrüchen, nach der Digitalisierung, nicht um Zuordnungen und Einordnungen, nicht um die Scheidung in Fortschritt und Rückschritt, nicht um Traktate und Deklarationen, auch nicht um die rechte linke Gesinnung oder das gute neue Medium, sondern darum geht, ob die wirkliche und einzige Errungenschaft der Moderne, die riskante Entbindung einer autonomen ästhetischen Subjektivität, noch einmal einen Weg gefunden hat, eine Welt zu gestalten und damit jene Souveränität der Kunst gegenüber allem Betrieb zu behaupten und durchzusetzen, die diese allein rechtfertigt. Solches entscheidet sich aber, wenn überhaupt, nicht von Richtung zu Richtung, nicht von Mode zu Mode, nicht von Diskurs zu Diskurs, nicht von Kontext zu Kontext, nicht von Netz zu Netz, auch nicht von Moderne zu Moderne, sondern immer nur: von Fall zu Fall.»[11] Die folgenden Architekturauffassungen bieten dazu in ihrer spezifischen Ausprägung konkrete Ansätze.

1 Buchrezension «Architektur in Deutschland», Architektur Aktuell Nr. 209, 11-1997, S. 34
2 Günther Feuerstein: Visionäre Architektur. Wien 1958/1988, Berlin 1988, S. 8/9
3 Wilfried Wang, in: Gerd de Bruyn: Zeitgenössische Architektur in Deutschland 1970–1996, Basel 1997, S. 7/8
4 Gerhard Matzig: Für immer alt? Süddeutsche Zeitung 26.1.1998, S. 13
5 Kees Wartburg: Moderne statt Postmoderne, Szene Hamburg 1-1998, S. 26
6 Bauwelt 10-1998, S. 488
7 MVRDV, El Croquis 86/1997, S. 8
8 Gerd Zimmermann: Die andere Architektur. Bauen in der DDR, in: Gerd de Bruyn: Zeitgenössische Architektur in Deutschland 1970–1996, Basel 1997, S. 21
9 deutsche bauzeitung db 3-1998, S. 10
10 Heinrich Klotz: Nach der «Wende», in: Helge und Margret Bofinger: Junge Architekten in Europa, Stuttgart 1983, S. 164
11 Konrad Paul Liessmann: Von Tomi nach Moor. Ästhetische Potenzen – nach der Postmoderne, Kursbuch 122: Die Zukunft der Moderne, Dezember 1995, S. 32

Seduced into Experimentation

"It seems strange that Germany would open its gates to the world's architects but that German architects have rarely succeeded in building outside the borders of their own country."[1] Failure is connected with inability. Is that the reason German architects fail in European competition? Or – a fine but important nuance – is it because, leaving aside the rarity of being invited to a competition, they can't participate to start with due to bureaucratic reasons? Those who have been harmed need do nothing else to merit scorn. It may just be the simple fact that nowhere else is it as easy to open an architectural office, irrespective of nationality, than in Germany. This is undoubtedly a great opportunity for German architects, leaving aside the resulting tough competition. Yet the excellent work conditions for foreign architects in Germany shouldn't lead to a transformation of the unique architectural openness of Germany into the reverse, nor should it lead to a rating of the importance of German architects using this highly unsuitable scale as a method of appraisal. In order to do so, the exchange of architectural ideas would also have to be internationally set at a scale of 1:1 outside of Germany. However, this isn't the case. The preliminary Austrian opinion from 1997 therefore has to be complemented by the ten-years-older and still unrealized utopia by Günther Feuerstein for the city of Vienna: "In the future it will become more and more necessary to allow the country lads and the Tyroleans and even – God forbid! – the Anglo-Saxons and the Germans to come to the city and build. Berlin did it, and there the discussion has indubitably experienced a boom."[2]

Young German architects find themselves – a little-noticed fact – in an environment of oppressive competition. There are two reasons for this. In the tradition of the big international architectural expositions – Stuttgart Weissenhof development 1927, Berlin Interbau 1957, Berlin IBA 1987, IBA Emscher Park – Germany, according to Wilfried Wang, has become an international architectural stage. "Meanwhile, there is hardly a single important designer in the world who hasn't been allowed to realize some of his ideas here. [...] There is probably no other country that has such a density of buildings by European and North American architects."[3] For quite some time, this theme hasn't been just about the big cities, the prominent tasks, the internationally operating clients. The Californian Frank O. Gehry, for example, is also talked about in the northern German province after his success with Vitra, in towns with a population between 40,000 and 60,000 that nobody really needs to have heard of. However, this comment, like the arbitrary Austrian example, should not be misinterpreted. The question is not whether to restrict this fertile architectural exchange or even whether it should be terminated. What should be wished for, rather, is that the example becomes the rule. This aspect is of importance in this context because it is a determining factor in the working environment of young architects who have to contend with international competition. By the way, and it couldn't be otherwise expected given the described international background, the young German architects aren't necessarily German in the sense of the law; it's not even necessary for them to have been born in Germany. In fact, the selection presented in this book includes Switzerland, the Netherlands, Poland and the former Yugoslavia as countries of origin.

The second obstacle can be found in the deficiency of the instruments of the competitions which in the past have offered the best opportunity for graduates to earn a level of distinction. According to European law, a regional restriction of open competitions isn't possible even for small building tasks. Starting from commissions with a value of 200,000 ECU, the invitation must go out throughout Europe or – as is more frequently the case – the flood of participants is rigorously contained through limited competitions or specific invitations due to cost considerations. It's not the innovative potential of an office that counts but, under the best scenario, the professional experience of the participants. Without resorting to the final aid – the scales of justice, the divine verdict of a drawing – the large and more experienced offices always have an advantage. Those who have solved a similar task in the past can practice repetition and convention. It's no surprise that many young architects no longer can nor even want to participate in such competition procedures or pre-selections. The attempt to create equal opportunity throughout Europe has led to the opposite in practice. Young architects aren't being sponsored but discriminated against.

The consequence is a spiritual standstill that doesn't explode only because enough international contributions provide some movement. Absent this fresh breeze, the drawbacks becomes obvious. Take, for example, the city of Munich where, according to the Süddeutsche Zeitung, "only those who at least can prove some personal relationship with Ludwig I have a right to contribute to its design."[4] Contrary to this, Szene Hamburg, the Hamburg scene magazine, celebrates the breakthrough of a new generation that, with the creativity of an alert time, achieves fresh triumphs against the old-fatherly conservatism of the brick barons. "This generation of young architects, which has been working for a number of years with an increasing rate of success throughout Germany, is about to replace the guild of the sixty-year-old architectural masons who were instrumental in establishing the miserable reputation of German architects abroad with their conservative complacency and artistic rheumatism, and who have allowed the cities to become places of boredom."[5]
The most recent architectural ranking of Bauwelt, the second of its kind,[6] may not document a breakthrough of young architects, but it at least chronicles a strong infiltration. At least a dozen young architects rank among the Top 50. Günter Behnisch, born 1922, and Josef Paul Kleihues, born 1933, are followed on rank 3 by Christoph Ingenhoven, born 1960,

after a steep ascent from rank 21. Large-scale orders such as the RWE high-rise in Essen, the Stuttgart main station or the 250m tall Wan Xiang International Plaza in Shanghai underscore the pretension and self-assertion of this office. In the competition for the Frankfurt Commerzbank, Christoph Ingenhoven didn't fail with his 31 years against the triumphant Norman Foster, but against the client, who was tempted by this architect's reputation and not by the jury's decision to allow both award winners make revisions. In 1991 this inglorious outcome of the procedure caused quite a stir. Whether the bank followed the right instinct with its investment remains doubtful. Generally, the building isn't considered one of Foster's most outstanding works. How could it be, with such a global flood of orders?

This perfect example of the fears and obstacles that prominent clients can throw onto the paths of young architects in Germany demonstrates how elusive success could be even at the beginning of the decade. In the face of the double decision concerning Florian Nagler in the case of the German Expo-Pavilion in Hannover, the necessary openness toward architecture as a renewal and risk seems to have become more tangible. We can only hope that this is so. In the recently decided competition procedure for the headquarters of the Bayerische Rückversicherung in Munich, the young generation of architects had already prevailed. A similar change of direction can be noticed with the German Architectural Award. In the past, the winners were always far beyond the age of 50: Günter Behnisch 55 and 71, Fritz Auer and Carlo Weber 56 and 55, Joachim Schürmann 55 or 65, Uwe Kiessler 58. Only Doris and Ralph Thut (34/36) stood out in this circle in 1979 as foreign contributions, as did Hans Hollein (49) in 1983. The change in generation among the German award winners was marked by the Munich architects Markus Allmann, Amandus Sattler and Ludwig Wappner only in 1997.

And still we are far beyond the Dutch conditions. The newcomers who currently cause the greatest stir in Holland, MVRDV, were able to tackle their largest project, the office building Villa VPRO, at the age of 28 and 34 – following the motto "let's give them a chance and see what comes of it" In Holland, young architects already have the chance for a realization even if they have not yet proven their abilities. Only in this way do experiments and experiences become possible. Furthermore, the societal and economic situation in the Netherlands is quite different. MVRDV: "Holland has a specific situation – it has an enormous population density, quite a healthy economy and a big demand for housing that leads to large building production at relatively low costs. So in absolute terms, within that growing amount there's also a bigger chance of finding interesting projects. Besides, people are starting to realize that it's worthwhile to invest in architecture in general..."[7]

The spectrum of current buildings and projects introduced in this book, however, has a surprising range of types: from the university for applied sciences to the university library, from the gymnasium and shopping center to the station and therapy center, from the villa, high-rise and Expo-pavilion to the kindergarten, school, town hall, museum, church and cemetery, from the industrial building to the main administration and social housing. Aside from the new buildings, there are also extensions, heightenings, renovations, urban condensations and additions. Despite all of the problems young architects face – as compared to the established offices – in their attempt to assert themselves, this reveals a tremendous potential for development – a lot of times taken more seriously by the international specialized press than by the German press (see Architektur Aktuell/Vienna) – that will have to be considered in the future. Still, the architectural development in the old western federal states dominates the developments occurring in the eastern new states of Germany. Thus far, a counterweight – measured only in terms of architectural quality – has not (yet) been established here. But perhaps the next volume by Rudolf Stegers one year from now will be able to uncover a different assessment of this situation. Right now, nothing can really be added to Gerd Zimmermann's assessment: "The real psycho-political defect was the far-reaching oppression of subjectivity, the abolition of the architect, so to speak, which caused the raging facelessness and weakness of expression of what has been built."[8]

Rather than making a statement, this book's title instead poses two questions: when are architects "young," and when are they "German"? It makes little sense to hold on to nationalities on an international stage. Therefore, the "German" architect basically exists only geographically. And the same necessarily happens to "German" architecture, a late consequence of the German past with clearly positive omens. Even Norman Foster is surprised that he is converting the Reichstag in Berlin. In this respect, the criteria for selection was the requirement that the architects live and work in Germany – and have realized several projects, as well. Concerning age, it has become a habit to expand the youth of the architect to the magical number of 40, and – due to pure coincidence – this just happens to accurately apply in this case: the range of age, really unavoidable with several partners in a single office, spans from 35 to 47 years. Being young wasn't bound to an age limit in this broad research. What was decisive was the documentation of all the different sophisticated approaches as individually as possible in light of current realizations. The geographic proportion – Berlin, Hamburg, Stuttgart and Munich with two offices each, Hannover, Cologne, Darmstadt with one – resulted from the sought-after architectural demand as did the age structure. The search field was larger by far. About 50 offices made it to the final selection. A series of prominent names were left out as there are extensive monographs already in existence or in progress, or because there were no current projects. In other, mostly younger offices, the number of the projects didn't suffice for a documentation of a development for the reasons given.

Still, the question about the human conditions of young, "revolutionary" architecture isn't without any wit. In the first year after the first architectural ranking in Bauwelt, the candidates are looking around and making comparisons, also with regards to the age-performance-relationship. Adolf Loos started building the house at Michaelerplatz as a young architect – around 40 – according to this scale, Le Corbuiser built the Weissenhof houses, Villa Stein and drew the palace for the League of Nations; Aldo Rossi tackled the new San Cataldo cemetery in Modena and Norman Foster started with the administration building in Ipswich. Today, the theoretical advances of young architects have become rare. At the age of 36, Le Corbusier published his collected works from "L'Esprit Nouveau" under the title "Vers une architecture", at age 38 Adolf Loos wrote "Ornament und Verbrechen", and at 41 Robert Venturi wrote "Learning from Las Vegas." When the first issue of *Archigramm* was published, Peter Cook was 25 years old.

The dynamic adjective "young" doesn't generally stand for "fresh" and "new", but also for "immature", "callow" and "inexperienced." And herein may lie one of the basic misunderstandings, not of the German language, but the German architecture or its present audience. Compared to other nationalities, especially the Dutch, one can only wish for more trust in the engagement of the young German architects, and more publicity aside from the proven architectural successes like the German Architectural Award 1997. Without the ideas and buildings by young architects, some important chapters of German architectural history would not have been written. Fritz Höger opened his office at the age of 20 and built the Chile House at 35. Walter Gropius started his own business at age 27 – three years older than Oswald Mathias Ungers and two years older than Alvar Aalto in the beginning – and in the same year built the Fagus Works together with Adolf Meyer. Erich Mendelsohn started the Einstein Tower at 30; Rudolf Schwarz, the Corpus Christi Church in Aachen at 31; Ungers built his own house at the age of 33. Mies van der Rohe drew his spectacular glazed high-rise buildings at 34, the age that Hans Scharoun had attained when he participated in the Stuttgart Weissenhof development, when Bruno Taut built his glass house and when Hans Kohlhoff tackled the housing block at the Berlin Museum. Mies van der Rohe realized the Barcelona pavilion at the age of 42; Hugo Häring had reached the same age when he built Garkau Estate, as did Le Corbusier at the time of his Villa Savoye. Josef Paul Kleihues started the Berlin urban clean-up at age 36; the Luckhard brothers began their villas at Rupenhorn at age 38; Ernst May, the Römerstadt in Frankfurt at age 41; Gottfried Böhm built the pilgrimage church in Nevige with 43; Egon Eiermann realized the handkerchief weavery Blumberg directly after the end of the war at age 45. At that same age, Günter Behnisch started the Munich Olympics buildings and Frei Otto was three years his junior. This reorganization of architectural history according to career criteria also outlines the most important contemporary and historical starting points of German architecture. To say it right away: national points of reference play a relatively minor role for the architects presented in this book.

So what is a young architect? The revolutionary of change? Guiseppe Terragni built his masterpiece – Casa del Fascio – at the age of 28 and the Novocomum apartment block at 23. There are also the counter-examples. Frank O. Gehry realized his own house, the incunabula of Deconstructivism, only at 49; Emil Steffann was past 50 when he started his own business as a freelance architect; Karljosef Schattner was 65 after his work as a docent master builder. Why do architects in Germany always have to wait until they are older in order to be able or allowed to build? Is the training not practice-oriented enough? Do the established architects, including the foreign contributors, leave too little space for development to themselves given the tense economic situation? Or do the clients place their bets too much on security? To some younger people, a 40-year-old architect already seems ancient. "But how are the truly young architects doing? Those below 30? They are being trained en masse, but in a "market" that is firmly in the hands of well-established circles and that awards access only to those who bear the promise of an increase in reputation, they hardly have any chance at all." [9] It's a fact that the architecture association within their federal structure doesn't even know the true number of these architects. The Federal Office of Statistics may show that there are about 105,000 registered architects in Germany (and twice as many unregistered ones), and each architect has fewer than 1,000 inhabitants to service. But they can't tell you anything about the age structure, because the association doesn't even maintain an overall statistical compilation, which would be the only valid one. Independent from this, an architectural paradise cannot be expected until young architects not only fill out the statistical data base but are also allowed to actually build.

The unique openness in Europe towards architectural questions leads to varied personal contacts in Germany (studies and office work abroad) and to an especially intense exchange of different, in part completely, contrary approaches and opinions. In this respect, the points of reference of this architectural laboratory within Germany, at first glance opaque, reach as far as the United States. The result of this architectural open-mindedness cannot be – as a law of nature – a uniform formal language. This multi-lingual disadvantage is, however, opposed by the immense advantage of unhindered experimentation.

In no case can a clear dependency of "students" on dominating "teachers" be diagnosed. Surprisingly, there are hardly any connections with Günter Behnisch, but there is also only a very small following for the safe foundations of Oswald Mathias Unger, Gottfried Böhm, Karljosef Schattner or Frei Otto. And still, they, like many other idols, are a part of the imperative wealth of experience.

The biographies of the twenty architects documented here show important connections with, among others, the following architects: Hinrich and Inken Baller, Bangert-Jansen-Scholz-Schultes, Werner Düttmann, Johann Eisele and Nicolas Fritz, Hardt-Waltherr Hämer, Hans Kollhoff, Peter C. von Seidlein, Joachim Schürmann, Rudolf Wienands... But just as many great international architects oppose them: Raimund Abraham, Carlo Aymonino, Norman Foster, Johannes Gsteu, Haus-Rucker-Co, Friedrich Kurrent, Richard Meier, Gustav Peichl, Boris Podrecca, Fabio Reinhart, Dolf Schnebli, Peter Wilson... Three fourths of the twelve offices are actively engaged in university work. Two thirds of the offices exhibit strong relations with other countries in the professional development of their founders, which has a significant correlation with an engagement as a university teacher.

Among the preferred German architectural faculties, the following dominate: TU Munich, TU Berlin, TU Braunschweig and Stuttgart University. The other schools mentioned (TH Karlsruhe, TH Darmstadt, GH Kassel, FH Hamburg, Städelschule Frankfurt...) are opposed by equally important universities in Switzerland, the United States, Austria, England, the Netherlands and Italy. The continuing strong presence of ETH Zurich is therefore no wonder. What is surprising are the other experiences at universities abroad, aside from the Architectural Association in London: the Academy For Fine Arts in Vienna, the Gerrit Rietveld Academy in Amsterdam, Rome University, Harvard University Cambridge/USA, Virginia Polytechnic Insitute Blacksburg/USA, Illinois Institute of Technology Chicago.

In the search for a complex and innovative spatial language that doesn't just remain a pictorial language after the experience of Post-Modernism, Deconstructivism and Berlin Reconstruction, the field of search is consciously expanded in terms of space and time, an internationally-oriented open scene that even revives utopian perspectives of the past with new instruments. Constructive, ecological, technological and artistic focal points can't be denied; an architecture that takes complexity seriously, however, does change with each of its conditions and handicaps. A fear expressed in 1983 by Heinrich Klotz hasn't become reality: "As pleasantly full of ideas the young generation of architects may appear to be, one has to fear as much that a new uniform style will be established that will begin dominating and hindering the inventive forces because a new dress will already exist before the new form has come into being."[10] The pluralism reestablished with every concrete individual case on the following pages isn't the result of a search for the new dogma but reveals the existing diversity; it isn't a pretense but is deeply anchored. The tectonics of the images and identities stands next to the urban tectonics. Konrad Paul Liessmann – born in 1953 – who teaches philosophy at Vienna University has described this phenomenon in a very tangible way: "It is possible that, where the power of aesthetics is truly endangered – after Post-Modernism, after the changes, after digitalization – the question is not one of differentiation into progression and regression, and not about tractates and declarations, and not about right vs. left nor the good new medium, but about whether the true and only achievement of Modernism, the risky delivery of an autonomous aesthetic subjectivity, has once again found a way to design a world and thus, against all odds, to maintain and accomplish the very sovereignty of art – which alone justifies the latter. Something like this, however, is decided – if at all – not from movement to movement, not from fashion to fashion, not from debate to debate, not from context to context, not from network to network, and not from Modernism to Modernism, but always and only: from case to case."[11] The following architectural attitudes offer concrete approaches to this with their specific characteristics.

1) Book review "Architektur in Deutschland", Architektur Aktuell no. 209, 11-1997, p. 34.
2) Günther Feuerstein: Visionäre Architektur. Vienna 1958/1988, Berlin 1988, pp. 8–9
3) Wilfried Wang, in: Gerd de Bruyn: Zeitgenössische Architektur in Deutschland 1970–1996, Basel 1997, pp. 7–8.
4) Gerhard Matzig: "Für immer alt?" Süddeutsche Zeitung 26 January 1998, p. 13.
5) Kees Wartburg: "Moderne statt Postmoderne", Szene Hamburg 1–1998, p. 26.
6) Bauwelt 10–1998, p. 488.
7) MVRDV, El Croquis 86/1997, p. 8.
8) Gerd Zimmermann: Die andere Architektur. Bauen in der DDR, in: Gerd de Bruyn: Zeitgenössische Architektur in Deutschland 1970–1996, Basel 1997, p. 21.
9) deutsche bauzeitung db 3–1998, p. 10.
10) Heinrich Klotz: Nach der "Wende", in: Helge and Margret Bofinger: Junge Architekten in Europa, Stuttgart 1983, p. 164.
11) Konrad Paul Liessmann: Von Tomi nach Moor. Ästhetische Potenzen – nach der Postmoderne, Kursbuch 122: Die Zukunft der Moderne, December 1995, p. 32.

Bernd Albers

Stadt aus Bausteinen

Bernd Albers entfaltet in seinen in kraftvollen Ziegelsteinmauern auftretenden, den öffentlichen Raum markant definierenden Projekten und ersten Bauten in Berlin eine große Leidenschaft für die europäische Stadt in ihrer historisch fundierten Ausprägung. Architektur ist für ihn auch akribische Spurensuche in einer bis zur wissenschaftlichen Recherche reichenden Dimension. Gesucht ist der ortsspezifische Bezug zur Tradition der Stadt bis hin zum authentischen historischen Stadtgrundriß – auch dann, wenn über diesen die Entwicklung längst hinweggegangen und zwischen verschiedenen historischen Zeitschichten nur schwer auszuwählen ist. Die Architektur gewinnt damit eine utopische Dimension jenseits ihres eigenen Metiers, allein auf den Stadtraum und die ihn bildende Struktur bezogen. Das architektonische Stückwerk parzellenbezogener Einzelprojekte wird zugunsten einer die Stadt insgesamt planenden und wiederherstellenden Gesamtbetrachtung aufgegeben bzw. durch entsprechende städtebauliche Regeln präjudiziert. Eine solche «sukzessive Reurbanisierung», wie sie Bernd Albers für Leipzig anläßlich des Wettbewerbs für das neue Kunstmuseum vorsieht, hat den großen Nachteil, nur über funktional noch gar nicht belegbare Festlegungen weit in die bauliche Zukunft der Nachbargrundstücke hinein realisierbar zu sein. Für den Umbau Berlins im Rahmen der «Kritischen Rekonstruktion» ist die Komplexität weit größer, der zeitliche Ablauf nur in Generationen zu denken. Ungeachtet des Berliner Streits um die «Reaktion als Fortschritt», den Friedrich Nietzsche schon im Vorgriff lapidar mit dem Hinweis darauf kommentierte, daß vergangene Phasen der Menschheit immer dann heraufbeschworen würden, wenn die neuen Richtungen dem zuwenig

Überzeugungskraft entgegenstellen könnten, bleibt eine Faszination, die mit dem Hinweis auf moderne Gegenmodelle ohne ästhetische Fesseln – in Eichstätt von Karljosef Schattner (*1924), in Monte Carasso von Luigi Snozzi (*1932) – nicht ganz aufzulösen ist. Dies gilt besonders für die bislang leider nicht realisierte Neuformulierung des Stuttgarter Platzes in Berlin, einen «Idealstadtfetzen» (Ulrich Conrads) in labyrinthischer Wirrnis. Unabhängig von der Frage nach dem Realitätsgrad und der Durchsetzbarkeit des «Planwerks Innenstadt Berlin» mit seinem nachvollziehbaren Ziel, das bislang wenig effektiv und wenig ästhetisch genutzte historische Zentrum Berlins durch identitätsstiftende urban gestaltete Stadtstraßen, Uferpromenaden, Plätze, Stadtparks, Quartierparks und Gartenhöfe einerseits nur fragmentarisch, andererseits aber nachhaltig zu reaktivieren, geht es um die Bildfähigkeit von Stadtarchitektur, ihren funktionalen und formalen Beitrag zur Urbanität der Stadt, um eine anschaulich in die Zukunft verlängerte Stadtentwicklung ohne vorgetäuschte historische Fassaden. In dem zur Zeit größten Stadterweiterungsgebiet Berlins fern des historischen Zentrums, der Wasserstadt Spandau, deutet sich die formale Kraft einer steinernen, Stadt bildenden und abbildenden Architektur bereits an. Bernd Albers variiert den Rationalismus seiner Stadtarchitektur nicht schematisch, sondern bezieht sich jenseits der den öffentlichen Charakter der Straße betonenden Gleichförmigkeit der Fensterfolgen feinsinnig auf die neu realisierte Nutzungsmischung von Wohnung, Büro und Handel in ein und demselben Gebäude. Ohne die Plastizität und Vielfalt vergleichbarer Großformen im Hamburg oder Wien der 20er Jahre liegt in der architektonischen Reduktion die Verheißung, Stadt neu und intensiver zu erfahren.

City of Stone

In his first projects and buildings in Berlin, which strikingly define the public space with their mighty brick walls, Bernd Albers unfolds a great passion for the quintessential European city and its historically homogeneous characteristics. To Albers, architecture is also a meticulous search for artifacts in a manner that verges upon scientific research. What he is searching for is the locally specific relationship with the tradition of the city, even going so far as to include the authentic historical ground plan of the city – even if it has long been disregarded by the subsequent development and choosing now between the different historical layers has become a rather arduous task. Through this, architecture gains a utopian dimension beyond its own field, referring only to the urban space and the block structure forming it. The architectural patchwork of parcel-related single projects is abandoned in favor of an overall observation that plans and restores the city in its entirety, or is prejudiced by the pertinent design rules. Such a "successive re-urbanization," as Bernd Albers proposed for Leipzig at the occasion of the competition for the new art museum, has the great disadvantage of being achievable only far into the architectural future of the neighboring properties through functional determinations that cannot yet be determined. For the conversion of Berlin – against the background of the "critical reconstruction" – the complexity is greater by far; the temporal procedure can be thought of only in terms of generations. Leaving aside the dispute in Berlin over "reaction as progress," which Friedrich Nietzsche, in advance, had already banally commented upon with his remark that past phases of humanity would always be conjured up if the new directions are not able to confront them with an adequate force of conviction,

there remains a fascination that cannot completely be eliminated through the hint at modern counter-models without aesthetic chains – in Eichstätt by Karljosef Schattner (*1924), in Monte Carasso by Luigi Snozzi (*1932). This applies especially to the reformulation of the Stuttgarter Platz in Berlin, which, unfortunately, hasn't been realized thus far – an "ideal urban fragment" (Ulrich Conrads) within a labyrinth of incoherency. Independent of the question about the realism and the potential for realization of the "Planwerk Innenstadt Berlin," which intends, on the one hand, a fragmentary reactivation, and on the other, a permanent reactivation of the historic center of Berlin – thus far under-utilized in the sense of efficiency and aesthetics – through identity-creating, urbanistically designed city roads, riverside promenades, squares, urban parks, quarter parks and garden courtyards, the question, really, is the pictorial ability of urban architecture, its functional and formal contribution to the urbanity of the city, a tangible urban development that projects into the future without any pretentious historic facades. In what is currently the largest urban extension area of Berlin – the Wasserstadt Spandau, far away from the historic center – the formal power of an architecture of stones forming and depicting the city is hinted at. Bernd Albers doesn't vary the rationalism of his urban architecture in a schematic way but subtly refers to the newly realized commingled utilization of apartments, offices and trade within a single building in a way that transcends the homogeneity of the window sequences which enhance the public character of the street. Without the plasticity and variety of the comparable large-scale projects in Hamburg or Vienna during the '20s, the architectural reduction implies a promise to experience the city in a new and more intense way.

Berlin Wasserstadt
Spandau 1998.

Villa Köln Marienburg 1996

Im Rahmen der für architekturinteressierte Laien und kunstsinnige Bauherren gedachten Ausstellung "Houses for Sale" dient der fiktive Entwurf für ein Stadthaus im Villenviertel Köln Marienburg, einem der nobelsten Viertel der Stadt, der Positionsbestimmung der Architekten wie dem Verhältnis von Architektur und Kunst. Das Grundstück liegt in einer Straße mit vielen Backsteinvillen unmittelbar neben der Kunstgalerie Gmurzynska von Diener & Diener. Der zweigeschossige Kubus, durch den zentralen Eingang in seiner für eine Villa typischen Symmetrie betont, signalisiert mit geschoßhohen gleichförmig angeordneten Fenstern den urbanen Standpunkt des Hauses wie seiner Bewohner. Insofern entwickelt sich diese Villa als Refugium der Großstadt dialektisch. Die Öffentlichkeit der Wohnstraße wird durch eine strenge Baustruktur räumlich definiert und in der großformatigen Befensterung des Hauses thematisiert. Gleichzeitig finden sich dieselben Raumqualitäten und Fensteröffnungen identisch auf der Gartenseite wieder, dienen hier aber dem privaten Rückzug, ohne in die übliche Gemütlichkeit umzuschlagen. Die Bewohner sind aufgefordert, die neutrale Wohnstruktur wie ein nach den Regeln des Architekten gestimmtes Instrument individuell zum Klingen zu bringen. Das Gartenhaus ist als Wintergarten, Badehaus oder Bibliothek vielfältig nutzbar. Der kiesbedeckte Hof zwischen Gartenhaus und Wohnraum, mit einem langgestreckten Wasserbecken im Zentrum, läßt an festliche Gesellschaften ebenso denken wie an privates Familienleben. So wie das gesamte Haus ein klares Bild zeigt, aufgebaut auf nur einem verglasten bzw. offenen Element, wird auch die Bepflanzung rund um die Gesamtanlage in einen Rahmen verwiesen. Konkrete Bildhaftigkeit und abstrakte Struktur sind ohne Vorrang ausgewogen.

Villa Cologne Marienburg 1996

In the context of the exhibition "Houses for Sale", intended for amateurs interested in architecture and clients with a sense for art, the fictitious design for a townhouse in the villa quarter Cologne Marienburg – one of the finest addresses in town – serves to determine the position of the architects and the relationship between architecture and art. The property is located on a street that hosts many brick villas, and is situated directly next to the Gmurzynska art gallery by Diener & Diener. The two-story cube, its typical villa symmetry enhanced by the centrally positioned entrance, signals the urban position of the house and its inhabitants with floor-to-ceiling windows that are evenly arranged. This villa, as a refuge from the big city, develops in a dialectic way in this regard. The public character of the residential street is defined spatially by a strict architectural structure and is made a theme in the large format of the windows. At the same time, the same spatial qualities and window openings reoccur on the garden side; however, here they serve the private retreat without developing into the usual coziness. The inhabitants are challenged to evoke an individual sound from this neutral structure which has been tuned according to the architect's rules. The garden house can be used in multiple ways – a winter garden, a bath house or a library. Between the garden house and the main house, the graveled yard with a long water basin at its center encourages the contemplation of festive parties as well as private family life. As the house shows a clear picture, established on the basis of only one glazed or open element, the plantings around the entire compound are placed into a clear framework. The concrete pictorial nature and abstract structure are evenly balanced.

1. Lageplan.
   Site plan.
2,3. Grundrisse.
   Ground plans.
4. Straßenfront.
   Street facade.
5. Blick in den Gartenhof.
   View of the garden yard.
6. Gartenfront.
   Garden facade.

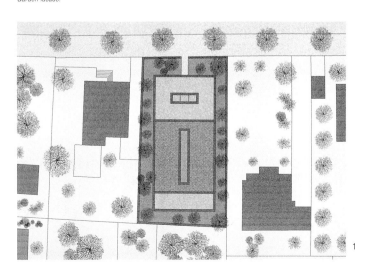

1

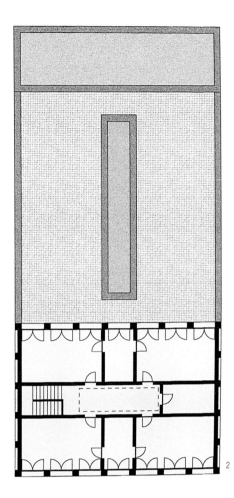

2

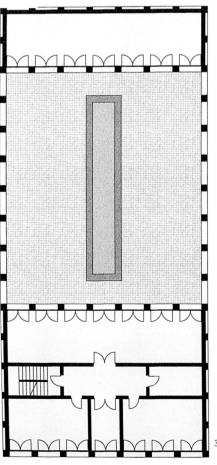

3

18

4

5

6

Wohn- und Geschäftshaus Berlin Wasserstadt Spandau 1994–1998

Zwischen Charlottenburg und Spandauer Forst, unmittelbar an Havel bzw. Spandauer See angrenzend, entsteht auf einer 206 Hektar großen Industriebrache nördlich der Zitadelle das mit Wohnraum und Infrastruktur für 34.000 Menschen größte Stadterweiterungsgebiet von Berlin. Leitgedanke der städtebaulichen Konzeption (Hans Kollhoff/Helga Timmermann, Christoph Langhof, Klaus Zillich, 1989) ist ein ökologischer, kompakter Stadtumbau mit einer von der Lage am Wasser bestimmten Atmosphäre. Ausgangspunkt waren darum nicht Flächennutzungsplan und Straßenschema, sondern das markante urbane Bild der zukünftigen Wasserstadt, das sich aus den Stadträumen, den Plätzen, den Wegen, Parkanlagen und Gebäudekonfigurationen entwickelt. Der vorgegebene Gestaltungskanon forderte für die orthogonal geordneten Straßenfronten blaubunte bis rote Klinker und naturbelassene Holzfenster. Das zum See geöffnete, von innen erschlossene «U» setzt die urbanistische Grundkonzeption der komplementären Welten von Stadt und Natur formal und außenräumlich um. Das Wohnen am Havelufer wird mit einer markanten Gemeinschaftsterrasse oberhalb der Tiefgarage und privaten Wintergärten ebenso deutlich thematisiert wie der urbane Straßenzug, zu dem sich die erdgeschossigen Läden orientieren. Die französischen Fenster entlang der Straße bleiben in Maß und Rhythmus gleichförmig, während die Fenster auf der Gartenseite sich in gleichbleibenden Klinker-Passepartouts scheinbar spielerisch der Auseinandersetzung mit funktionalen Kriterien stellen. Die strukturale Strenge der symmetrischen Großstruktur bleibt dennoch prägendes Ordnungsprinzip.

Apartment and Office Building Berlin Wasserstadt Spandau 1994–1998

Between Charlottenburg and Spandauer Forst, in the immediate vicinity of the Havel and Lake Spandau, the largest urban extension of Berlin, with apartments and an infrastructure for 34,000 people, will be built on 206 hectares of abandoned industrial land north of the citadel. The guiding idea of the urban concept (Hans Kohlhoff/Helga Timmermann, Christoph Langhof, Klaus Zillich, 1989) is an ecological and compact city conversion with an atmosphere determined by the nearby water. The starting point was therefore not the zoning plan and street plan but the striking urban image of the future "Wasserstadt" (water city) that would develop out of the urban spaces, the squares, pathways, parks, and the configurations of buildings. The given design criterion called for blue to red colored brick and natural wood windows for the orthogonally structured street fronts. The U-form that opens towards the lake and develops from within realizes the basic urban concept of the complementary worlds of the city and nature in a formal and externally spatial way. Living at the banks of the Havel River is made a theme, with a striking common terrace above the underground parking and private winter gardens, as clearly as the urban street towards which the ground floor stores are oriented. The French windows along the street remain uniform in their scale and rhythm, whereas the windows on the garden side face the confrontation with functional criteria in a seemingly playful way in equal brick passe-partout. However, the structural strictness of the symmetrical large-scale structure still remains the decisive principle of order.

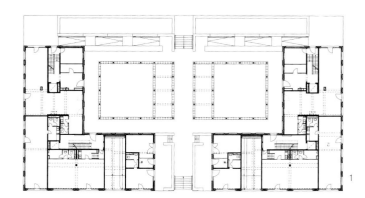

1

2

3

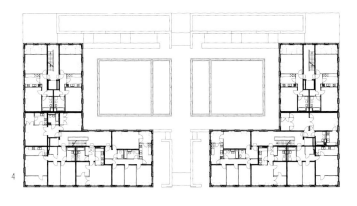

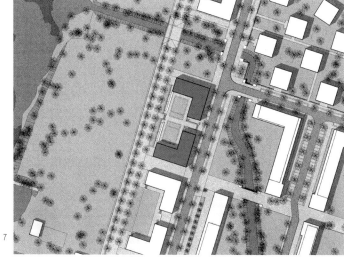

1. Läden Erdgeschoß.
   Stores on first floor.
2,5. Hofansicht und
   Längsschnitt.
   *View of the yard and
   longitudinal section.*
3. Gartenhof.
   Garden.
4. Wohnungen 1.–4.
   Obergeschoß.
   *Apartments on 2nd to
   5th floors.*
6. Straßenraum.
   Street space.
7. Lageplan.
   Site Plan.

Wohn-, Büro- und Geschäftshaus Berlin Wasserstadt Spandau 1994–1998

Entgegen der Generalplanung mußte das Gebiet Pulvermühle aufgrund seines längeren Planungsvorlaufs noch weitgehend als Wohnsiedlung konzipiert werden (Johanne/Gernot Nalbach, 1992), sieht aber teilweise eine Durchmischung mit erdgeschossigen Läden und Büronutzung auch in den Obergeschossen vor. Im Endausbau soll die Wasserstadt ca. 14.000 Wohnungen umfassen, aber auch 900.000 m² Bruttogeschoßfläche für Dienstleistungen und Gewerbe, 22 Kindertagesstätten, 6 Grundschulen, 3 Oberschulen, 3 Jugendfreizeitheime... Hinsichtlich der Balance zwischen Urbanität und Landschaft liegt das Ziel im spannungsreichen Wechselspiel, auch im Hinterland soll die Lage am Wasser spürbar bleiben. Einer fünf- bis siebengeschossigen Bebauung, Garant für die Wirtschaftlichkeit des Städtebaus, stehen die freien Uferzonen und Parklandschaften, aber auch vom ruhenden Verkehr weitgehend befreite Straßenräume als Pendant gegenüber. Der L-förmige Bau, dem zuvor dokumentierten südlich gegenüber, formuliert als freistehendes Volumen eine Straßenecke. Der formale Reiz der Massivität des Materials wird bei strenger Fensterfolge in wechselnden Leibungstiefen ausgespielt. Die französischen Fenster der Büros im ersten Obergeschoß sind steintief nach innen versetzt, die Fenster der Wohnungen darüber liegen, 40 cm zurückversetzt, innen bündig. Mit dem für eine gemeinschaftliche Dachterrasse zurückgenommenen fünften Obergeschoß wird die Figur des Hauses dramatisiert und im Zusammenspiel mit der Arkade des Erdgeschosses wie der horizontalen Verschiebung der Fensterfolge übereck die Schmalseite zur Hauptfront erklärt. Das Haus ist geprägt von seiner monolithischen Erscheinung, deren spezifische Ausprägung aus der Auseinandersetzung mit Raumprogramm und Bebauungsplan resultiert.

Apartment, Office and Commercial Building Berlin Wasserstadt Spandau 1994–1998

Contrary to the master plan, the Pulvermühle area, for the most part, had to be established as a residential development since the time of its planning (Johanne/Gernot Nalbach, 1992). But it still envisions a mixture of ground floor storefronts and offices on the upper floors. In the final development, the Wasserstadt will include not only 14,000 apartments, but also 900,000 m² gross floor space for services and trade, 22 day care centers, 6 primary schools, 3 high schools, 3 youth clubs, etc. When it comes to the balance between urbanism and landscape, the goal is a suspenseful interaction, and the waterfront location is to be felt even in the hinterland. The five to seven story development, which cedes to the economy of urban development, is counterbalanced not only by the free waterfront areas and parks, but also by the streets that are largely free of traffic. The L-shaped building situated to the south, opposite the above-documented structure, forms a street corner as a free-standing volume. The formal attraction of the materials' massiveness is fully played out in the differing reveal depths of the strictly arranged windows. The French windows of the second floor offices recede to the inside by the depth of a brick, and the windows of the apartments above recede by 40 cm and are even with the interior wall. The figure of the house is made even more dramatic with the receding of the sixth floor to make room for a communal roof terrace; with the interaction with the first floor arcade and the horizontal offset of the window sequence around the corner, the narrow side of the building is declared the main facade. The house is marked by its monolithic appearance, whose specific form results from the confrontation with the spatial program and the zoning plan.

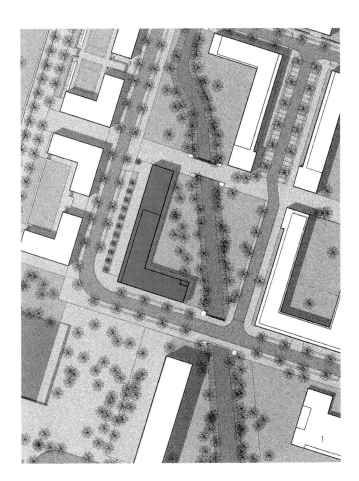

1

2

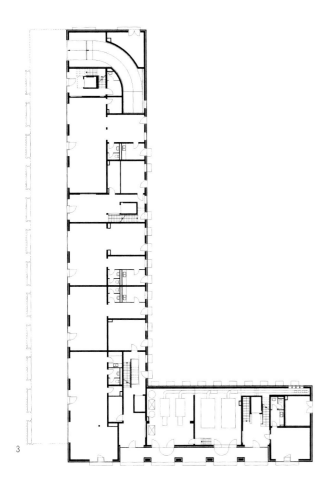

3

5

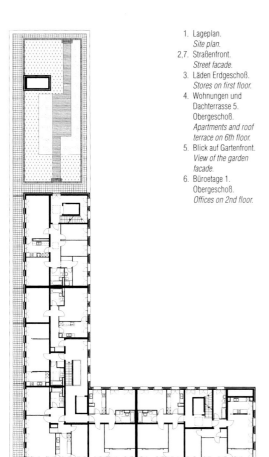

4

1. Lageplan.
   Site plan.
2,7. Straßenfront.
   Street facade.
3. Läden Erdgeschoß.
   Stores on first floor.
4. Wohnungen und
   Dachterrasse 5.
   Obergeschoß.
   *Apartments and roof
   terrace on 6th floor.*
5. Blick auf Gartenfront.
   *View of the garden
   facade.*
6. Büroetage 1.
   Obergeschoß.
   Offices on 2nd floor.

6

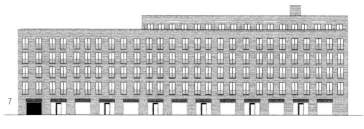

7

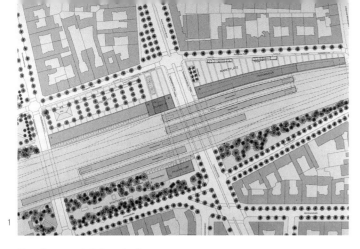

Turmhaus und Bahnarkaden
Berlin Charlottenburg
Stuttgarter Platz 1996

Straßen und Bahnanlagen schaffen die Basis für Städtebau. Mit den aktuellen Bauabsichten der Bahn ergibt sich am vormals bedeutenden Stuttgarter Platz die Chance, die Planungswunden der 60er Jahre zu heilen und aus der räumlich wenig markanten Abfolge unterschiedlicher Kiez-Biotope wieder eine großstädtische Platzanlage zu gewinnen. Der Typus des gründerzeitlichen Berliner Platzes baut auf klare Platzkanten, markante Gebäudesolitäre und ein symbiotisches Nebeneinander von steinernem Platz und grünem Park. Der Entwurf sieht darum im Norden eine urbane Bebauung des Bahndamms mit Arkaden und einem Turmhaus vor, im Süden einen Stadtgarten mit Freizeitqualitäten. Die Bahnarkaden, aus der Thematik und dem Maßstab der Berliner S-Bahn-Bögen entwickelt, lassen mit dem Turmhaus ein Spannungsfeld entstehen, das den Platz in seinem schwierigen Zuschnitt signifikant kennzeichnet und optisch weit in den Stadtgrundriß einbindet – nach Süden bis zum Adenauerplatz am Kurfürstendamm, nach Norden bis zum Luisenplatz am Charlottenburger Schloß. Funktional verknüpfen die mit Läden besetzten Bahnarkaden den Verkehr von U-Bahn, S-Bahn und Regionalbahn. Die großzügige Platzfigur erlaubt die Anlage eines Marktplatzes und eines Stadtplatzes, Anlaufstation für Bus und Taxi, vor allem aber Adresse für den neuen Büro- und Hotelturm. Der janusköpfige Turm verkörpert als architektonisches Zeichen die neue Identität des Stuttgarter Platzes am eindringlichsten. Seine bauliche Figuration zielt auf eine ebenso einfache wie einprägsame Form. (Wettbewerb, 1. Preis)

Tower House and Railway
Arcades Berlin Charlottenburg
Stuttgarter Platz 1996

Streets and railroad tracks create the basis for an urban development. The current plans of the railroad company create the opportunity for the once important Stuttgarter Platz to heal the wounds of the planning that took place during the '60s and to once again reestablish an urban square out of the spatially rather unimpressive sequence of different district biotopes. Following the Gründerzeit (years of rapid industrialization and expansion) style, the Berliner Platz is characterized by clear edges, striking solitary buildings and a symbiotic coexistence of the stone-covered square and the green park. Therefore, the design plans for an urban development of the railway embankment with arcades and a tower house in the north, and a municipal park with leisure qualities in the south. The railway arcades were developed from the theme and scale of the Berlin tramway arcs and, together with the tower house, create a suspenseful field that to a large extent determines the square with its difficult layout and visually integrates it far into the city's ground plan – in the south to Adenauerplatz at Kurfürstendamm, in the north to Luisenplatz at the Charlottenburg Castle. Functionally, the railway arcades – occupied by stores – connect the traffic of the subway, the tram and the regional railway. The generous figure of the square allows for the establishment of a market square and a city square, the target points for busses and taxis and, above all, the address for the new office and hotel tower. As an architectural symbol, the Janus-faced tower embodies the new identity of the Stuttgarter Platz most vividly. Its architectural configuration is directed towards a form that is as simple as it is impressive. (Competition, 1st prize)

4

5

1. Lageplan.
   Site plan.
2. Stadtgarten südlich der
   Bahnlinie.
   *Municipal park south
   of the railroad tracks.*
3. Platzfront mit
   Hochhaus.
   *Facade facing the
   square with high-rise
   building.*
4. Bahnarkaden von
   Osten.
   *View from the east of
   the railway arcades.*
5. Blick aus der Kaiser-
   Friedrich-Straße von
   Norden.
   *View from the north of
   Kaiser-Friedrich-
   Straße.*
6. Schnitt Bahnarkaden
   mit S-Bahn-Zugang.
   *Section railway arcades
   with train access.*

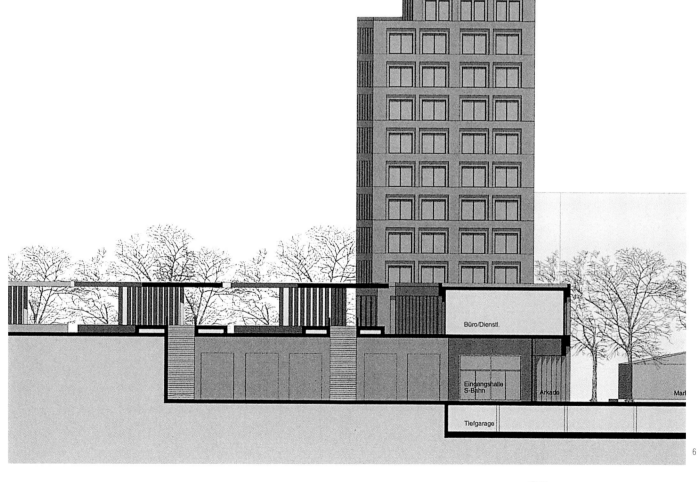

Büro/Dienstl.

Eingangshalle
S-Bahn

Arkade

Mar

Tiefgarage

6

25

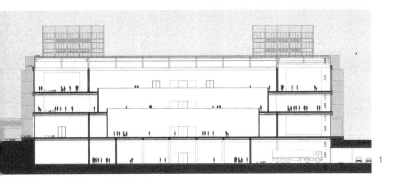

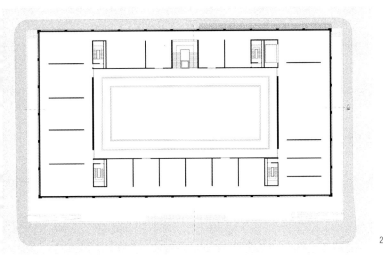

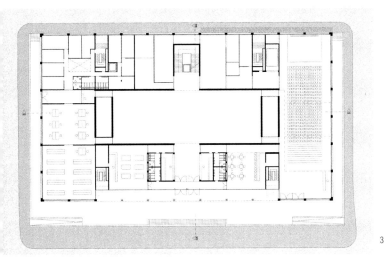

Museum der bildenden Künste
Leipzig 1997

Das Museum in innerstädtischer Lage soll zu einem Anziehungspunkt für Touristen und Bürger gleichermaßen werden. Die Schwierigkeit der Aufgabe lag vor allem darin, den Bau einerseits in die nördliche Innenstadt einzupassen, andererseits aber dessen zentrale Bedeutung angemessen zu verdeutlichen. Vorgeschlagen wird eine sukzessive Reurbanisierung auf Basis des nach und nach wieder sichtbar gemachten historischen Leipziger Stadtgrundrisses. Das neue Museum gliedert sich so als eigener Baublock in den Kontext der neuen Textur ein. Mit der wiedergewonnenen Böttcherstraße, an der der Haupteingang angeordnet ist, erhält das Museum eine eindeutige und prägnante Adresse. Ein flacher Sockel mit eingeschnittenen Rampen und Treppen weist auf die besondere Bedeutung des Gebäudes hin. Langfristig ist im südlichen wie im östlichen Anschluß an blockhafte Bebauungen entlang der Baufluchten gedacht. Diese städtebauliche Zielvorstellung kann mittelfristig in einer Differenzierung des Bodenbelags wie durch freistehende Stangen entlang der Baufluchten zum Ausdruck gebracht werden. Der nördlich anschließende Baublock soll zeitgleich mit dem Museum entstehen. Mit der zentralen, über Dach belichteten Halle des Kunstmuseums werden nicht nur internationale Wechselausstellungen möglich, sondern im Sinne eines Kulturhauses publikumswirksame kulturelle Veranstaltungen verschiedener Art. Foyer, Museumscafé und Museumsladen sind im unmittelbaren Anschluß an eine zentrale Säulenhalle separat nutzbar. Die Lichtdecke im zweiten Obergeschoß läßt in der aus Stahlprofilen und Glastafeln entwickelten Fassade Raum für dunkle, mit den Künstlernamen bedruckte Glasscheiben. (Wettbewerb, 7. Rang)

Museum of Fine Arts
Leipzig 1997

The museum in an inner city location is to become an attraction for tourists and for the residents of the city, as well. The difficulty of the task was, above all, the integration of the building into the northern inner city on the one hand, and on the other, to appropriately clarify its central importance. The proposal is a successive reurbanization on the basis of the historic ground plan of Leipzig that will once again be made visible in separate phases. The new museum thus integrates itself as a separate block into the context of the new texture. With the main entrance at Böttcherstrasse, it receives a clear and poignant address. A flat base with cut-in ramps and steps points out the special meaning of the building. For the future, block-like developments adjoined to the north and south have been planned along the alignment of the buildings. This urban goal can be expressed in the interim with a differentiation of the floor coverings and free-standing rods along the alignment of the buildings. The block adjoining the north is to be established at the same time as the museum. The central sky-lit lobby of the art museum not only enables changing international exhibitions but also many different types of cultural events attractive to a wide range of audiences. Adjoining a central columned hall, the lobby, the museum café and the museum store can be utilized separately. The third-floor skylight ceiling, developed from steel profiles and glass panels, leaves space in the facade for dark glass panes imprinted with the artists' names. (Competition, 7th place)

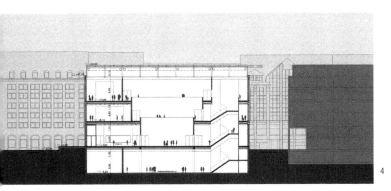

1,4. Schnitte.
      Sections.
2. Erdgeschoß.
      First floor.
3. Obergeschoß.
      Upper floor.
5. Zentrale Ausstellungshalle.
      Central exhibition hall.
6. Städtebauliches Konzept.
      Urban concept.
7. Perspektive Eingangsfront.
      Perspective entrance facade.

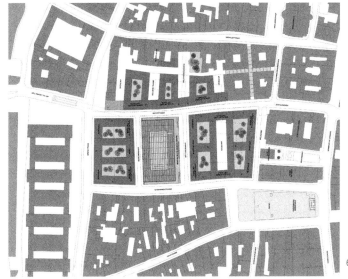

27

Markus Allmann
Amandus Sattler
Ludwig Wappner

Symbole ohne Vorgeschichte

Markus Allmann, Amandus Sattler und Ludwig Wappner, im Alter von kaum vierzig Jahren gegen 483 Mitbewerber und sehr prominente Konkurrenz mit dem Deutschen Architekturpreis 1997 ausgezeichnet, bevorzugen in ihrer Architektur klare Linien, leichte schwebende Baukörper, einfache Geometrien, bei aller Reduktion ausdrucksstarke Materialien und changierende Materialschichtungen. Dabei widersetzen sie sich den formalistischen Innovationen, die in Ermangelung einer klaren architekturtheoretischen Orientierung auf dem Wege eines immer schneller rotierenden Architekturmix über kurzlebige Collagen zu haben sind. Vielmehr versuchen die Architekten, ihr mentales Bildarchiv zu löschen, um möglichst unvoreingenommen, zunächst weniger kreativ als analytisch, das Wesen der konkreten Aufgabe und Situation umfassend zu erschließen. Um alle Eigenarten, Bedingungen, Ziele und Varianten der Aufgabe auszuschöpfen, nur scheinbar stichhaltige Sachzwänge, vordergründige Gebäudetypologien und unberechtigte Funktionalismen aber auf der Strecke zu lassen, wird der eigentliche Entwurfsprozeß, die Klärung der Beziehung zwischen Funktion und Form,

möglichst lange hinausgezögert. Dieses in der Soziologie unter dem Stichwort «pragmatisches Modell» beschriebene Verfahren wurde Ende der 60er Jahre von dem Soziologen Norbert Schmidt-Relenberg für Architektur und Städtebau propagiert (Ders.: Soziologie und Städtebau, Stuttgart 1968), führte allerdings in der konkreten Umsetzung damals nicht zu Architektur, sondern dank einer aus den Zeitumständen zu erklärenden Überbewertung von Mitbestimmung und Flexibilität zu deren Auflösung. Die Methode ist dennoch schlüssig, wenn auch unter «kreativen» Architekten in ihrer Wissenschaftlichkeit wenig gebräuchlich. Abstrakte Analysen und Konzepte im Vorfeld kommen ohne das Medium Zeichnung aus, geht es doch darum, Aufgabenstellung und Zielsetzung sprachlich zu präzisieren. Das Ziel der Architekten liegt darin, das Wesen der Bauaufgabe zeitbezogen und eigenständig umzusetzen, ohne formal zu begründende Umschweife oder modische Anleihen. An die Stelle der Leidenschaft für eine Form tritt so das pragmatische Modell, das in Bezug auf einen Modellgegenstand – das geforderte Gebäude – mit Hilfe von Erkenntnis- und Zieldaten eine logisch vereinbarte und vor allem «sinnvolle» Modellaussage formuliert – nicht im Sinne eines Abbildes der Realität, sondern im Sinne eines vorgestellten Idealbildes bzw. utopischen Zukunftsbildes. Der kreative Prozeß bewegt sich damit in den Grenzen der theoretischen Analyse und Synthese, verlangt aber Intuition und Phantasie schon vor den ersten architektonischen Aussagen in Form von Entwurfsskizzen, kann die Modellaussage doch grundsätzlich nicht aus einer logischen Ableitung resultieren. Den konkreten architektonischen Ergebnissen ist ihr analytischer Entstehungsprozeß nur insofern anzusehen, als die Reduktion der Form in ihrer inhaltlichen Verankerung zu überraschend unverbrauchten, neuen Thesen und Formulierungen auch der Architektur führt. Kargheit und Sachlichkeit der Erscheinungsform werden nachrangig zugunsten von ebenso inspirierten wie inspirierenden Gebäuden. Allgemein gültige Bautypologien wie Bürohaus (Hauptverwaltung Bayerische Rück, 1. Preis), Kirche, Schule und Friedhof wechseln mit der Struktur auch ihr Gesicht. Erläuterungsberichte werden nicht im Anschluß an die Formfindung nachgeschoben, sondern markieren einen Neubeginn.

Symbols without a history

In their architecture, Markus Allmann, Amandus Sattler and Ludwig Wappner, who before even having reached their forties had won the German Architectural Award 1997 against 483 competitors, some of them very famous, prefer clear lines, light, floating building volumes, simple geometry, expressive materials despite all reduction, and changing layers of materials. They stood up against the formalist innovations available through short-lived collages along the path of an ever more quickly rotating architectural melange resulting from the lack of a clear architectural-historical orientation. The architects attempt, rather, to delete their mental image archive in order to explore the true essence of the concrete task and situation without prejudice – at first, not so much in a creative way but more in an analytical way. In order to optimally use all specifics, conditions, goals and variations of the task and to leave behind the only seemingly important factual restrictions, superficial building typologies and unjustified functionalism, the real design process, the clarification of the relationship between function and form, is delayed as long as possible. This procedure, described in sociology under the term "pragmatic model," was propagated in the late '60s by the sociologist Norbert Schmidt-Relenberg for architecture and urbanism (Soziologie und Städtebau, Stuttgart 1968). However, it did not lead to concrete realizations of architecture back then but rather to its dissolution, if one considers the overvaluation of the co-determination and flexibility that was defined by the conditions at the time. And yet, the method is logical, although not very practical among the "creative" architects because of its scientific approach. Preliminary abstract analyses and concepts can do away with drawing as a medium, since the real point is to precisely phrase the task and goals. The goal of the architects is to realize the essence of the building task in a contemporary and distinctive way without any detours based on formalities or fashionable appropriations. The pragmatic model thus takes the place of the passion for form; it formulates a logical and, above all, "sensible" paradigmatic statement through knowledge and goal oriented data with reference to a model object – the required building – not in the sense of a mirroring of reality, but in the sense of an imagined ideal image or utopian future image. The creative process moves within the limitations of the theoretical analysis and synthesis, but it requires intuition and fantasy even before the first architectural statements are made in the form of design sketches, because the model statement principally can't result from a logical derivation. The analytical creative process can be seen in the concrete architectural results only in as far as the reduction of the form – in its contextual anchoring – leads to surprisingly fresh and new theses and formulations of the architecture, as well. Scarcity and factuality of the appearance become subordinate to buildings that are as inspired as they are inspiring. With the structure, the generally valid building typologies – such as the office building (main administration Bavarian Rück, 1st prize), the church, the school and the cemetery – also change their countenance. The explanatory reports are not added after the form has been found, but demarcate a new beginning.

Herz Jesu Kirche
München
Neuhausen
1996–1999.
*Herz Jesu Kirche
Munich Neuhausen
1996–1999.*

Gymnasium mit Dreifachturnhalle Flöha/Chemnitz 1992–1996

Der Standort im Auenbereich der Flüsse Zschopau und Flöha westlich der Stadt führte dazu, auf Erdgeschoß und Untergeschoß weitgehend zu verzichten. Die Schule schwebt in strenger Formation, dennoch fragil und luftig als aufgeständerter Ring 4 m über dem Gelände – transparent und elegant. Lediglich im Norden berührt der Bau mit weniger als einem Drittel der Ringfläche (Lehrerzimmer, Verwaltung) seinen Untergrund. Unter einer nach Süden orientierten Schrägverglasung in den Ring eingestellte Kuben nehmen die zentralen Funktionen auf (Bibliothek, Speisesaal, Kunst- und Musikräume). Die hier angeordnete Eingangshalle mit ihrer tribünenartigen Treppenanlage bildet das Herzstück der Schule: wettergeschützte Pausenhalle, Aula und Treffpunkt. Geometrisches Zentrum des zweigeschossigen Rings aus umlaufenden Schulklassen ist ein Pausenhof von 68 m im Durchmesser. Selbst die wie Gangways ausgeklappten Treppenhauszugänge unter dem Gebäuderund berühren den Boden nicht. Die Symbolik sozialer Gemeinschaft und Kommunikation innerhalb und außerhalb der Gebäudegrenzen ist poetisch in Szene gesetzt. Die Fernsicht reicht bis zum Erzgebirge, aufgedruckte Entfernungsangaben auf der Gebäudeunterseite setzen internationale Städte in Bezug zum Kreismittelpunkt: «ein Monument des Sozialen ohne Monumentalität» (Deutscher Architekturpreis 1997), alltagstauglich und gebrauchstüchtig – ohne dekonstruktivistischen, demokratisch fundierten Tanz der Bauelemente. So läßt sich das Konzept bis zum Detail auch mit lapidaren praktischen Erwägungen des Schulbetriebs vertreten. (Wettbewerb, 1. Preis)

High School with Triple-Use Gymnasium, Flöha/Chemnitz 1992–1996

The location – west of the city in the meadow area of the rivers Zschopau and Flöha – leads to a design that, for the most part, makes do without a basement and ground floor. The school floats in a strict formation. And yet, it is fragile and airy, a circular post-and-beam construction hovering 4 meters above the grounds – transparent and elegant. On the north side, the building touches the ground with less than one third of the circular surface (teacher's room, administration). The central functions (library, cafeteria, art and music rooms) are fulfilled by cubes installed into the ring below the sloped glazing oriented towards the south. The entrance lobby with its stage-like staircase system forms the heart of the school: it is a weather-protected recess hall, aula and meeting point. The schoolyard, with a diameter of 68 meters, forms the geometric center of the two-story ring consisting of wraparound classrooms. Even the stairway accesses, looking like gangways beneath the building circle, do not touch the ground. The symbolism of the social community and communication, both inside and outside the building boundaries, is poetically put on stage. The view extends to the Erzgebirge, and distances imprinted on the underside of the building provide the center of the circle with a reference to international cities: "a monument to the social, without monumentality" (German Architectural Award 1997), fit for every-day-use and highly functional – without a deconstructivist, democratically conceived dance of building elements. The concept can thus be defended in its details even within the banal practical considerations of the school life. (Competition, 1st prize)

1

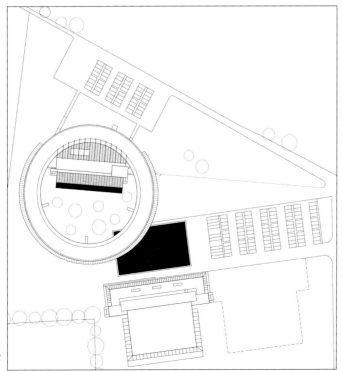

2

3

1. Atrium.
   Atrium.
2. Lageplan.
   Site plan.
3. Pausenhalle.
   Recess hall.
4. Innerer Gebäudering.
   Inner building ring.
5. 1.Obergeschoß.
   Second floor.
6. Querschnitt.
   Cross section.

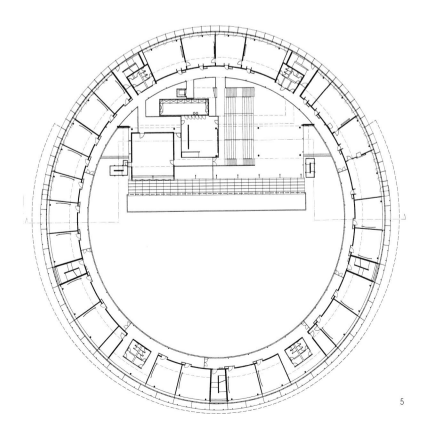

5

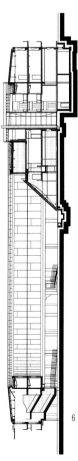

6

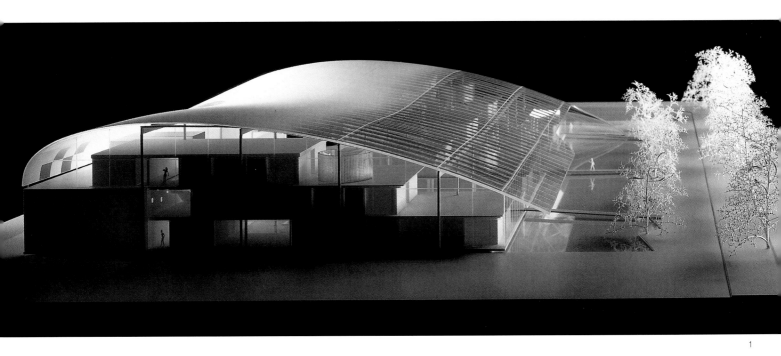

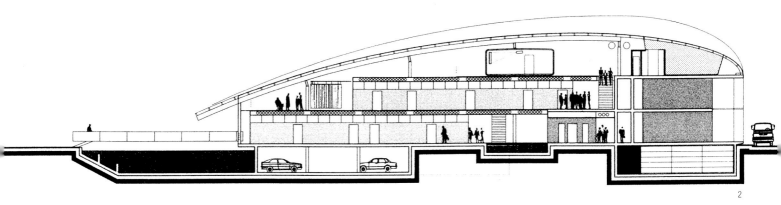

Labor- und Bürogebäude Bärlocher München Unterschleißheim 1996

In einem stadtnahen Landschaftsraum kann sich das Projekt lediglich auf die Lärmbelastung der umschließenden Verkehrswege, seine Orientierung und die vorhandenen topographischen Elemente beziehen. Ein straßenbegleitender Lärmschutzwall wird genutzt, um den Verkehrslärm über das gebäudeumhüllende Glasdach hinweg abzuleiten. Bei drei Geschossen entwickelt sich die Charakteristik der Doppelfassade im wesentlichen horizontal, der Baukörper wird nach den Gesetzen der Aerodynamik zu einer Tragfläche geformt. Lediglich die lärmabgewandte Fassade nach Nordwesten wird für spätere Erweiterungen (mit identischer Fassade) aus der doppelt dynamischen Stromlinienform ausgenommen. Mit einer hochwertigen 2-Scheiben-Wärmeschutzverglasung

als Außenhaut (planebene Module) und einer voluminösen, als interne Dispositionsfläche wie als lärmgeschützter Freiraum nutzbaren Zwischenzone greift die überraschende Umkehrung des Prinzips Doppelfassade in die Organisation des terrassenartig nach Süd-Westen orientierten Gebäudes ebenso komplex ein wie in dessen Klima- und Energieplanung. Ab einer Außentemperatur von 0°C sollen die Wärmeverluste selbst an trüben Tagen durch solare und interne Energiegewinne gedeckt werden können. Eine Luftheizung könnte auf die unvermeidlichen starken Schwankungen der Raumtemperatur am schnellsten reagieren. Flächendisposition und Büroorganisation lassen sich – bis hin zu variablen Bürotiefen – als «atmender Organismus» ausbilden. Die Hülle bleibt in Form und Dimension unverändert, ihr Innenleben, offen auch für Kultur und Kunst, wandelt sich dagegen kontinuierlich.

Bärlocher Laboratory and Office Building Munich Unterschleissheim 1996

In a landscape close to the city, the project can only refer to the noise of the surrounding traffic routes, its orientation, and the existing topographical elements. A noise barrier along the street is used to divert the traffic noise past the glass roof encasing the building. The main attribute of the double facade is its essentially horizontal character in this three-story building; the volume is shaped like a wing, following the laws of aerodynamics. Only the northwest facade is turned away from the noise and is excluded from the dynamic streamlined shape to allow for the possibility of an extension at a later time(with an identical facade). With high-quality, double-pane insulating glass for the outside shell and a voluminous interstitial zone usable

as an internal disposition space and as a free area protected from the noise, this surprising reversal of the double facade principle influences the organization of the building, oriented towards the southwest in a terrace-like manner, in a way that is just as complex as its influence on the interior climate control and energy planning. From an outside temperature of 0°C onward, the heat loss is compensated even on overcast days by solar and internal heat gains. An air heating system can most quickly react to the unavoidably strong fluctuations of the room temperature. The characteristics of the surface and the organization of the offices can be formed as a "breathing organism" – including flexible office depths. The shell remains unchanged in its form and dimensions, but its inner life – accessible for culture and art –changes continuously.

32

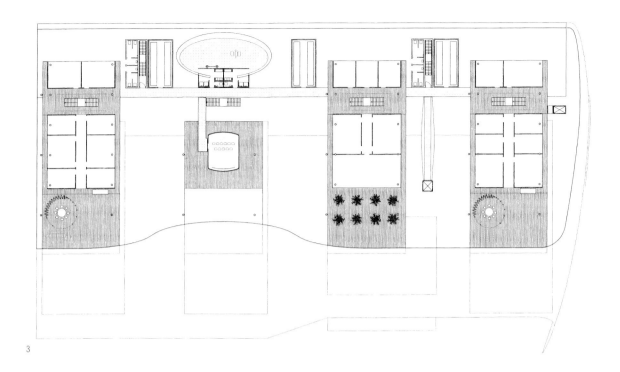

3

1. Seitenfront für Erweiterungen.
   Side facade for extensions.
2. Querschnitt.
   Cross section.
3. 2. Obergeschoß.
   Third floor.
4. Modell von Süden.
   Model from the south.

4

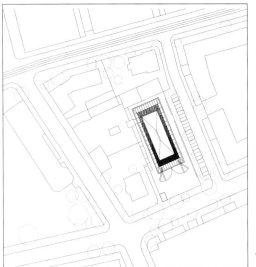

1

Herz Jesu Kirche München Neuhausen 1996–1999

Nach dem Verlust der aus der Holzkonstruktion eines Kinos in den 50er Jahren entwickelten Notkirche bei einem Brand im Jahr 1994 entsteht der lange umstrittene Neubau in derselben markanten städtebaulichen Situation der Jahrhundertwende unweit von Schloß Nymphenburg – in einer traditionsbewußten Gemeinde. Den Kirchenraum bilden zwei diaphane ineinandergestellte Hüllen mit gegenläufigen Materialwirkungen. Dazwischen liegt der Kreuzweg. Der äußere Glaskubus, physischer und thermischer Gebäudeabschluß, transportiert das Licht in kontinuierlich veränderter Intensität, Farbe und Brechung – in beiden Richtungen, tagsüber und nachts. Die innere Hülle aus Lärchenholzlamellen, deren Abstände sich zum Altar kontinuierlich weiten, begrenzt den Kirchenraum dagegen im Zusammenspiel mit der zum Altar gleichgerichtet abnehmenden Transparenz der Glashaut zunehmend virtuell. Ähnlich changierend wechselt der Betonboden der Kirche von einer rauhen zu einer glatten, reflektierenden Oberfläche. An der Grenze zum Altar entsteht in der Gesamtwirkung der Materialströme ein metaphysischer Raum. Der auf der Gegenseite als Objekt eingestellte Emporenkasten wirkt in der gegenläufigen Materialstimmung dagegen fast so massiv und irdisch wie das gebäudehohe Eingangstor. Dieses Tor, das synonym zum Tor hinter dem Altarbereich die gesamte Front zu einer Willkommensgeste stilisiert, kann je nach Jahreszeit und feierlichem Anlaß in verschiedenen Positionen fixiert werden. Im einen Fall schließt die Außenhülle den Kirchenraum thermisch und akustisch ab, im anderen verbinden sich Vorhalle und Kirchplatz zu einem gemeinsamen Raum. Der Glockenturm wiederholt das Motiv Materialüberlagerung und -verdichtung mit Hilfe von Metallgeweben. (Wettbewerb, 1. Preis)

Herz Jesu Church Munich Neuhausen 1996–1999

After the loss of the temporary church, developed from the wood construction of a '50s movie theater, after a fire in 1994, the long-disputed new building is to be erected in a striking turn-of-the-century urban location, near Nymphenburg Castle, in a community that remains highly aware of tradition. The church is formed by two diaphanous shells set into one another with opposing material effects. Between them is the cloister walk. The outer glass cube, both the physical and thermal termination of the building, transports the light, continuously changing in intensity, color and refraction, in both directions – during the day and at night, as well. The interior shell of lark wood lamella, the interstitial spaces of which continuously increase towards the altar, terminates the church in an increasingly virtual way due to the interaction of the decreasing transparency of the glass shell as it approaches the altar. The concrete floor of the church changes in a similar way, from a rough surface to a smooth, reflecting surface. A metaphysical space is thus created through the overall effect of the flow of materials at the border of the altar. In contrast, the pulpit on the opposite side, installed like an object and, with its opposing material atmosphere, almost has an effect that is as massive and earthly as the entrance gate, which is as high as the building. This gate, which stylizes the entire front into a welcoming gesture, synonymous to the gate behind the altar, can be fixed in different positions, depending on the season and the celebration. In one case, the outside shell closes off the church space acoustically and thermally. In another, the anteroom and church square unite into a single common space. The bell tower repeats the motif of the material layering and condensation with the help of metal grid web. (Competition, 1st prize)

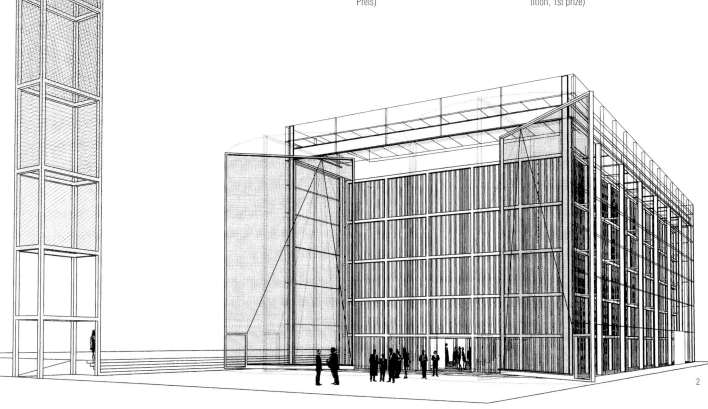

2

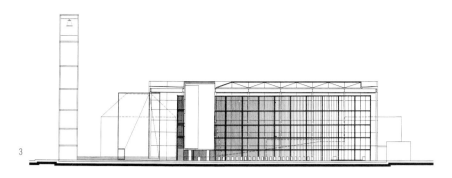

3

1. Lageplan.
   Site plan.
2. Perspektive.
   Perspective.
3. Längsschnitt.
   Longitudinal section.
4. Erdgeschoß.
   First floor.
5. Modell.
   Model.

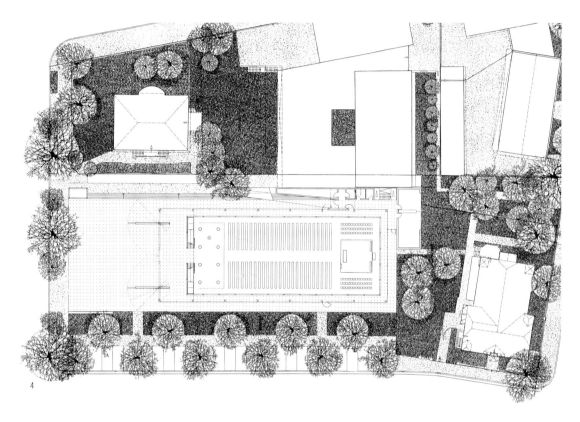

4

5

35

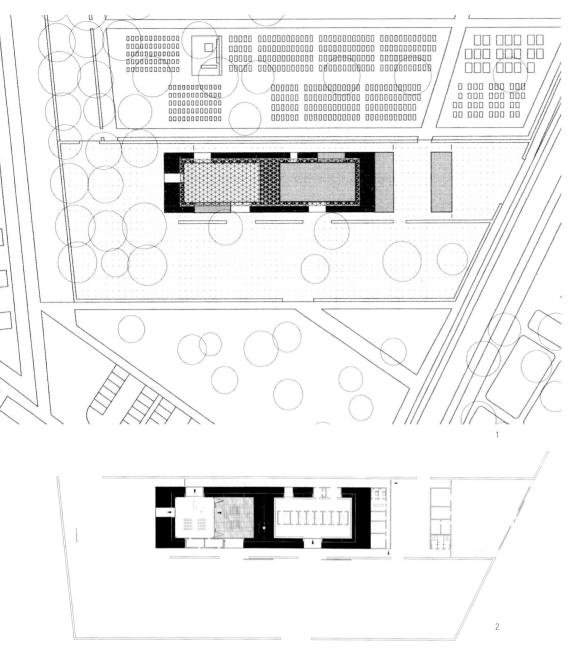

1

2

Aussegnungs- und Aufbahrungshalle Friedhof München Riem 1997

Die Gebäude entwickeln sich analog zum landschaftsplanerischen Konzept. Der Übergang zwischen den Baumreihen und den Gräbern ist kontinuierlich und stufenlos. Stufenloses Ineinanderübergleiten, die schlüssige Metapher für permanenten Wandel und für den dialektischen Zusammenhang zwischen Leben und Tod, wird auch in der Ausformung der beiden Friedhofsbauten zum Ausdruck gebracht. Ein Kokon aus patiniertem Kupferdrahtgewebe, das seine Dichte im Verlauf des Gebäudes variiert, schließt Aussegnungshalle und Aufbahrungshalle zusammen. Die Leichenhalle liegt als massives Sichtbetonvolumen unter einem weitmaschigen Kokon, die Gebäudegrenzen verlieren so in wechselnden Schattenwürfen ihre klaren Konturen. Im Bereich der gläsernen Aussegnungshalle wird die äußere Hülle dagegen dichter angelegt, als Sichtschutz und Sonnenschutz läßt sie nur gefiltertes Tageslicht passieren. Der gleiche Schleier überzieht den witterungsgeschützten Vorplatz, der mit der Aussegnungshalle durch eine faltbare Fassade verbunden werden kann. Ein Wasserbecken, das beide Gebäude umschließt und den Weg der Toten von dem der Lebenden trennt, unterstreicht als zusätzliche imaginäre Hülle den kontemplativen Charakter dieser Architektur. (Wettbewerb, 3. Preis)

Benediction Hall and Mortuary Munich Riem Cemetery 1997

The buildings are developed analogously with the landscaping concept. The transition between the rows of trees and the graves is continuous and smooth. This smooth transition, the logical metaphor for the constant change and the dialectic connection between life and death, is also expressed in the shape of the two cemetery buildings. A cocoon of stained copper wire webbing, which changes in density as it traverses the length of the building, connects the benediction hall and mortuary. The mortuary is placed beneath a cocoon having a wide grid size as a massive, fair-faced concrete volume. The borders of the building thus loose their clear outlines in the continuously changing cast shadows. In the area of the glassed-in benediction hall, the outer shell becomes more dense and, in its function of providing privacy and, protection from the sun, it allows only filtered daylight to pass through. The same veil covers the weather-protected forecourt, which can be connected with the benediction hall via a foldable facade. A water basin encircling both buildings and separating the path of the dead from that of the living enhances, like an imaginary shell, the contemplative character of this architecture. (Competition, 3rd prize)

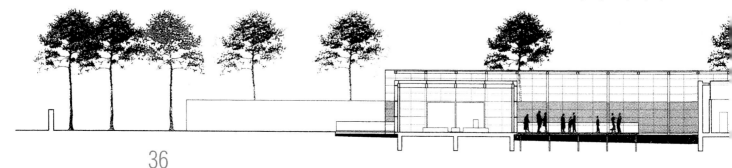

3

1. Lageplan.
   Site plan.
2. Grundriß.
   Ground plan.
3. Modell.
   Model.
4. Längsschnitt.
   Longitudinal section.

4

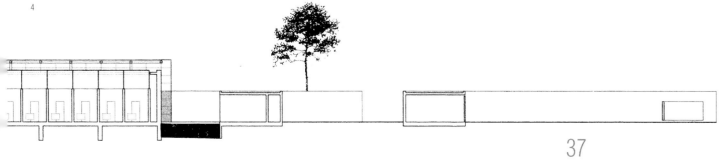

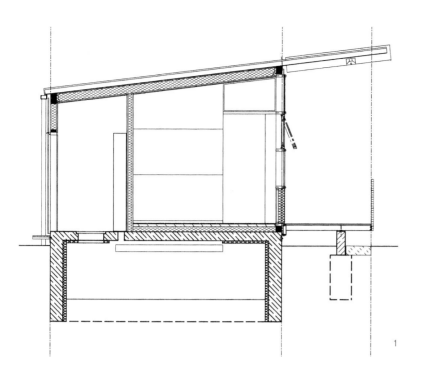

1

Wertstoffhof München Lerchenau 1995–1997

Im Zuge einer Reform der früheren Sperr-müll-Sammelstellen errichtet die Stadt München seit mehreren Jahren Wertstoffhöfe. Als integraler Bestandteil einer neuen Kultur des Sammelns, Trennens und Verwertens dokumentieren diese Anlagen den Begriffswandel vom «Müll» zum «Wertstoff». In den bevorzugten städtischen Randlagen bzw. Industriegebieten bleibt die Einbindung in einen übergreifenden baulichen Kontext regelmäßig unmöglich. Darin liegt die Chance, einen eigenständigen Typus mit hoher Wiedererkennbarkeit zu entwickeln. Vier schmale Einzelbauten gleicher Traufhöhe in einem begrünten Passepartout markieren die Seiten einer rechtwinkligen Fläche, die alle Gebäude doppelt erschließt – innen wie außen. Zentrales Element des so gebildeten Hofes ist eine überzogen pittoreske Bauminsel mit hochstämmigen Kiefern, die den rauhen, industriellen Charakter der Anlage im Sinne der Wertstoff-Philosophie kontrastierend bzw. zielführend in Zweifel zieht. Die in ihrem Volumen ähnlichen Gebäude unterscheiden sich je nach Funktion in ihrer ökonomischen Bauweise: ein Holzständerbau mit Glasfassade für das Personalgebäude, eine Stahlhalle mit Profilglasfassade und Wellblech-Vorhang für das Lager, eine Betonkonstruktion mit Stahltoren für den Problemmüll. Die Wertstoff-Container in den Zwischenräumen werden dreiseitig mit Gitterrosten umhüllt und durch ein Blechdach geschützt. Korrespondierend zum grellen Orange der Container setzt die Farbgebung der Gebäude neben der reinen Materialaussage punktuell auf die Signalwirkung von Leuchtfarben.

Recycling Center Munich Lerchenau 1995–1997

In the course of a reform of the former bulky refuse centers, the city of Munich has been establishing recycling centers for the past couple of years. An integral component of the new culture of collecting, separating and recycling, these centers document the change in paradigm from "waste" to "recyclable material". In the preferred peripheral urban locations or industrial areas, the integration into an encompassing architectural context is ordinarily impossible. This, however, offers the possibility to design an independent type with a high-recognition value. Four narrow buildings, with identical eave heights and established as a passe-partout, limit the sides of a rectangular surface that provides double access to all buildings – inside and outside. The central element of the yard formed in this way is an exaggerated, picturesque island of trees with tall pines which, in the sense of recycling philosophy, raise doubts about the rough industrial character of the complex in a contrasting and targeted way. Depending on function, the buildings differ in their economical design, though they are all similar in volume: for the staff, a post-and-beam structure with a glass facade; a steel hall with profiled glass facade and a hung corrugated metal sheet facade for storage; a concrete structure with steel gates for problem waste. The recycling containers in between them are surrounded on three sides by metal grids and protected by a sheet metal roof. Corresponding to the bright orange color of the containers, the buildings' coloration, aside from the visual appearance of the different materials, includes the signaling effect of bright neon colors.

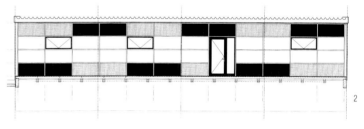

2

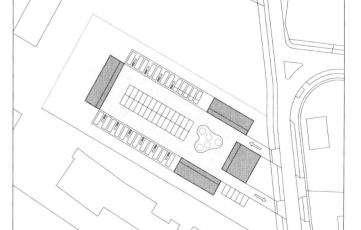

3

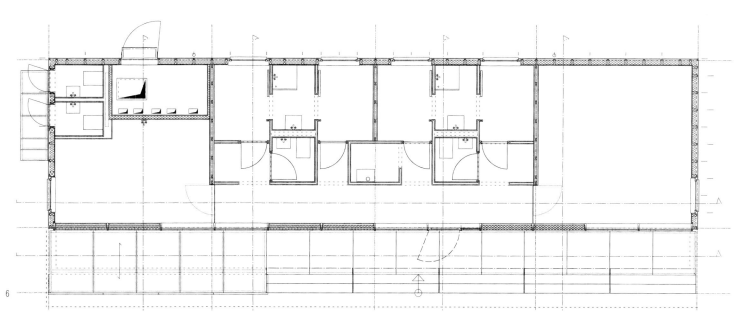

Georg Augustin
Ute Frank

Engagierte Formationen

Ute Frank und Georg Augustin stellen soziale Leitbilder in den Mittelpunkt ihrer Arbeit, verstärken dieses gesellschaftspolitische Engagement darüber hinaus aber in überzeugenden architektonischen Gesten und städtebaulichen Formationen. Anknüpfend an die Berliner Erfahrungen der behutsamen Stadterneuerung und der sozialen Partizipation entspricht diese Architektur in idealer Weise sehr unterschiedlichen Anforderungen: auf Langfristigkeit ausgelegte, ökonomische moderne Bauweisen, stadt- und sozialräumliche Qualitäten, urbane Durchmischung der Funktionen, Integration von Sonderwohnformen für Alte, Behinderte und Kranke, aber auch – und nicht zuletzt – eine ausdrucksvolle moderne Architektursprache, die sich nicht darin erschöpft, das innere Funktionsgefüge nachzuzeichnen. Diese architektonische Offensive der sozialen Verpflichtung des Bauens vermittelt in gewisser Weise zwischen dem sozialen Rationalismus des jungen Aldo Rossi (1931–1997) und der partizipatorischen Architektursprache von Ralph Erskine (*1914). Der Bezugspunkt liegt damit in beiden Fällen im Zeitraum 1968/69 bzw. in den 70er Jahren, wenn man auf die Realisierung von Rossis Gallaratese und Erskines Byker Wall abhebt. 1982 wagte Julius Posener anläßlich der Verleihung der Ehrendoktorwürde der Universität Hannover die Perspektive: «Der Weg führt zu Ralph Erskine». Seine Prognose schien sich jedoch mit dem Aufbruch von Postmoderne, High-Tech, Dekonstruktivismus, Neo-Rationalismus, Minimalismus und einigen anderen formalen Ausprägungen keineswegs zu bewahrheiten. Und dennoch wurde mit dem weniger spektakulären Weg des Teils der Berliner IBA, für den Hardt-Waltherr Hämer verantwortlich zeichnete, in den 70er und 80er Jahren durch die intensive und kontinuierliche Beschäftigung mit der Altbausubstanz eine Brücke geschlagen, die heute zu neuen Lösungen des Wohnungsbaus auf der Basis der am Bewohner, nicht an der Utopie orientierten Arbeit von Ralph Erskine führt. Den schlüssigen Beleg für diese Argumentation liefert der zwei Wohnblöcke umfassende soziale Wohnungsbau in Berlin Lichtenberg. Mit einer aus den Dimensionen der umgebenden Plattenbausiedlung resultierenden Steigerung auf acht Geschosse wird aus städtebaulichen Gründen selbst die abschirmende Geste des Byker Wall neu in Szene gesetzt. Die Architektur selbst ist geradliniger, weniger populistisch und regionalistisch, deutlich weniger traditionell, ornamental und malerisch. Es gibt die Farbigkeit und den Abwechslungsreichtum des Byker Wall: changierende Blautöne auf den geputzten Wänden der Obergeschosse, Holz im Wechselspiel mit Sichtbetonfertigteilen, als verfahrbare Sonnenschutzlamellen vor den Loggien und im Innenbereich der Loggien, aber trotz einer Vielfalt von 60 Grundrißvarianten spielt die Architektur nicht Dorf, eine Oase, sondern thematisiert die Stadt – auch im Motiv einer zweigeschossigen Sockelzone, die nicht wie bei Rossi als Leerraum reine Kunst bleibt, sondern dem Wohnen dient. Die Architekten hatten nicht schon unmittelbar nach dem Hochschulabschluß das eigene Büro im Visier, ihren ersten Bauten sieht man diese Lebens-Erfahrung und Detail-Kenntnis an. Ihre Formensprache ist selbstverständlich genug, um nicht reine Kunst zu sein, aber auch ungewöhnlich genug, um den Alltag des Wohnens nicht in akademischem Funktionalismus, nicht durch das Gesetz der Serie zu fesseln.

Engaged Formations

Ute Frank and Georg Augustin place social models at the center of their work; however, they enhance this socio-political engagement with their convincing architectural gestures and urban formations. Connecting with the careful urban renewal and social participation of the Berlin experience, this architecture ideally conforms with very differing requirements: modern economic ways of building, designed for long-term use, urban and social spatial qualities, urban blend of functions, integration of special living forms for the aged, the handicapped and for those with debilitating disease but also – and not least – an expressive modern architectural language that doesn't exhaust itself in redrawing the inner functional organization. This architectural offensive of the social responsibility of architecture mediates, in a certain way, between the social rationalism of young Aldo Rossi (1931–1997) and the participatory architectural language of Ralph Erskine (*1914). In both cases, the point of reference is the time frame of 1968/69, and of the '70s if the focus is placed on the realization of Rossi's Gallaratese and Erskine's Byker Wall. In 1982 Julius Posener, on the occasion of receiving an honorable doctorate from Hanover University, ventured to express this perspective: "The way leads toward Ralph Erskine." With the dawn of Postmodernism, High-Tech, Deconstructivism, Neo-Rationalism, Minimalism and a couple of other formal forms, his prognosis, however, proved to be not at all correct. And yet a gap was bridged with the less spectacular path that the section within the Berlin IBA followed under the guidance of Hardt-Waltherr Hämer during the long period between 1975 and 1990 through the intense and continuous occupation with the old building substance; today, this bridge has led to new solutions for apartment architecture on the basis of Ralph Erskine's work, which is oriented towards the inhabitants rather than towards utopia. The conclusive proof for this debate is supplied by the two apartment blocks of the comprehensive social housing project in Berlin Lichtenberg. With an increase in height to eight stories conforming to the dimensions of the surrounding slab construction development, even the shielding gesture of the Byker Wall is, on an urban basis, placed in a new light. The architecture itself is more straight-forward, less populist and regionalistic and, clearly, less traditional, ornamental and painterly. The coloration and rich variety of the Byker Wall are there: changing shades of blue on the plastered walls of the upper stories, wood interacting with fair-faced concrete panels, movable sun shade louvers in front of and inside the loggias. But despite the great variety of 60 ground plan versions, the architecture does not pretend to be a village, nor an oasis, but it makes the city the theme – this is also true in the two-story base zone motif, which, contrary to Rossi, does not remain pure art as a empty space but serves actual living purposes. The architects did not aim to establish their own office right after completing their diplomas, and their first buildings clearly communicate this life-experience and a profound knowledge of details. Their formal language is self-understood enough not to be pure art, but it is also unusual enough to refrain from handcuffing the every-day-living with an academic functionalism or the law of the series.

Aufstockung Haus Scherer Berlin Grunewald 1992–1993/98

Bei ihrer Aufstockung der vor 25 Jahren im Grunewald errichteten Doppelhaushälfte erkennen die Architekten erst das Erscheinungsbild nach Patinierung der offenen Holzschalung aus unbehandeltem Robinienholz als endgültig an – fünf Jahre nach Abschluß der Bauarbeiten. Denn gestalterisch bestand das Ziel der Materialwahl darin, den neuen Aufbau von der kubisch verschachtelten Moderne der 70er Jahre im Material zwar abzusetzen, aber nicht in Patinierung und Farbton. Dieser Zustand ist jetzt erreicht. Die leichte Fassadenhaut der wiederum leichten Konstruktion auf dem Dach hat sich dem schweren Backsteinkleid farblich sehr gut angeglichen. Beide Materialien werden nun mit Anstand und von identischer Startlinie aus gemeinsam altern. Die Bauaufgabe war

aus der Not der neu eingezogenen Bauherren entstanden, unter sehr hohen alten Bäumen wenigstens mit ihren beiden Arbeitszimmern zur Sonne vorzustoßen. Konstruktiv erwies sich der Bestand als so ausgefuchst kalkuliert, daß die Aufstockung ein eigenes Tragwerk benötigte – von einer Ringkonstruktion aus durch alle Etagen: unsichtbar. Ein Endoskop und die Kanäle einer Warmluftheizung spielten dabei keine geringe Rolle. Auf dem begehbaren obersten Dach sorgen Röhrenkollektoren einerseits für die Verschattung der Dachhaut, andererseits für das Aufheizen des verschatteten Gartenpools im Sommer. Viel Aufwand für zwei Räume, aber gewonnen hat das ganze Gebäude. Nicht zuletzt durch ein paar gehobelte Bretter und ein paar Fallarmmarkisen. Ein in der Fassade verborgener Abstellraum und ein in die Brüstung einzuhängendes Tablett sorgen für fröhliche Feste auf dem Dach unter Bäumen.

Heightening Scherer House Berlin Grunewald 1992–1993/98

In the case of the heightening of the semi-detached house built 25 years ago in Grunewald, the architects considered the exterior appearance of the building to be finished only after the raw, untreated Robinia wood formwork was finally stained – five years after the construction work had been completed. In terms of design, the choice of materials had the goal of clearly distinguishing the new structure from the '70s cubist modernism; however, it was felt that this should not apply to the structure and color. Now this condition has been realized. The light facade shell of the lightweight construction on the roof has adapted very well to the heavy brickwork skirt. Both materials will now age with dignity, starting at a common point. The building had arisen from the needs of the clients, who had just moved

into the house. They wanted their offices to rise above the tall, old trees and glimpse the sun. Constructively, the existing structure turned out to be so precisely engineered that the heightening required a new supporting structure – invisibly taking a ring structure through all levels. An endoscope and the channels of a hot air heating system played a rather important part in this. Atop the roof (which can be walked on), tube collectors provide, on the one hand, the indispensable protection from the sun. On the other hand, during the summer they provide heat for the pool in the shady garden. This may seem like a rather large undertaking for the sake of two additional rooms, but the whole house has gained from it, not least because of a few planed wooden planks and a couple of retractable awnings. A storage space hidden in the facade and a shelf that can be attached to the parapet guarantee happy parties on top of the roof beneath the trees.

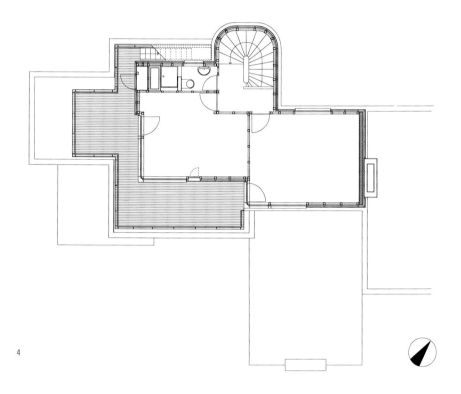

4

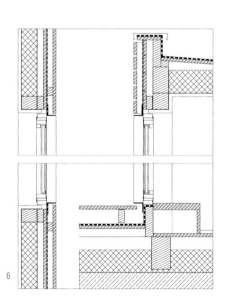

6

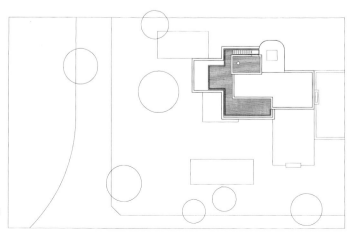

5

1. Straßenfront.
   Street facade.
2. Dachterrasse am Arbeitszimmer.
   Roof terrace adjoining the office.
3. Aufstockung von Osten.
   Heightening seen from the east.
4. Grundriß Aufstockung.
   Ground plan heightening.
5. Lageplan.
   Site plan.
6. Fassadendetail.
   Detail facade.

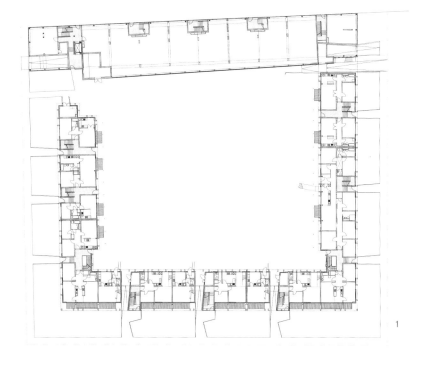

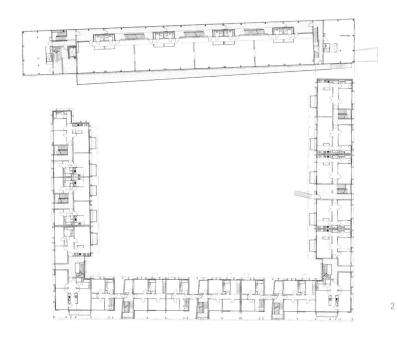

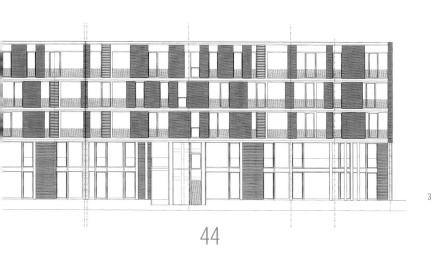

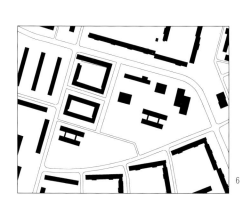

7

Sozialer Wohnungsbau mit Ladenzeile und Büros Berlin Lichtenberg 1992–1997

Die brachgefallene Fläche eines ehemaligen Bauhofs stellt heute im Rahmen einer geplanten «Infrastrukturinsel» die einzige größere Nachverdichtungsmaßnahme in einer bestehenden Berliner Plattenbausiedlung aus DDR-Zeiten dar. In der weiteren Umgebung zeigt das Wohngebiet Friedrichsfelde Süd in einzigartiger Weise die wesentlichen städtebaulichen und gebäudetypologischen Entwicklungsschritte vom Beginn der 50er Jahre bis heute, in einem vielschichtigen außenräumlichen Netz verwoben. Im Nebeneinander verschiedener Baualter und Gebäudetypen mit der vielfältigen Vegetation einer ehemaligen Gartenkolonie wird ein Spannungsverhältnis von Dichte und Weite, Klein- und Großräumigkeit erreicht, das der vorhandene indifferente Wohnungsbestand im Detail nicht realisieren konnte. Dennoch wird der Dialog mit den Plattenbauten aufrechterhalten und äußert sich bei der nordorientierten urbanen Straßenrandbebauung in der gefalteten Glashaut der Laubengangwohnungen eines achtgeschossigen Brückenkopfes sogar in der Übernahme formaler Details. Die blockartigen Zusammenschlüsse, wegen des hohen Grundwasserpegels mit einem Hochparterre ausgestattet, bilden zwei Innenhöfe, die über zweigeschossige Durchgänge in einem filigranen zweigeschossigen Sockel zugänglich bleiben. In dieser den Straßenraum prägenden, sehr lebendigen Sockelzone sind Wohnungszugänge, Badezimmerfenster und Abstellräume hinter einer horizontalen Verschalung aus unbehandeltem Robinienholz verborgen. Die in drei verschiedenen Blautönen ihren unterschiedlichen Lichtverhältnissen angepaßten massiven Obergeschosse darüber geben wie ihre Nachbarn ihre innere Organisation auch dann nicht preis, wenn es sich innerhalb von 60 Varianten und verschiedenen Sonderwohnformen einmal um grundrißgleiche Typen handeln sollte. (Wettbewerb, 1. Preis)

Social Housing with Stores and Offices Berlin Lichtenberg 1992–1997

The fallow area of an erstwhile farm represents the only larger condensation measure within the framework of a planned "infrastructure-island" within the confines of an existing Berlin slab construction development dating from the old GDR. Nearby, the housing quarter Friedrichsfelde South uniquely reveals the essential urban and architectural typological stages of the development – from the early '50s up to the present – interwoven in a diverse spatial network. The juxtaposition of different architectural periods and building types, combined with the diversity of vegetation of a former garden colony, creates a suspense of density and broadness, of small and large spatial sections, that could not be fully realized in detail by the existing indifferent structures. And yet, the dialog with the slab constructions is maintained and is expressed in the urban roadside development oriented towards the north, and even in the adaptation of formal details in the folded glass shell of the balcony-access apartments in an eight-story bridgehead. The block-like joints, designed with an elevated first floor level due to the high groundwater level, form two courtyards that remain accessible via two-story passageways in a filigree two-story base. In this lively zone that determines the street space, apartment accesses, bathroom windows, and storage spaces are hidden behind horizontally-mounted, untreated Robinia wood panels. The massive upper stories, adapted to the various light conditions through the use of three different shades of blue, also don't reveal their interior organization, despite the fact that at one point the layouts were similar for all 60 versions and various special apartment types. (Competition, 1st prize)

8

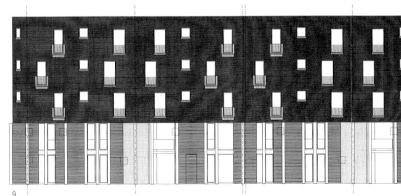

9

1. Grundriß Erdgeschoß.
   Ground plan first floor.
2. Grundriß 1.Obergeschoß.
   Ground plan second floor.
3. Straßenfront nach Süden.
   Street facade facing south.
4. Laubengang.
   Gallery access.
5. Sockelzone.
   Base.
6. Lageplan.
   Site plan.
7. Ladenzeile, Büros und Laubengangwohnungen.
   Stores, offices and gallery access apartments.
8. Sraßenfront mit Loggien von Westen.
   Street facade with loggias seen from the west.
9. Gartenfront nach Norden.
   Garden facade facing north.

1

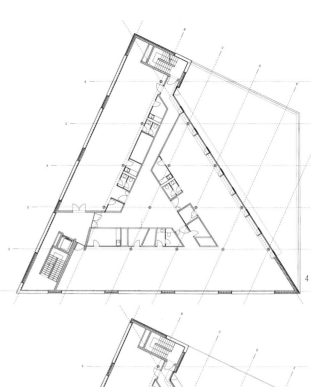

4

2

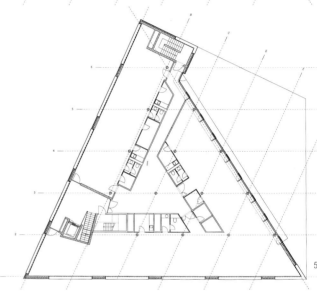

5

3

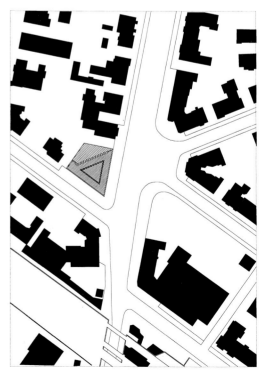

6

Büro- und Geschäftshaus Berlin Karlshorst 1995–1998

Karlshorst ist geprägt durch eine homogene Baustruktur nach der zur Zeit seiner Erschließung geltendenden Vorort-Bauordnung. Der Bereich nördlich der Bahn, rund um den Bahnhof, hat mit den hier angesiedelten zentralen Funktionen im Gegensatz zur villenartigen Bebauung im Süden städtischen Charakter. Im Zuge der weiteren Verdichtung dieses örtlichen Zentrums wird das vorhandene Gleichmaß der Dichte nicht erhalten bleiben können, die spezifische offene Bauweise in Doppeleinheiten mit markanten Ecksituationen an Straßeneinmündungen soll das Ortsbild jedoch weiterhin bestimmen. Im Vorgriff auf die geplante städtebauliche Entwicklung realisiert der Neubau bereits eine über das noch ortsübliche Maß hinausgehende bauliche Dichte, fügt sich aber mit den typischen Doppelhauslängen (35 bis 40 m) in die vorgegebene Struktur ein. Der 5 m tiefe «Vorgarten» wird nach üblicher Praxis zur Ausdehnung kleinteiliger Ladenstrukturen in den Straßenraum genutzt. In anderen Dimensionen des Solitärs praktizieren die Architekten Einordnung in einem exakten Maßstabssprung durch Verdopplung. Der an der Straßenecke spitz zulaufende Bau zeigt seiner Nutzung folgend in den Obergeschossen gleichförmige langformatige Fensterfelder, die als Kastenfenster konzipiert sind, spielt jedoch nach festen Regeln mit deren Anordnung und Zwischenräumen. Das System verdeutlicht eine betongraue Sandstein-Fassade in nur scheinbar wildem Verband. Die traditionelle Fassaden-Ordnung der benachbarten Altbauten wird damit in eine dynamische überführt. Die vor einer Terrasse zurückspringenden Obergeschosse der Gartenseite sind bodentief verglast.

Office and Commercial Building Berlin Karlshorst 1995–1998

Karlshorst is marked by a homogeneous building structure according to the local building regulations applicable at the time of its development. The area north of the railroad, around the station with its central utilities, has an urban character that stands in stark contrast to the villa-like structures to the south. At the occasion of the condensation of this local center, the existing balance in the density could not be maintained. However, the specific open building style of the double-units, with striking corner situations at the intersections, continues to determine the local image. The new structure, preceding the planned urban development, already realizes an architectural density exceeding the current local scale, but it is integrated into the given structure with the typical double-unit length (35 to 40 meters). The front garden is 5 meters deep and, following the traditional practice, functions as an extension of the small shop structures into the street space. In other dimensions of the solitary structure, the architects practice integration into the environment with an exact 1:2 ratio. The building assumes a pointed form towards the street corner and, according to its utilization, shows equally shaped, long window surfaces on the upper floors, conceived as box windows. However, following established rules, it plays with their organization and with the interstitial spaces. The system clarifies a concrete gray limestone facade in a seemingly wild pattern. The traditional facade order of the adjoining old structures is thus transformed into a dynamic one. The upper floors on the garden side are set back from a terrace and have floor-to-ceiling glass facades.

7

1. Gardenfront.
   Yard facade.
2, 3, 7. Straßenfront.
   Street facade.
4. 2.Obergeschoß.
   Third floor.
5. 4.Obergeschoß.
   Fifth floor.
6. Lageplan.
   Site plan.
8. Ansicht Straßenfront.
   Elevation street facade.
9. Ansicht Gartenseite.
   Elevation garden side.

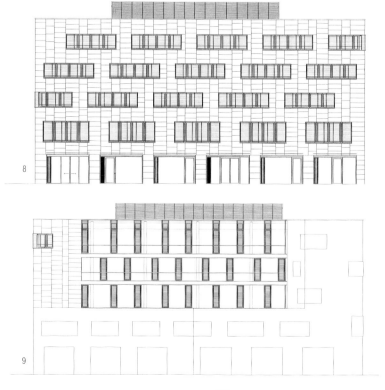

8

9

Kindertagesstätte Berlin Spandau
1996–1998

Eingepaßt in die städtebauliche Struktur des neuen Wohngebiets entwickelt sich die Kindertagesstätte, Bestandteil eines städtebaulichen Vertrags zwischen Stadt und Investor, auf kleinem Grundstück als langgestreckter dreigeschossiger Kubus. Im Hinblick auf die passive Nutzung der Sonnenenergie und um die erhebliche Länge der Gebäudefront ohne Verluste für den knappen Freiraum formal zu gliedern, werden die nach Vormittags- und Nachmittagsbetrieb unterschiedenen Funktionen von Kindergarten und Hort entsprechend ihrer bevorzugten Orientierung gegenläufig angeordnet. Der nördlich an die Eingangshalle anschließende Gebäudeteil öffnet sich nach Westen, sein Pendant auf der anderen Seite dagegen unter gegenläufigem Pultdach nach Osten. So stoßen auf beiden Langseiten unvermittelt zwei sehr konträre Fassaden aufeinander, die die Gruppenräume von den Nebenräumen funktional wie formal absetzen. Je zwei Gruppenräume, zu einer pädagogischen Einheit gekoppelt, befinden sich im Drittelspunkt des Gebäudes. Die verbleibenden Flächen dienen an den Kopfenden als Nebenräume, im Zentrum als Erschließungshalle. In Erd- und Dachgeschoß variieren Küche, Büro und Mehrzweckraum dieses einfache Grundschema. Die Flure weiten sich perspektivisch und ihrer Nutzerfrequenz folgend zur Halle. Dieser Vorgabe entsprechend wurden Treppe, Aufzug und Windfang spielerisch verdreht. In den offenen Fassadenfeldern (Holzfenster, Holzpaneele) werden die Dach- und Deckenvorsprünge jeweils durch zwei gegenläufig-schräge Stahlstützen abgefangen. Die an der östlichen Grundstücksgrenze notwendige Stützmauer wurde mit einfachen Mitteln zum Spielhaus ergänzt. (Wettbewerb, 1. Preis)

Day Care Center Berlin Spandau
1996–1998

The day-care-center is integrated into the urban structure of the new quarter and is a component of the urban contract between the city and the investor. It is developed on a small property as a long, three-story cuboid. Considering the passive use of solar energy, and in order to formally structure the considerable length of the building's front without any loss of the scarce space around it, the various kindergarten and day-care functions and activities that take place during the mornings and afternoons are positioned according to the different times of the utilization of the spaces. The part of the building adjoining the north side of the entrance lobby opens up towards the west; its counterpart on the other side opens towards the east beneath an opposing shed roof. On both long sides, two very dissimilar facades suddenly confront one another, setting off the group rooms from the side rooms both functionally and formally. Two group rooms on each floor, coupled into pedagogical units, are located in the third point of the building. The remaining spaces serve as side rooms at the head ends and, in the center, as an access lobby. On the first and upper floors, a kitchen, office and multi-purpose room vary this simple layout. The hallways, according to their frequency of use, expand their perspective as they approach the lobby. The stairs, elevator and foyer were playfully woven following these conditions. The roof and ceiling projections are held by two opposing, slanted steel supports in the open facade fields (wooden windows and panels). The necessary supporting wall on the eastern property border was turned into a playhouse through simple means. (Competition, 1st prize)

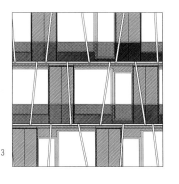

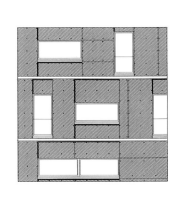

3

8

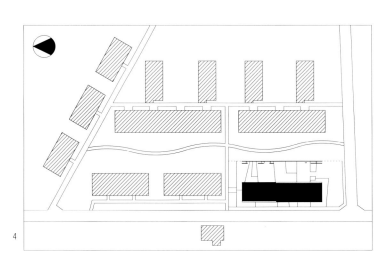

4

9

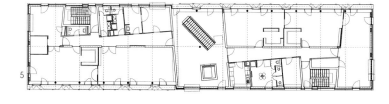

5

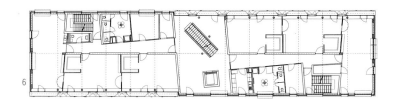

6

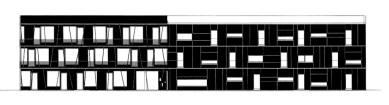

7

1. Straßenfront.
   Street facade.
2. Arbeitsmodell.
   Model.
3, 9. Fassadenausschnitte.
   Facade openings.
4. Lageplan.
   Site plan.
5, 6. Dachgeschoß und
   1.Obergeschoß.
   *Roof floor and second
   floor.*
7. Ansicht Straßenseite.
   Elevation street side.
8. Treppenhalle.
   Stairway hall.

Landesvertretung Rheinland-Pfalz Berlin Tiergarten 1997

Im Übergang der Friedrichstadt zum Tiergarten, auf dem Areal der ehemaligen «Ministergärten», errichten die Bundesländer Niedersachsen, Rheinland-Pfalz, Saarland und Schleswig-Holstein ihre Landesvertretungen in enger Kooperation und Nachbarschaft (gemeinsame Tiefgarage). Die Vertretung von Rheinland-Pfalz sollte ausdrücklich die besondere Offenheit des Landes zum Ausdruck bringen. Daß dem siegreichen Entwurf laut Jury ausgerechnet «jener Esprit fehlt, der dem Gebäude auch weit über die Jahrtausendwende hinaus eine zukunftsweisende Selbstdarstellung ermöglicht», stellt nicht weniger als das gesamte Wettbewerbswesen in Frage. Der fünfte Preis präsentiert baukörperlich einen einfachen fünfgeschossigen Kubus, der sich auf besonders komplexe Art und Weise auf allen fünf Fassaden öffnet –

dank Atrium auch im Dach. Die Südfassade der Eingangsfront, wie die Nordseite völlig in Glas aufgelöst, erhält nach dem Prinzip Kastenfenster eine zweite Schicht aus Glaslamellen. Der damit gewonnene Wintergarten wird in den Obergeschossen zu einer Orangerie für Rebstöcke. Die Längswände im Bauwich sind zwar weitgehend geschlossen, bilden aber hinter ihrer offenen Holzschalung den über drei Geschosse reichenden Innenhof deutlich ab. Organisatorisch entwickelt sich das im Zentrum über Dach belichtete Foyer wie eine Passage über zwei Ebenen und eröffnet einen weiten Ausblick in den Garten. Oberhalb der Repräsentationsräume gruppieren sich die Verwaltungs-, Gäste- und Wohnbereiche, durch luftige Verbindungsstege kurzgeschlossen, um ein als Gartenhof genutztes Atrium und öffnen sich nach außen wie nach innen. (Wettbewerb, 5. Preis)

Representative Offices of Rhineland-Palatinate Berlin Tiergarten 1997

At the transition between Friedrichstadt and Tiergarten, on the grounds of the former "Ministers' Gardens", the states of Lower Saxony, Rhineland-Palatinate, the Saarland and Schleswig-Holstein, in close cooperation (a common underground park house was included), erected their Representative Offices. The offices of Rhineland-Palatinate were specifically designed to represent the distinct openness of this state. According to the jury, the awarded design "lacks that esprit that would allow the building to present itself in a path breaking way far into the next millenium." This statement would seem to question nothing less than all competitions. The fifth prize winner presented a simple, five-story cuboid that opens up on all five facades – the atrium in the roof, as well

– in an especially complex manner. The south face of the entrance structure is entirely glazed, as is the north facade, and receives a second layer of glass lamellae according to the box window principle. The resulting winter garden becomes an orangery for vines on the upper floors. The long walls facing the interstitial space between the two neighboring buildings are closed for the most part; however, behind their open wood shuttering they clearly reflect the inner courtyard reaching through three stories, lit in the center via the roof, develops like a gallery across two levels and opens up a wide view into the garden. The areas for administration, guests and apartments are grouped above the representational rooms around an atrium used as a garden yard and accessible via airy connecting bridges; they open towards both the outside and inside. (Competition, 5th prize)

1

2

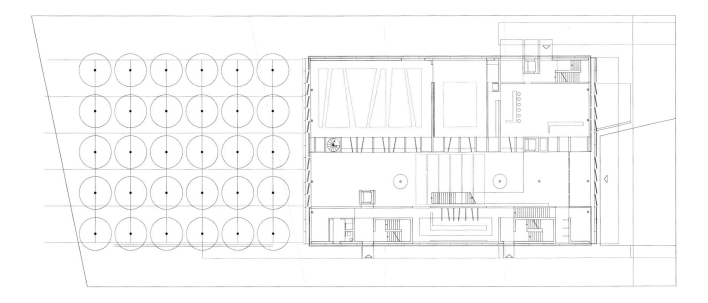

3

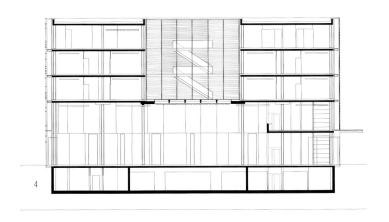

4

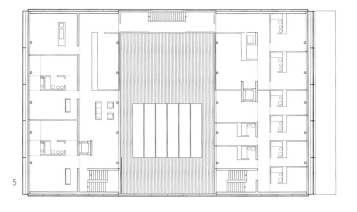

5

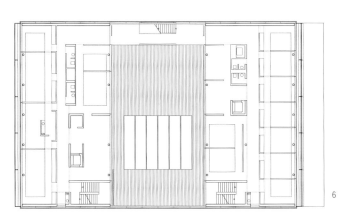

6

Konstruktive Raumgefüge

Jelena Bozic und Peter Cheret denken ihre Entwürfe konstruktiv und suchen nach einer «tragenden» Struktur im Sinne von Tragwerk aber auch Plattform oder Bühne, die der gestellten Aufgabe Raum und Spiel läßt, sich über viele Zwischenschritte zu ihrer architektonischen Lösung zu entwickeln. Spätere Nutzungswechsel müssen sich nicht gegen die Struktur des Hauses durchsetzen, sondern sie sind konstruktiv vorprogrammiert. Die Konstruktion formuliert die Spielregeln der Architektur, dominiert als Strukturform vielleicht sogar den Baukörper konstruktiv. Weitgespannte und dennoch sehr wirtschaftliche Dachkonstruktionen erlauben eine freie und flexible Positionierung von Zwischenwänden. Der Entwurf ist von Beginn an räumlich, bezieht alle Dimensionen ein. Entwerfen und Konstruieren beeinflussen sich simultan. Dazu kommt eine ausgeprägte Vorliebe für Holz als konstruktiven, aus ökologischen und ökonomischen Gründen aber auch symbolischen Werkstoff – bis hin zur Ausprägung und Gestaltung eines Kirchenraums samt Altar. Der inzwischen demontierte und eingelagerte Pavillon der Internationalen Gartenbauausstellung 1993 in Stuttgart besteht mit Blick auf das schmale Budget fast vollständig aus Furnierschichtholz, dessen spezifische Eigenschaften gleiche Oberflächen für Boden, Wand und Decke erlauben. Der große Reiz dieser Architektur liegt darin, daß sie konstruktiv anschaulich und selbsterklärend ist. Die Materialwahl reduziert sich auf Holz und Glas, Konstruktion und Finish sind identisch. Man fragt sich unwillkürlich, warum dieser konstruktive Sachverstand noch nicht mit großer architektonischer Wirkung die Produktion von Fertighäusern bestimmt, die erst mit diesem einfachen Instrumentarium tatsächlich als solche zu bezeichnen wären. Doch die Antwort liegt auf der Hand: Erstens sollen Fertighäuser nicht aussehen wie Fertighäuser bzw. industrielle Fabelwesen, und zweitens sollen sie schon gar nicht billig sein. Gerade auf diesem Gebiet, der architektonisch veredelten «Armut», liegt aber eine Stärke dieser Architektur. Sturmholz findet darin ebenso seinen Platz wie nach Katalog abrufbare Telegraphenmasten, Lärmschutzwände und Nagelplattenbinder. Der traditionelle Baustoff Holz wird dabei für eine Moderne herangezogen, die nur in Skandinavien und den USA ohne Voreingenommenheit gegenüber der Tradition von Material und Konstruktion möglich war. Auf dieser Ebene haben Charles Moore (1925–1993), Robert Venturi (*1925) oder Charles Gwathmey (*1938) und Robert Siegel (1939) in Deutschland, auch aufgrund anderer Bauvorschriften, erst in jüngster Zeit Resonanz gefunden. Nicht nur pittoreske Mißverständnisse, auch die Angst «moderner» Architekten vor konventionellen Bauweisen und Bauformen bildeten in dieser Entwicklung des Holzbaus in Deutschland die Hindernisse. Architektonisch gehen die Architekten von traditionellen Typologien aus: beim Pavillon von der Orangerie, beim Gemeindezentrum in Heilbronn vom Kloster bzw. den westlichen Vorbereichen der frühchristlichen Basilika (Atrium, Peristyl, Aula, Narthex). Diese Bilder, die Erinnerungen wachrufen und im Fall der Kirche bei aller Sachlichkeit und Moderne der «Kuppel» als sakrale Würdeformen verstanden werden, dienen als typologische Interpretationsmuster, nicht als Stilvorlagen. Gerade der lange verkannte Werkstoff Holz erreicht damit eine Reduktion und Prägnanz der Form, die andere Baustoffe oft nur im Verbund mit anderen realisieren können.

Constructive spatial structures

Jelena Bozic and Peter Cheret "think" their designs constructively and are searching for a "supporting" structure, not only in the sense of a load-bearing structure but also in the sense of platform or stage, which leaves enough space and play to the presented task in order to develop into its architectural solution by way of many interstitial steps. Any later changes in utilization need not fight against the structure of the house, but are constructively pre-programmed. The construction formulates the rules of the architectural game, perhaps even to the point of dominating the building volume constructively as a structural form. Broadly expansive yet very economic roof constructions allow for a free and flexible positioning of separating walls. From the beginning, the design is spatial and includes all dimensions. Designing and constructing simultaneously influence one another. Additionally, there is a clear preference for wood as a constructive material not only for ecological and economical reasons but also for symbolic reasons – for example, the design of a church space and altar. The pavilion of the international garden exposition 1993 in Stuttgart – meanwhile dismantled and stored – consists almost completely of relatively inexpensive wood veneer due to the small budget; its specific properties provide the same surfaces for the floor, walls and ceiling. The great attractiveness of this architecture is that it is self-explanatory in a clear and constructive way. The choice of material is reduced to wood and glass; the construction and the finish are synonymous. The question instinctively rises: why doesn't this constructive understanding determine the production of prefabricated houses with a great architectural effect – certainly, the first buildings to utilize these simple instruments would really deserve the name prefabricated. But the answer lies close at hand: first, prefab houses are not supposed to look like prefab houses or industrial fairy tale beings, and second, they should certainly not be cheap. But it is exactly in this field where one of this architecture's strengths can be found: the architecturally ennobled "poverty." In it, all kinds of materials find a place: storm wood, telegraph poles that can be ordered by catalog, noise protection walls, steel mending plates. Wood, the traditional building material, is used for a Modernism that had been possible – without any prejudices against the tradition of material and construction – only in Scandinavia and the United States. On this level, Charles Moore (1925–1993), Robert Venturi (*1925) or Charles Gwathmey (*1938) and Robert Siegel (*1939) have only recently met with approval in Germany; this is also due, in part, to the changing building regulations in that country. The development of wood construction in Germany was hindered by picturesque misunderstandings and the fear of "modern" architects executing conventional building styles and forms. Architecturally, the architects presume traditional typologies: in the case of the pavilion, it was the orangerie, in the case of the community center in Heilbronn, the monastery or the western antechambers of the early Christian basilica (atrium, peristilium, aula, narthex). These images – evoking memories and, in the example of the church, despite all factuality and Modernism of the "cupola", understood as dignified sacred forms – serve as typological samples for interpretation and not as stylistic examples. The long ignored material, wood, thus reaches a reduction and poignancy of form that can be only realized by other materials when used in connection with one another.

Tragwerk, Kirchenraum
Gemeindezentrum
Heilbronn Sontheim
1994–1998.
*Supporting structure,
church space
community center
Heilbronn Sontheim
1994–1998.*

Peter Cheret
Jelena Bozic

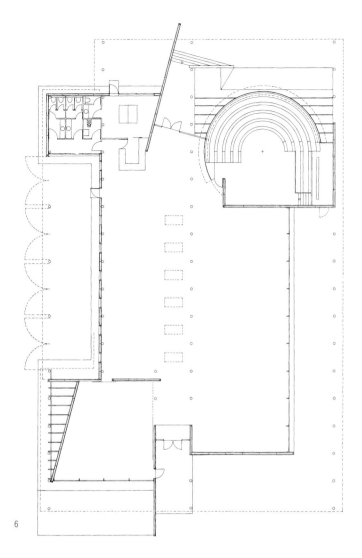

6

Deutsches Landwirtschaftsmuseum Stuttgart Hohenheim 1992–1994

Ein Haus, welches zweimal gebaut wurde. Während der Internationalen Gartenbauausstellung IGA 1993 diente dieselbe expressivelementare Konstruktion, durch eine dünne Glas-Membran und vorgelagerte Stützen eng mit ihrer Umgebung verzahnt, zunächst als Landespavillon von Baden-Württemberg. Danach wurde der 1.000 m² große Ausstellungs-Pavillon zerlegt und einige Kilometer entfernt auf dem Gelände der Universität Hohenheim wieder aufgebaut: zum Deutschen Landwirtschaftsmuseum. Der erste Standort, ein englischer Garten des 19. Jahrhunderts, war ebenso prägend für den Entwurf wie die bauphysikalisch konsequent als Temporärbau entwickelte Konstruktion. Dennoch wirkt der Bau nach seiner Translozierung, in ganz anderer Umgebung und Orientierung auf Dauer angelegt, ebenso ursprünglich und selbstverständlich. Wie bei einer großen, scheinbar offenen Remise, typologisch dem transitorischen Charakter des Pavillons/ Museums besonders nah, wird der Bau geprägt von seiner markanten Konstruktionsart. Der konstruktiven Ausdruckskraft gelingt es, alles Provisorische abzustreifen und Raum fundamental zu begründen. Die lange vergessene Mastenkonstruktion, bei der Rundhölzer (Telegraphenmasten aus Sturmholz) punktuell mit Beton im Boden verankert werden, entwickelt sich auf einem Achsmaß von 3 m. Rohe Nagelplattenbinder tragen Boden und Dach unverkleidet, stellen sich – ohne dekonstruktivistischen Mehraufwand – expressiv zur Schau, machen den Bau konstruktiv durchschaubar. Traditionelle Bauweisen, intelligent umgesetzt, transportieren die architektonische Idee ebenso raffiniert wie ökonomisch und nicht zuletzt ökologisch. (Wettbewerb, 1. Preis)

German Agricultural Museum Stuttgart Hohenheim 1992–1994

A house that was built twice. During the International Gardening Exhibition IGA in 1993, the same expressively elementary construction that is tightly linked with its environment through a thin glass membrane and columns first served as the pavilion representing the state of Baden-Württemberg. After that, the 1.000 m² exhibition pavilion was dismantled and later reassembled on the grounds of Hohenheim University a few kilometers away: there, it became the German Agricultural Museum. The first site, an English garden from the 19th century, was as decisive for the design as the engineering of the structure as a temporary building. And yet, even after its translocation to a totally different environment and orientation, the building still has an effect that is just as original and self-understood. The building is characterized by its striking construction method, typologically close to the transitory character of the pavilion/museum and somewhat like a large, open shed. The expressive constructive power manages to do away with all that is provisorical and to put space on a fundamental basis. The long forgotten mast construction, where round wood columns (telephone poles made of trees felled by storms) are anchored with concrete at regular points in the ground, develops on a unit spacing of 3 m. Raw plank frames support the floor and roof without any facing and present themselves expressively – without a deconstructivist "extra effort" – making the building's construction understandable. Traditional building methods realized in an intelligent way transport the architectural idea as cleverly as they do economically and, not least, ecologically. (Competition, 1st prize)

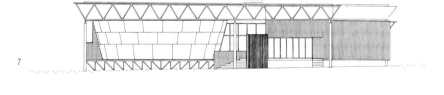

7

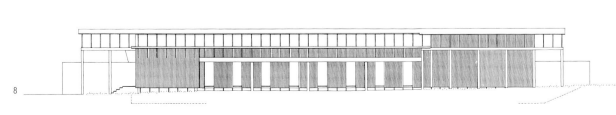

8

1. Ausstellungsbetrieb.
   Exhibition management.
2. Ausstellungsraum.
   Exhibition space.
3. Vortragsraum.
   Lecture room.
4. Blick von Osten.
   View from the east.
5. Anschluß der Glasfassade.
   Adjoining glass facade.
6. Grundriß.
   Ground plan.
7. Ansicht von Osten.
   East elevation.
8. Ansicht von Norden.
   North elevation.

Ausstellungspavillon Windkraftwerk Heroldstatt/Ulm 1994

Das Informationszentrum für erneuerbare Energien, das in der örtlichen Presse schnell als «Raum-Schiff» galt, soll auf einer Hochfläche der schwäbischen Alb am Fußpunkt einer Windkraftanlage in freier Landschaft entstehen. Aus dem rauhen Klima und dem in exponierter Lage nicht unerheblichen Windangriff ergab sich ein aerodynamischer Baukörper, der mit seinen äußeren Bedingungen ebenso symbolträchtig und expressiv spielt wie mit seiner internen Zweckbestimmung. Eine aus Polygonzügen gebildete windschnittige, spitz zulaufende Grundfigur dient im Erdgeschoß als in der Mitte geteilter Ausstellungs- und Vortragsraum. Im Zentrum des Geschehens entwickelt sich auf einem frei eingestellten Oberdeck ein zweites, zur umgreifenden Dachkonstruktion wiederum offenes Geschoß. Hier befinden sich, über eine Spindeltreppe vom Foyer aus erreichbar, weitere Ausstellungsflächen und ein offener oder auch abgeschirmter Konferenzbereich. Alle Nebenräume liegen im Untergeschoß. Der selbsttragende Raumabschluß, der ohne Unterscheidung von Wand und Dach einem Schiffsrumpf ähnlich aus hölzernen Spanten entsteht, formt eine sich nach oben verjüngende, kuppelartige Halle. Die Spanten werden aus etwa 10 cm starkem Furnierschichtholz geschnitten. Die lamellenartig aufgebaute Außenhaut besteht in den Dachflächen aus patiniertem Kupferblech, in den Fassadenflächen aus Glaselementen. Dem technischen Fortschritt wie ökologischen Materialien und Bauweisen verpflichtet, findet die Architektur ein positives Bild für den ökologisch sinnvollen Einsatz von Windkraftanlagen.

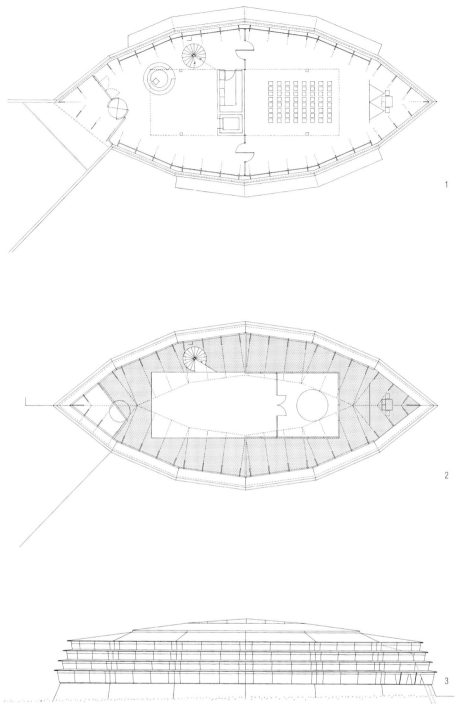

1

2

3

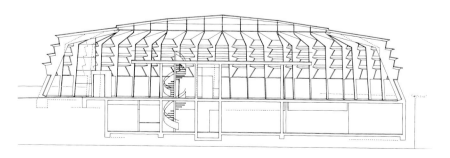

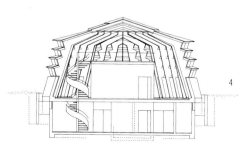

4

5

6

Exhibition Pavilion Wind Power Plant Heroldstatt/Ulm 1994

The information center for renewable energy sources, quickly labeled a "space-ship" by the local press, is to be realized in an open landscape on a high plateau of the Swabian mountains at the foot of a wind power plant. An aerodynamic building volume resulted from a consideration for the rugged climate and the strong winds of the exposed site; it plays with its outer conditions as symbolically and expressively as with its internal function. An aerodynamic, pointed primary form shaped by polygonal struts serves as an exhibition and lecture room that is divided through the middle on the ground floor. In the center of events, a second floor – open to the surrounding roof construction – develops on a freely installed upper deck. Here, accessible from the lobby via a spiral staircase, additional exhibition spaces and an open or shielded conference area can be found. All side-rooms are located on the basement level. The self-supporting termination of the space is created from wooden ribs, without any differentiation from the wall and roof, similar to a ships hull, and forms a tapered, cupola-like hall. The ribs are cut from approximately 10 cm thick laminated veneer. The trellis-like layered outer shell consists of pre-patinate copper sheets on the roof surfaces and glass elements on the facade surfaces. Dedicated to technological progress and the utilization of ecological materials and building methods, the architecture finds a positive image to symbolize the ecological and sensible use of wind power plants.

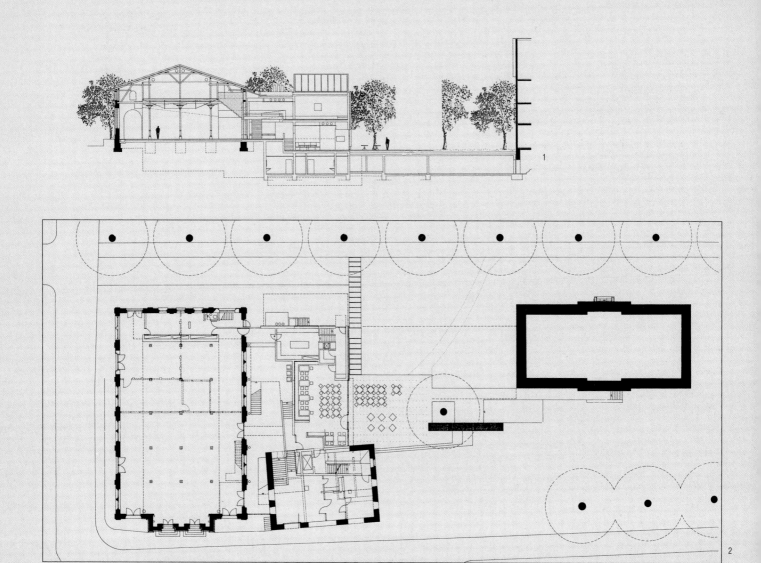

1

2

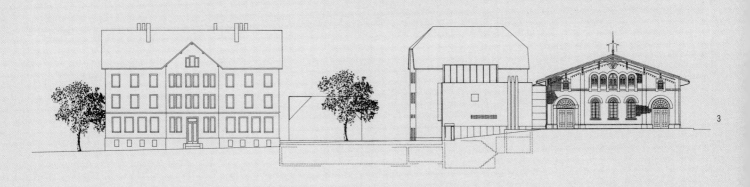

3

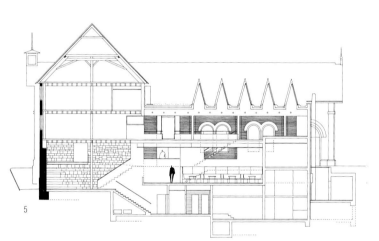

Sanierung und Erweiterung Kulturzentrum Giengen an der Brenz/Ulm 1991–1995

Ziel des Wettbewerbs war, Getreideschranne, Eichamt und Grabenschule, ein am Stadtrand im Bereich der Stadtmauer vorhandenes historisches Ensemble, zu revitalisieren. Dies gelingt im ersten (vorerst nur innerhalb der Schranne realisierten) Bauabschnitt mit einem zwischen den beiden Denkmälern Schranne und Eichamt positionierten Kubus, der den nach Abriß eines Gasthauses zweiteiligen Komplex zu einem dreiteiligen, funktional verbundenen Ensemble erweitert. Der Neubau wird dabei von außen lediglich als winkelförmiger Anschluß an die Altbauten erlebbar, durch Glasfugen auf Distanz gehalten, aber in seiner modernen Ausdrucksweise nicht unterdrückt. Ein steiles Sheddach ordnet sich in die vorhandene vielfältige Dachlandschaft ein oder gibt sich – seitlich betrachtet – als Pendant zu den historischen Dach- und Giebelreitern aus. Ebenso spielt die Ornamentik der Ziegel-Fassade auf historische Ursprünge an, ohne ihren modernen Charakter zu verleugnen. Restaurant, Festsaal und das im Dachgeschoß der Schranne untergebrachte Museum werden über das ehemalige Eichamt erschlossen. Das Foyer macht die ursprüngliche Nachbarschaft von Schranne und Eichamt deutlich und vermittelt zwischen den unterschiedlichen Ebenen mit einer reizvollen, den Verdrehungswinkel des Eichamts aufgreifenden Komposition aus scheinbar zufällig verstreuten Treppenläufen. Da die Saaldecke des Festsaals auf den beiden Längsseiten geöffnet wurde, wird der weiträumige Hallencharakter der Schranne betont, die Konstruktion durchschaubar. Die damit verlorenen Museumsflächen werden im Obergeschoß des Neubaus unterhalb des Sheddachs ersetzt und wie die Räume von Volkshochschule und Stadtbibliothek über eine Rampe am nördlichen Saalende angebunden. (Wettbewerb, 1. Preis)

Restoration and Extension Cultural Center Giengen on Brenz/Ulm 1991–1995

The goal of the competition was the revitalization of the granary, the weights and measures office and the Graben school; an existing historic ensemble at the old town ramparts. It is achieved in the first building phase (so far realized only within the granary) with a cube placed in between the two monuments – the granary and the weights and measures office. After the demolition of a guesthouse, it extends the twofold complex into a threefold, functionally connected ensemble. The new building can be experienced from the outside only as an angular connection to the old structures and is kept at a distance through glass joints; however, it is not oppressed in its modern expression. A steep shed roof integrates itself into the existing multiple roof landscape or – if seen from the side – presents itself as a kind of counterpart to the historic roof and gable spires. The ornamentation of the brick facade also alludes to the historic origins without denying its modern character. Situated on the attic level of the granary, the restaurant, the hall and the museum are developed through the former weights and measures office. The lobby clarifies the original neighborhood of the granary and weights and measures office and mediates between the different levels with an attractive composition of seemingly haphazardly spread staircases that refer to the contorted angle of the weights and measures office. Because the ceiling of the hall has been opened on both longitudinal sides, the spacious character of the granary hall is enhanced and the construction becomes understandable. The museum space that is lost as a result is relocated on the upper floor of the new building below the shed roof and is connected to the northern hall termination – as are the spaces of the adult education center and municipal center – via a ramp. (Competition, 1st prize)

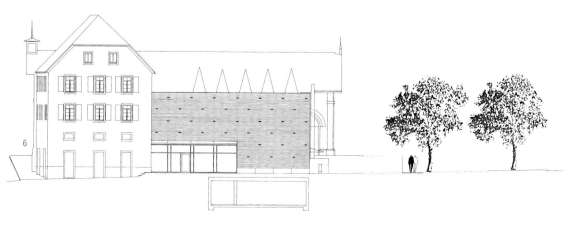

1. Längsschnitt Gesamtanlage.
   Longitudinal section of the complex.
2. Erdgeschoß.
   First floor.
3. Ansicht von Norden.
   Elevation from the north.
4. Längsschnitt Getreideschranne.
   Longitudinal section granary.
5. Querschnitt Gesamtanlage.
   Cross section of the complex.
6. Ansicht von Osten.
   Elevation from the east.

Kindergarten Reutlingen Schafstall 1995–1996

Der Kindergarten für drei Gruppen liegt im Herzen eines Neubaugebiets, das vorwiegend Geschoßwohnungsbau zeigt. Das abfallende Gelände erforderte ein Hanggeschoß in Ortbeton, hier liegen der Hauptzugang und ein Mehrzweckraum, der auch extern zu nutzen ist. Für den Bau mit besonderen Anforderungen an eine kostengünstige Planung waren die Erstellungskosten bindend festgeschrieben. Um den Anforderungen von Kindern zu genügen und den Bauunterhalt langfristig zu begrenzen, lag die Strategie der Architekten darin, den Standard für den Innenausbau dennoch möglichst hoch anzusetzen. Wesentliche Einsparungen erlaubten das Tragwerk und die Gebäudehülle, für die nach der Vorgabe industrielle Vorfertigung und leichte Montage die Möglichkeiten des Holzbaus genutzt wurden. Der Hauptorientierung nach Südosten folgend, löst sich der Baukörper mit freistehenden Massivholzstützen skelettartig auf und schafft einen fließenden Übergang zwischen Gruppenraum und Außenraum. Für die Decke über dem Sockelgeschoß wurden Spannbeton-Hohldielen eingesetzt. Die Tragkonstruktion des begrünten Daches besteht aus Nagelplattenbindern im Achsmaß von 1,25 m. Zur Aussteifung des Gebäudes dient eine Scheibe aus Flachpreßplatten, neben Rundholzstützen übernehmen Wände in Holztafelbauweise die Lastabtragung. Der einzige Luxus der Architektur liegt in der elementaren Ästhetik von Holz und Holzkonstruktion wie im Einbeziehen des Konstruktionsvolumens innen und außen.

1

2

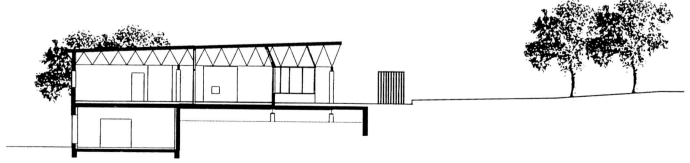

3

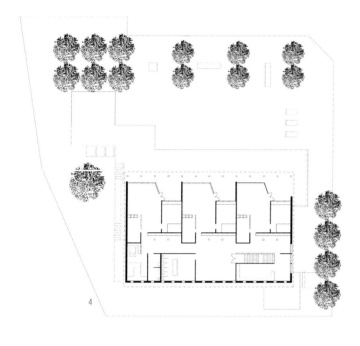

4

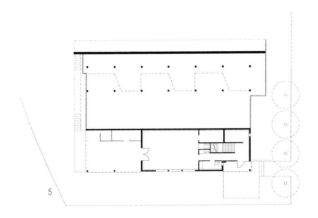

5

6

7

Kindergarten Reutlingen Schaf-stall 1995–1996

The kindergarten for three groups is located in the center of a new development that is mainly characterized by apartment units. The sloped property required a suspended level made of in-situ concrete that houses the main access, and a multi-purpose room that can also be accessed and utilized from outside. For a building having special requirements in terms of a cost-efficient planning, the construction costs were predetermined and binding. In order to meet with the needs of the children and to limit the maintenance cost of the building in the long term, the architects' strategy was, however, to set the standard for the interior design as high as possible. The supporting structure and building shell that were realized using the possibilities of wood construction, adhering the precondition of industrial prefabrication and ease of assembly, achieved essential savings. Following the main orientation towards the southeast, the building volume dissolves into free-standing, massive wood columns, skeletal in appearance, and creates a flowing transition between the group room and the outside space. Hollow, pre-stressed concrete panels were used for the ceiling above the base floor. The supporting structure of the planted roof consists of nailed plank framing with a unit spacing of 1.25 meters. A flat, press-board panel serves to stiffen the building structure, and wood panel walls together with round wooden columns transfer the load. The only luxury of the architecture is the basic aesthetics of wood and wood construction, as well as the integration of the construction volume on the inside and outside.

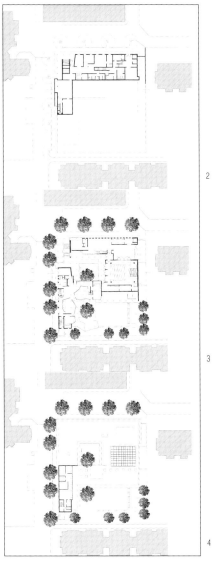

1. Kirchenraum.
   Church space.
2. Sockelgeschoß.
   Base floor.
3. Erdgeschoß.
   First floor.
4. Obergeschoß.
   Upper floor.
5. Übergang von Aussen
   nach Innen.
   *Transition from the
   outside to the inside.*
6. Altar.
   Altar.
7. Schnitt.
   Section.

Katholisches Gemeindezentrum Heilbronn Sontheim 1994–1998

Sontheim-Ost ist ein neuer, baulich sehr heterogener Stadtteil Heilbronns, in dem viele katholische Bürger Rückkehrer aus Polen, Rumänien und der ehemaligen Sowjetunion sind. Das schon außen einer klösterlichen Stille verpflichtete Gemeindezentrum mit Kindergarten, Gymnastik- und Gemeinderäumen markiert neben seinem evangelischen Pendant und dem Supermarkt die Ortsmitte – weltabgewandt als in sich ruhender Pol. Zwar öffnet sich der in heimischen Muschelkalk gekleidete, die Geländebewegung nutzende Bau an seiner quasi in den Alltag der Bewohner ragenden zweigeschossigen Gebäudeecke zu einer eindeutigen Willkommensgeste. Aber unter dem baldachinartig freigestellten Dach sind im Sockelgeschoß nur die vor allem der Jugendarbeit gewidmeten Gemeinschaftsräume direkt erreichbar. Rundsäulen aus Furnierstreifenholz deuten hier bereits eine von außen nach innen variierte Materialwahl von harten zu weichen Oberflächen an. Zu den um ein Atrium versammelten zentralen Funktionen Gemeindesaal, Kirche und Kindergarten führt eine breite Treppenanlage bzw. eine schmale Rampe, deren beider Aufgabe Zugang und Distanz zugleich ist. Der Weg zur eigenen Innenwelt im Sakralraum beginnt bereits hier. Ruhe und Schönheit eines klösterlichen Innenhofs mit Kreuzgang formulieren mit dem Kreuz, einer Sitzbank und einer Linde die nächsten Stationen der Besinnung. Die Reduzierung der allgegenwärtigen medialen Bilderflut erreicht in der Kirche, die sich in den Hof erweitern läßt, ihren Höhepunkt. Neben dem nach Osten orientierten, von den Architekten gestalteten Altar bestimmt den weitgehend geschlossenen Raum eine auf vier Stützen ruhende Holzkonstruktion, die, aufgebaut aus einzelnen tragenden Scheiben, in der Summe eine das Zenitlicht zelebrierende Kuppel formt. (Wettbewerb, 1. Preis)

Catholic Community Center Heilbronn Sontheim 1994–1998

Sontheim-East is a new, architecturally heterogeneous district of Heilbronn, where many catholic immigrants from Poland, Romania and the former Soviet Union live. The community center with a kindergarten, gymnastics and community rooms is dedicated to the serenity and silence of a monastery as can already be seen on the outside; it marks the center of town – next to its Protestant counterpart and the super market – as a pole resting within itself, turned away from the world. The building, clad with regional limestone, uses the movement of the grounds and opens up into a clear, welcoming gesture at its two-story corner that literally reaches into the every-day-life of the residents. But beneath the baldachin-like free-standing roof on the ground floor, only the communal rooms, which are mainly dedicated to youth work, are directly accessible. Round columns made of parallel strand lumber already hint at a choice of materials that varies from hard surfaces on the outside to soft on the inside. A wide staircase or a narrow ramp lead to the central functions of the community hall, the church and the kindergarten arranged around an atrium; their task is access and yet, at the same time, keeping some distance. The next stations of contemplation are formulated by the quietness and beauty of a monastery courtyard with a cloister walk, a cross, a sitting bench and a linden tree. The reduction of the omnipresent flood of images reaches its climax in the church which can be extended towards the yard. The mostly closed space is determined – aside from the altar designed by the architects and oriented towards the east – by a wood construction resting on four columns which, built from separate supporting panels, in its sum forms a cupola celebrating the light of the zenith. (Competition, 1st prize)

5

6

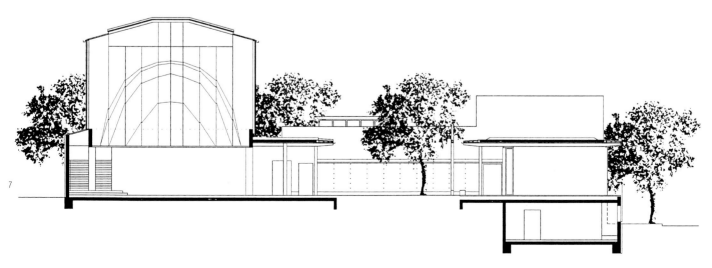

7

Hansjörg Göritz

S-Bahnhof (EXPO
2000) Hannover
Nordstadt 1996–1997.
*Suburban train station
(EXPO 2000) Hannover
Nordstadt 1996–1997.*

Ordnung nach Archetypen

Hansjörg Göritz denkt und entwirft in eindrucksvollen Bildern, nimmt diesen aber jeden oberflächlichen Zeitbezug. Im Zwiespalt zwischen dem als notwendig erachteten Rückzug aus der Schnellebigkeit einer medien- und neuigkeitenbesessenen Gesellschaft, der darin gipfelt, die Nachrichtenflut architektonischer Bilder für sich selbst weitgehend zu unterbinden, und dem Verlangen, in die Gedankenlosigkeit des Bauens ordnend einzugreifen, fällt die Durchsetzung idealtypischer Gegenbilder, die vor größerem Publikum wiederum nur über den Auftritt in den Medien gelingen kann, naturgemäß schwer. Mit großer Hartnäckigkeit beharrt der Architekt dennoch darauf, dem Modebetrieb Architektur fundamentale Grundbausteine von philosophischer Dimension entgegenzustellen, dem Stadtbild Signale der Besinnung einzufügen. Für die Entschleunigung überhasteten Fortschritts kämpfend, propagieren die Bauten einen ethischen Utilitarismus, der zum Nutzen aller Menschen Rationalität, Reduktion und Dauerhaftigkeit über Willkür, Vielfalt und Verschleiß stellt. Für die architektonische Form fordert der Architekt Zeitlosigkeit, nicht um ideologischer Engstirnigkeit oder architekturhistorischen Verliebtheiten zu frönen, sondern um verantwortungsvoll für hohe Wertbeständigkeit und dauerhafte Brauchbarkeit Sorge zu tragen. Archaisch anmutende, damit auch formal wirksame Dauerhaftigkeit ist nicht zum niedrigsten Preis zu haben, denn sie muß das Triviale weit hinter sich lassen, um zu einer Kunst vorzustoßen, die Alltag und Gebrauch einschließt. Eine so tiefgreifende Auseinandersetzung mit dem Bauherrn gelingt vor allem im persönlichen Austausch und im kleinen Kreis. Je größer die Zahl derer ist, denen der Architekt seine unzeitgemäße Intensität der architektonischen Vertiefung abverlangt,

desto kleiner wird unter den gegebenen Bedingungen zu Zeiten überbordender Vielfalt, in der Meinungslosigkeit zur Meinungsfreiheit wird, die Chance zur Realisierung. Zu absonderlich scheinen auf den ersten Blick die ebenso asketisch wie luxuriös anmutenden Symmetrien und Zentralräume der Einfamilienhäuser, zu weltabgewandt das klösterliche In-sich-Gekehrtsein größerer Projekte hinter sicheren Mauern oder zu zwei Dritteln im Baugrund versenkt, zu fremd das begleitende Vokabular von Arche über Insula bis Zisterne. Der Werkkatalog ist darum spärlich, wenn es um eine Erfolgsbilanz nach Bausummen geht, reich aber in der Schlüssigkeit von Typologie und Tektonik. Jedes neue Projekt, gleich ob seine Durchsetzung gescheitert ist oder gelungen, fügt sich in dieses gezeichnete Gedankengebäude ein, ist darum nicht verloren, sondern bildet als weiterführende Manifestation eines Theoriegebäudes die Vorstufe für Folgeprojekte innerhalb derselben typologischen Kategorie. Der Architekt beschränkt sich damit, wiederum mit dem Vorteil größerer Intensität, auf wenige Themenzyklen, mindert in der von Ort und Bauaufgabe bestimmten typologischen Definition seinen spezifischen Entwurfsspielraum jedoch nicht. Die Festlegung gilt nicht einem traditionellen Formenrepertoire oder bestimmten Materialien, sondern allein einer elementaren, typologisch klaren Ausdrucksweise in moderner Diktion. Wenn Bezugspersonen zu nennen sind auf der Suche nach dem Ereignis absoluter Räume, dann Louis Kahn (1901–1974), Le Corbusier (1887–1965), Tadao Ando (*1941), Luis Barragán (1902–1988), Emil Steffann (1899–1968), nicht Karl Friedrich Schinkel (1781–1841), für den sich das neue steinerne Berlin begeistert. Wieviel formale Kraft und Eigenständigkeit in der Reduktion liegen kann, dokumentiert für die Expo 2000 der S-Bahnhof Hannover Nordstadt.

An order according to archetypes

Hansjörg Göritz thinks and designs in impressive images, but he removes from them any superficial reference to time. Torn between the withdrawal from the fast-paced lifestyle deemed necessary in a society obsessed with media and news, culminating in the suppression of the flood of architectural images as well as one possibly can and the desire to interfere in the thoughtlessness of architecture in an organizing way, the realization of ideal typical counter-images, which consequently can only be successful with a larger audience by tapping into the media consciousness, is naturally rather difficult. Still, the architect insists – with great determination – on opposing the fashionable architectural enterprise with fundamental elements of a philosophical dimension, to integrate signals of contemplation into the urban picture. Fighting for a decrease in the speed of the over-hasty progress, the buildings propagate an ethical utilitarianism that places rationality, reduction and durability above arbitrariness, variety and use for the benefit of all people. The architect demands timelessness for the architectural form, avoiding an indulgence in ideological narrow-mindedness or an adherence to any architectural historical preference, choosing rather to responsibly care for a highly durable value and lasting usefulness. The archaic, and thus, the formally efficient durability, is not available at the lowest price because it has to leave far behind anything trivial in order to advance to an art that includes daily life and use. Above all, such a deep confrontation with the client results in highly personal exchanges and a small intimate circle. The larger the number of those with whom the architect demands to become architecturally involved in his non-modern intensity, the smaller the chance

becomes for realization under the given circumstances and in a time of overwhelming variety, where not having an opinion actually becomes freedom of opinion. At first glance, the ascetic as well as luxurious symmetries and central spaces of the single-family homes seem too strange, the monastic self-contemplation of larger projects behind safe walls or with two thirds of their volume sunk into the ground seem too far removed from the world; the vocabulary used, ranging from Ark to Insula to Cistern, seems too foreign. Therefore, the list of works is rather short if one looks for a balance of success only in the number of realized buildings. But it is rich in the conclusiveness of the typology and tectonics. Every new project, whether its realization succeeded or failed, fits into this drawn mental structure and is therefore not lost but represents the preliminary step as a continuous manifestation of a theoretical structure for the following projects within the same typological category. The architect restricts himself to only a few theme cycles, again with the advantage of a greater intensity. But he does not reduce his specific range for play in his designs in the typological definition determined by location and building task. The commitment is not aimed at a traditional formal repertory or specific materials but rather only at an elementary, typologically clear expression in a modern diction. If any references are to be made in the search for an event of absolute spaces, these are Louis Kahn (1901–1974), Le Corbusier (1887–1965), Tadao Ando (*1941), Luis Barragán (1902–1988), Emil Steffann (1899–1968), and not Karl Friedrich Schinkel (1781–1841), who was so enthused with the new Berlin of stone. For Expo 2000, the train station Hannover Nordstadt documents just how much formal power and independence can be found in reduction.

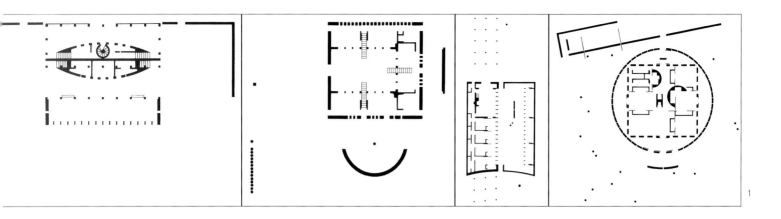

«Einraumhaus» Hannover Bemerode Seelhorster Garten 1996

Was könnte bei einem Einfamilienhaus faszinierender und zugleich schwieriger sein, als alle Wünche und Notwendigkeiten in einem einzigen, gemeinsamen Raum zu erfüllen? In einer langen Entwicklungsreihe von «Steinräumen» (Haus «Trennemoor» 1992, Haus Horstkotte 1993, Projekte Haus G und F 1994) folgt das im Rahmen eines Workshops entworfene Einraumhaus der Typologie des schlichten Rotstein-Körpers zwischen Hausbaum und Obsthain, wie sie das ursprüngliche niedersächsische Landschaftsbild mit seinen Bauernhöfen, insbesondere das niederdeutsche Hallenhaus als Einfirsthaus, vorgibt. Ohne Bezug zu einem konkreten Standort und Bauherrn geht es um den programmatischen Entwurf eines Prototypen, der sich vom Ideenzirkus rund um das Einfamilienhaus radikal distanziert: solide rote Ziegelmauern, gezielter Einsatz der Öffnungen, nachvollziehbare Fassadenschichtungen, ein hängendes begrüntes Dach, das seinen Gipfelpunkt in der Annäherung an den Außenraum jeweils am Auflager der Stirnseiten erreicht. Der langgestreckte, schmale Quader – selbst ein Stück bewohnte Wand – ordnet die Funktionen streng, aber logisch. Längs und quer ist das Durchwohnen jeweils in drei Schichten bzw. Zonen gegliedert. Dem Puffer der «dienenden Wand», einem gemauerten «Schrank» unterhalb der Treppen mit den Funktionszellen (Küche, Gästebett, WC/Bad, Abstellraum, Bibliothek...) folgt die ebenfalls hauslange, alles erschließende Wegschicht. Eine doppelverglaste Kolonnade öffnet die zentrale Halle mit Feuerstelle zum durch Nebengebäude abgeschirmten Gartenhof. Die als Emporen eingehängten Schlafbereiche sind systembedingt nur optisch, nicht akustisch abzuschirmen. Um die Raumwirkung nicht zu stören, sind grundsätzlich alle notwendigen Schränke in die Querwände integriert. So können die raumbeherrschenden Innenwände als Außenwände mit Öffnungen interpretiert werden.

"Single-Room-House" Hannover Bemerode Seelhorster Garten 1996

What could be more fascinating and more difficult and challenging in the case of a single-family-home than to attempt to fulfill all desires and necessities within the limitations of a single common room? In a long sequence of development of "stone spaces" ("Trennemoor" House 1992; Horstkotte House 1993; projects House G and F 1994), the single-room house designed during a seminar follows the typology of the simple red-brick volume between the tree and orchard, thus also following the example presented by the old farms of the original Lower-Saxon landscape, especially the lower Germany hall house as a single-gable house. Without any reference to a specific site or client, the design deals with a programmatic prototype that radically distances itself from the circus of ideas relating to the single-family home: solid red brick walls, a purposeful use of openings, understandable facade layers, a suspended planted roof reaching its peak in the approach to the outside space on the apex of each front side. The elongated, narrow parallelepiped – itself a section of lived-in wall – strictly but logically structures the functional elements. The living area is organized into three layers, or zones, in the length and width. The buffer of the "serving wall" – a masonry vault beneath the stairs containing the functional installations (kitchen, guest bed, WC/bathroom, storage, library...) is followed by the access path that develops everything along the entire length of the house. A double-glazed colonnade opens up the central hall with fire place towards the garden yard, which is protected by neighboring buildings. The bedroom areas, suspended like a gallery, can be protected visually but not acoustically due to the type of system used. In order to leave the spatial order undisturbed, all of the essential closets are integrated primarily into the transverse walls. Thus, the interior walls, which dominate the space, can be interpreted as exterior walls with openings.

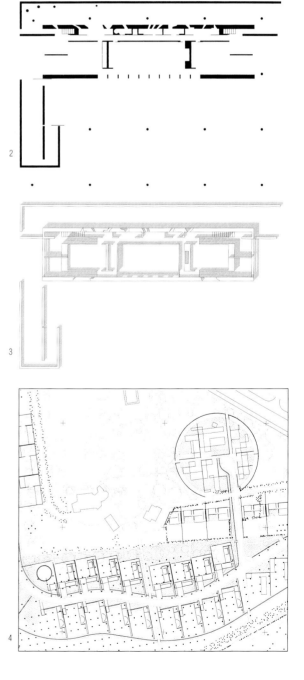

2

3

4

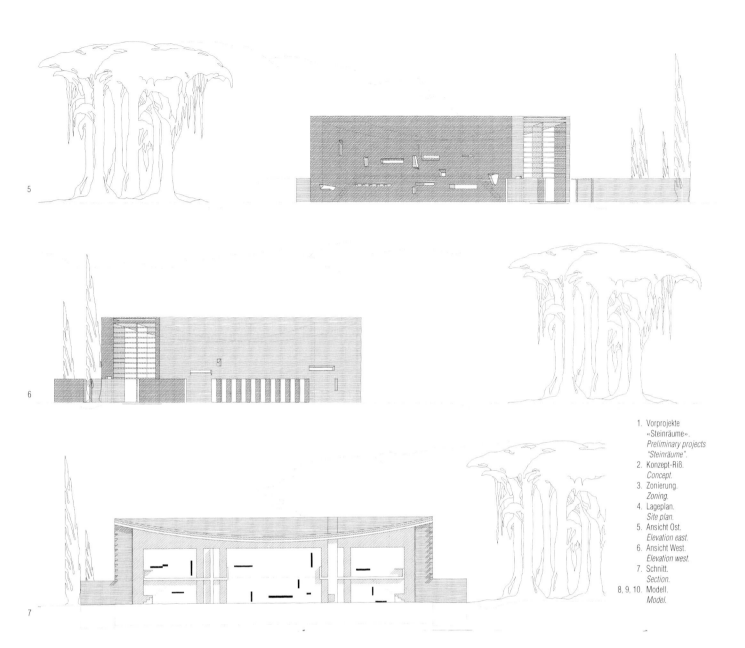

1. Vorprojekte
   «Steinräume».
   Preliminary projects
   "Steinräume".
2. Konzept-Riß.
   Concept.
3. Zonierung.
   Zoning.
4. Lageplan.
   Site plan.
5. Ansicht Ost.
   Elevation east.
6. Ansicht West.
   Elevation west.
7. Schnitt.
   Section.
8, 9, 10. Modell.
   Model.

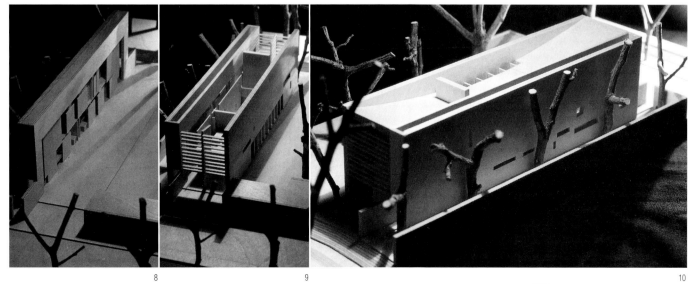

8   9

10

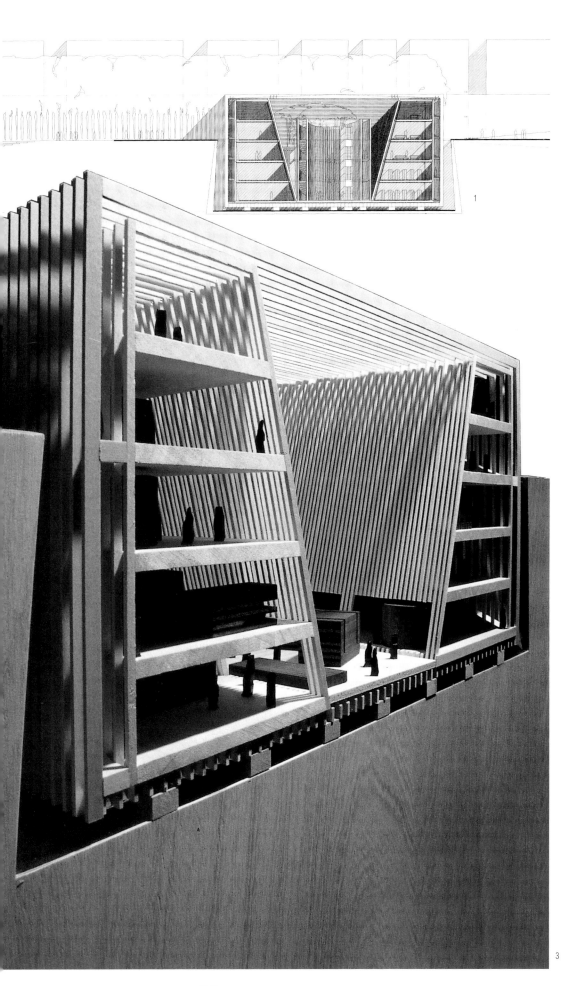

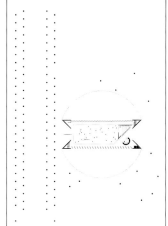

«Arche» Deutscher Pavillon
EXPO 2000 Hannover 1997

Die Wettbewerbsjury lobte das ganzheitliche
Konzept, die kraftvolle Eigenständigkeit des
sowohl städtebaulich raumschaffenden als
auch auf sich selbst reduzierten Solitärs, die
poetische und mystische Sprache, den hohen
Erinnerungswert, das intelligente Energiekon-
zept. Die Kritik am Wettbewerbsverfahren insgesamt, dem nach Sevilla zweiten der jüng-
sten deutschen Vergangenheit mit fragwürdi-
gem Endergebnis, sah Hangars, Raffinerien,
Museen, Messehallen und Autohäuser, aber
kein Zeichen für die Architektur am Beginn
des 3. Jahrtausends, bestaunt von 6000
Besuchern pro Stunde. «Mensch-Natur-Technik», «10 Jahre deutsche Einheit», «Insze-
nierung von Ereignissen, in deren Mittelpunkt
der Mensch steht»: Wie ist auf so wackliger
Vorgabe architektonisch Signifikanz zu
gewinnen? Noch dazu, wenn für die Nachnut-
zung der 56-Millionen-Mark-Investition
gleichzeitig Neutralität verlangt wird: für Verwaltung, Forschung, Lehre, Freizeit oder
Dienstleistung? Als primus inter pares definiert der deutsche Pavillon am Rand einer
Plaza den Eingang zu den anderen Weltaus-
stellungspavillons – die Grenzen der städtebaulichen Vorgabe auslotend, mit einem
Baukörper von maximal 132 x 65 x 20 m. In
diesem Fall taucht der Pavillon nach der Leit-
linie «am lauten Ort ist die Stille das Spektakuläre» als Arche bzw. «arca», Bewahrungs-
ort einer kostbaren Fracht, zu zwei Dritteln
25 m tief in einen Kiesgarten. Dabei
«schwimmt» er auf einer unterirdischen Wasserfläche, um über Frischluftbrunnen adiaba-
tisch abgekühlte Außenluft zu gewinnen und
das umgebende Erdreich wechselweise als
Thermolabyrinth oder Wärmespeicher zu nutzen. In totaler Holzwerkstoff-Konstruktion
spantenartig strukturiert, präsentiert die
Architektur nicht Bautechnologie, sondern
symbolischen Ein-Raum auch für Technologie. Nach unten in der Fläche zunehmende
Ausstellungsebenen begleiten einen mysti-
schen schiffsförmigen Lichtraum, der an seinem Boden zum Frachtraum wird, auch für
einen Garten (das Thema «Arche» bearbeitete
schon der Wettbewerbsentwurf Regenwaldhaus Hannover Herrenhausen 1995). Die in
der Überarbeitung vorgenommene Doppe-
lung der Außenschale für einläufige Treppen-
anlagen und eine den Erschließungssteg in
zentraler Position aufweitende Rotunde
erfüllten die Forderungen des Preisgerichts
zum Publikumsdurchsatz nicht. Statt Weg
war Erschließung gefragt. (Wettbewerb,
1. Ankaufsgruppe/5. Rang)

4

5

"Arche" German Pavilion
EXPO 2000 Hanover 1997

The holistic concept, the powerful independence of the solitary structure that creates
space in an urban sense yet is reduced to
itself, the poetic and mythical language, the
high value of memory, and the intelligent
energy concept were all praised by the competition jury. The critics of the competition
process as a whole, since Seville, the second
in recent German history with a questionable
result, beheld hangars, refineries, museums,
exhibition halls and car dealerships but no
clear direction for architecture at the beginning of the third millenium, and yet, it was
admired by 6000 visitors per hour. "Man-
Nature-Technology", "10 years of Germany's
unification", "staged events with man at their
center": how can an architectural significance
be achieved on the basis of such vague preconditions? Especially, when in addition, taking into consideration the future use of the
DM 56 million investment, neutrality is
required: for the administration, research,
teaching, leisure or services. As primus inter
pares, the German pavilion at the edge of a
plaza defines the entrance to the other World
Expo pavilions – plumbing the depths of the
urban precondition with a building volume of
a maximum 132 x 65 x 20 meters. In this
case, two thirds of the pavilion is submerged
into a gravel garden to a depth of 25 m following the motto "in a loud location, silence is
what's spectacular," like an ark or "arca," the
guardian of a precious freight. The building
"floats" on a subterranian water surface and is
provided with outside air adiabatically cooled
through a fresh air fountain; the surrounding
earth serves as a thermal labyrinth, or heat
storage. Constructed entirely as a wooden
framework structure, the architecture not only
presents building technology but a symbolic
single room for technology, as well. Exhibition levels, increasing in size towards the bottom, accompany a mystical ship-form light
space that becomes a freight room at its bottom and is also suitable for use as a garden
(the "ark" theme was already dealt with in the
competition design for the Regenwaldhaus
(rain forest house) Hannover Herrenhausen
1995). In the redesign, the doubling of the
exterior shell in order to accommodate the
single-flight staircases and a rotunda expanding the access bridge in a central position
didn't meet with the expectations of the jury in
terms of the movement of visitor traffic.
Instead of a path, a development was asked
for. (Competition, 1st purchase group/5th
place)

1. Querschnitt.
   Cross section.
2. Vorprojekt «Archen».
   *Preliminary project
   "Archen".*
3. Modell im Querschnitt.
   Cross section of model.
4. Blick von oben.
   View from above.
5. Zentraler Fracht- und
   Lichtraum.
   *Central freight and
   light room.*
6. Strukturprinzip.
   Structural principle.
7. Lageplan.
   Site plan.

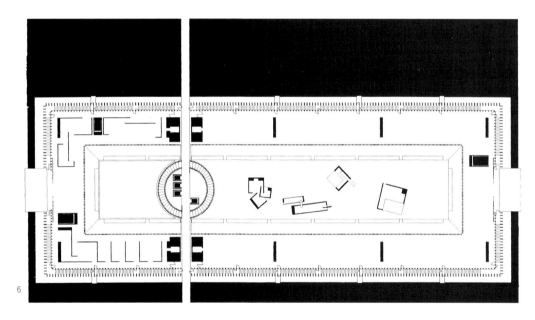

6

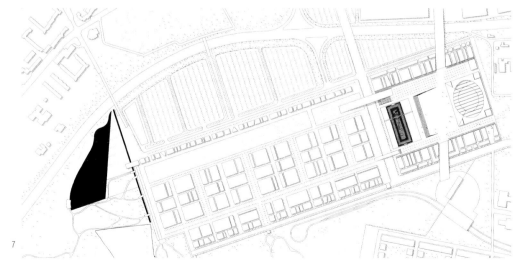

7

69

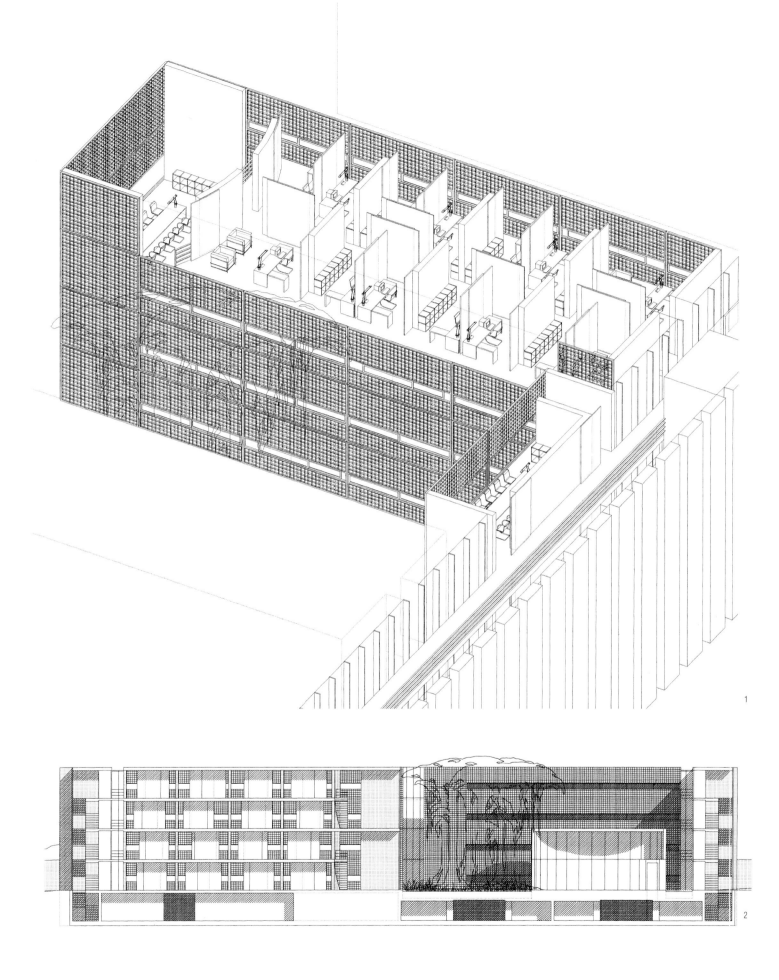

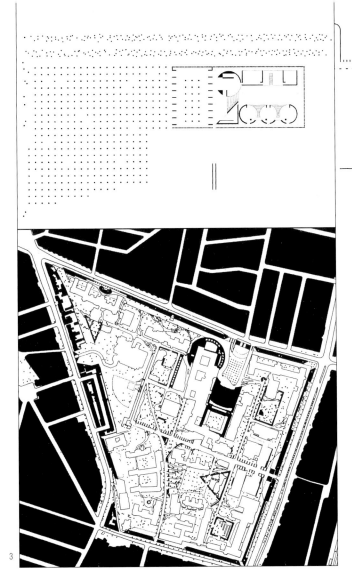

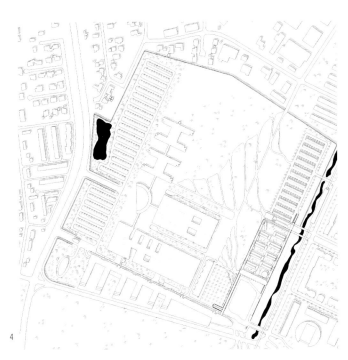

«New-Loft-System» Hauptverwaltung LBS Hannover Bemerode 1997

Innerhalb der Typologie des «hortus conclusus» (eine Vorstudie dazu war 1996 ein Projekt für ein Jugendzentrum in Oldenburg) sucht der Entwurf für die LBS-Hauptverwaltung an der südöstlichen Peripherie von Hannover, jenseits des Messeschnellwegs, auf eigenem, strikt abgeriegeltem, nach innen orientiertem «Claim» (70 x 140 m) nach Raum, Ökonomie, Ökologie und der daraus zu synthetisierenden Identifikation. Im Widerstreit mit jeder vordergründigen Interpretation des nach «außen offenen Unternehmens» lauten die Entwurfsthemen: Platz, Häuser im Garten, Service-Gebäude und Parken. Der wehrhafte äußere Mauerring aus rot durchgefärbten Betonschalungssteinen mit dazwischen angebrachten Glasmembranen erschließt wiederum weitgehend autonome Einzelgebäude, die als schmale, parallel angeordnete Querriegel ohne jede Brückenfunktion nur stegartig in den Garten vorstoßen und sich mit ihren Pendants gegenüber baukörperlich so verzahnen, daß in der inneren Struktur an jedes Bürogebäude ein Patio anschließt. Sondergebäude machen Sonderfunktionen in den Eckpunkten der Gesamtanlage oder bei Bedarf auch in den Patios markant deutlich. Die als «new lofts» interpretierten viergeschossigen Büro-Module, in der Länge variabel, sind über die zweigeschossigen Gemeinschaftszonen an ihrem Ende vertikal jeweils in zwei zweigeschossige Einheiten mit insgesamt 24 bis 32 Arbeitsplätzen unterteilt bzw. 12 bis 16 auf jeder Ebene. Rot durchpigmentierte Sichtbetonscheiben, durch verschiebbare Glaswände in ihrer Abschirmung zu verlängern, erlauben unterschiedliche Organisationsformen. Die Fassade aus weißen Glassteinen mit schmalen Fensterbändern fördert weniger das Abschweifen als das Arbeiten. (Wettbewerb, Ankauf)

"New Loft System" Main Administration Building Savings Bank LBS Hannover Bemerode 1997

Within the typology of the hortus conclusus (a preliminary study for it being a project for a youth center in Oldenburg in 1995), the design for the LBS main administration center at the southeastern border of Hannover, beyond the highway that leads to the fairgrounds, was seeking space, economy, ecology and the resulting synthesized identification on an individual, strictly closed-off "claim" (70 x 140 m) oriented towards the inside. Opposed to every superficial interpretation of the "enterprise open towards the outside", the design themes are: space, houses in a garden, service buildings, and parking. The weir-like exterior masonry ring made of red concrete formwork stones with interstitial glass membranes develops separate buildings that are for the most part autonomous. They project, like small bridges without any bridge function, as narrow, parallel transverse blocks into the garden and interlock with their counterparts' building volumes in the same way that a patio adjoins each office building inside the structure. Specific buildings strikingly clarify specific functions in the corners of the complex or, if necessary, in the patios as well. The four-story office modules, interpreted as "new lofts" and variable in their length, are vertically divided at their end via the two-story communal zones into two two-story units with either 24 to 32 or 12 to 16 workspaces on each level. Red-pigmented fair-faced concrete panels, which can be lengthened in their shielding effect with sliding glass walls, allow for different forms of organization. The white glass brick facade with narrow strips of windows fosters work rather than distraction. (Competition, purchase)

«Körper aus Glasblöcken» S-Bahnhof (EXPO 2000) Hannover Nordstadt 1996–1997

Durch eine Streckenkorrektur wurde für die Expo-Linie zwischen Flughafen und Messe-gelände ein neuer S-Bahnhof notwendig. Ursprünglich war vorgesehen, das für diesen weithin sichtbaren Bau im Rahmen eines Gut-achterverfahrens 1995 erarbeitete, modular angelegte Gestaltungskonzept als Corporate identity auf alle 9 Stationen anzuwenden, auch bei der Modernisierung bestehender Bahnhöfe. In ihrer Rationalität, Reduktion und Dauerhaftigkeit ist die Vorgabe für das Image der Expo-Linie beeindruckend – noch betont durch die städtebaulich prominente Lage zwi-schen einem weiten, vor Bahnhof und Brücke eingeschnürten Gleisfeld und dem Scheitel-punkt der die Gleise querenden Straßen-brücke. Sieben Meter Höhenunterschied zwi-schen der Straße und dem 210 m langen Mit-telperron werden zum Anlaß für Architektur. Ein Bahnhof aus Wand und Dach, Treppe und Lift, Bank und Uhr. Trotz unterschiedlicher Lastfälle ist das Dach als fünfte Fassade for-mal mit den Wänden identisch. Nur zwei Materialen und eine Farbe bestimmen das Erscheinungsbild des ohne Bahnsteigdach 40 m langen und 2.90 m schmalen Gebäudes: eigens gefertigte kobaltblaue Glassteine einer Florentiner Glashütte und nach Geheimrezep-tur dezent blau durchpigmentierter Sichtbe-ton. Dank ihrer archaischen Ausdruckskraft gerät die Einhausung von Treppe und Lift, mit architektonischen Mitteln zum «Empfangsge-bäude» mit Belvedere gesteigert, in der bun-ten Vielfalt ihrer trivialen Umgebung zum Sig-nal der Ferne. Das im Sonnenlicht und nachts weithin leuchtende Blau ist insofern nicht nur Bestandteil der Coporate identity. Es steht nicht zuletzt für Utopie, Sehnsucht, geistige Erkenntnis. Wie die Züge nicht ins Blaue fah-ren, sondern zu einer Expo unter dem Motto «Mensch-Natur-Technik», sollten Architekten nicht ins Blaue reden und bauen.

"Glasblock Volume" Suburbian train Station (EXPO 2000) Hannover Nordstadt 1996–1997

Due to a correction of the course of the tracks, a new train station became necessary for the Expo-line between the airport and fair grounds. Originally, the plan was to apply the modular design concept, which had been worked out in 1995, for this widely visible construction, as a corporate identity for all 9 stations, and to apply it also to the modern-ization of existing stations. The design for the image of the Expo-line is impressive in its rationality, reduction and durability and is additionally enhanced by the prominent urban location between a wide field of tracks in front of the station and bridge, and the apex of the road bridge crossing the tracks. The seven meters of elevation between the street and the 210 m long central platform gives cause for architecture – a station consisting of wall and roof, stairs and elevator, bench and clock. Despite having different structural require-ments, the roof, as a fifth facade, is formally identical to the walls. The appearance of the building, which is 40 m long and 2.90 m wide not including the platform roof, is determined by only two materials and one color: specially fabricated, cobalt-blue glass blocks from a Florence glazier, and fair-faced concrete unobtrusively tinted with blue pigment. Thanks to their archaic expressive force, the enclosure of the stairs and elevator, which can be evaluated through architectural means as a "reception building" with belvedere, becomes a signal of distance in the colorful variety of its trivial surroundings. The blue tone, res-onating far into the distance in the bright sun-light, and shimmering at night as well, is not simply a component of the corporate identity. Not least, it stands for utopia, desire, spiritual insight. Just as trains do not simply drive off into the blue but rather to an exposition titled "Man-Nature-Technology", so also should architects not speak and build into the blue.

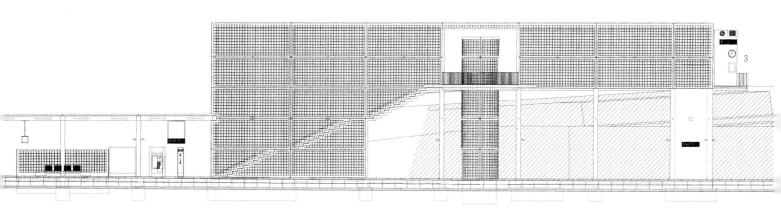

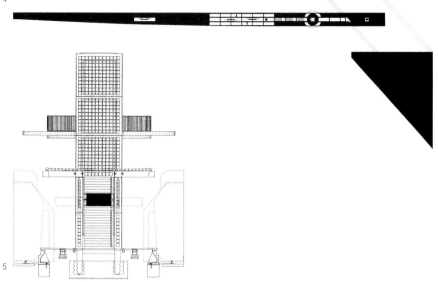

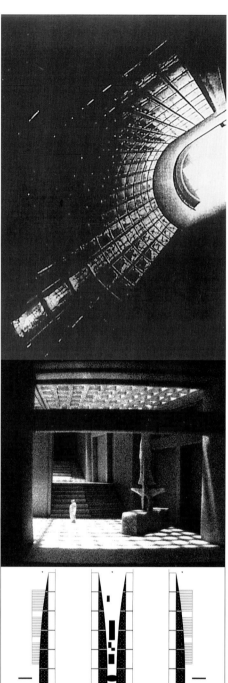

1. Blick vom Belvedere.
   View from the Belvedere.
2. «Laterne» nachts.
   "Lantern" at night.
3. Ansicht.
   Elevation.
4. Strukturprinzip.
   Structural principle.
5. Querschnitt/Ansicht.
   Cross section/ elevation.
6. Treppenhalle.
   Stairway hall.
7. Lageplan.
   Site plan.
8. Vorprojekte «Transparente Substanz – Substantielle Transparenz».
   Preliminary projects "Transparente Substanz – Substantielle Transparenz".

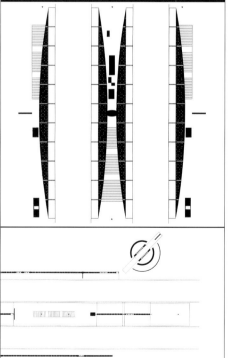

Andreas Hild
Tillmann Kaltwasser

Kompositionen des Alltäglichen

Andreas Hild und Tillmann Kaltwasser suchen und lösen ihre Aufgaben mit politischem Engagement. Markantes Beispiel dafür war 1996 die über Sponsoren finanzierte Kampagne «Sammeln ist Gold wert» in Landshut, bei der die Architekten für mehr Umweltbewußtsein in Sachen Wertstoff-Recycling warben. Die Architektur setzt Zeichen, die vor allem aus einer spezifischen Aufgabe, einer ebenso individuellen wie grundsätzlichen Fragestellung zu interpretieren sind, nicht im Zusammenhang einer den persönlichen Werkkatalog formulierenden Formensprache. Ausgangspunkt ist der (vor)gegebene Anlaß, das dafür notwendige unaufwendige Material, nicht die Frage nach einer überraschenden architektonischen Aussage. Das verbindende Element dieser Arbeiten ist die Methodik, das Operieren mit alltäglichen Vorgaben und einfachen, mitunter zweckentfremdeten Materialien und industriellen Halbzeugen, mit den fallspezifischen Bedingungen wie Tageslichtanforderungen, Konstruktionsgewicht, Einsatz von Standardmaßen und Regelzuschnitten, Preis-/Leistungsverhältnis von Fassaden, Budgetgrenzen. Das schließt sehr kleine, aber öffentlichkeitswirksame und das Stadtimage befördernde Objekte ein, wie eine plakative Wertstoff-Sammelstelle und ornamentale Bus-Haltepunkte in Landshut, die man eher als architektonische Aktionen bezeichnen möchte denn als Gebäude. Dennoch entstehen gerade aus dieser architektonischen Unvoreingenommenheit mit Realitätssinn grundsätzliche Statements, die vom Material bis zu Konstruktion und Städtebau Kritik üben an der Konvention des Bauens. Um zu treffen, arbeitet diese Kritik mit Naheliegendem, dem Allerweltsvokabular: Porenbetonplatten und Betonfertigteile jedweder Art, Lochblechfelder und Gitter aus Rippenstreckmetall, Aluminiumtafeln und -formteile, Acrylglas- und Corten-Stahl-Platten, Zinkbleche aus der Produktion von Klimakanälen... Die Reihe scheint unerschöpflich, die Wertigkeit von Produkten der Bauindustrie keineswegs schon festzustehen. Mit rein architektonischen Mitteln, mithin ohne konkreten Etatposten, wird der Nachweis geführt, daß die Konventionen des Bauens regelmäßig auf einem viel zu niedrigen künstlerischen Niveau angesiedelt sind. Noch mit dem unscheinbarsten Material und der einfachsten, modernen Gebäudesystematik lassen sich komplexe architektonische Kompositionen gewinnen. Dieser politische, das architektonische Bewußtsein auf möglichst breiter Front anregende Ansatz der Architektur bleibt auch dann erhalten, wenn der Materialeinsatz aufwendiger wird. Das wesentliche Instrument ist nicht plakative Signifikanz im Sinne Robert Venturis (*1925), auch nicht das Aufbrechen kompakter und darum wirtschaftlicher Raumkuben, sondern das zwei- oder dreidimensionale Arbeiten mit der die Architektur außen bestimmenden, «öffentlichkeitswirksamen» Materialkomponente. Das Ornament – gleich ob in einem sehr reduzierten Spiel der Fugen, ob im plastischen Verspringen der Fassadenelemente oder in der totalen Verfremdung historischer Motive des 19. Jahrhunderts – ist dabei eine der Möglichkeiten, die bei geschickter Planung nichts kosten, aber große Wirkung haben. Ein Sozialer Wohnungsbau in Kempten wird auf diesem Weg dank Kunststoff und Aluminium ein modernes Haus in einer künstlichen Mahagoni-Hülle. So nähern sich in überraschender Weise Moderne und Ornament, obwohl darin seit dem Diktum von Adolf Loos (1870–1933) – vorgetragen 1908, publiziert 1913 – jahrzehntelang ein «Verbrechen» gesehen wurde.

Compositions of the commonplace

With political engagement, Andreas Hild and Tillmann Kaltwasser are searching for and solving their tasks. One striking example was the sponsored campaign in 1996 "Recycling is worth gold" in Landshut with which the architects advertised an increased environmental awareness with regards to recycling. The architects set signals that could be interpreted, above all, out of a specific task, a question that is as individual as it is basic, and not in the context of a form language that structures the personal catalog of works. The starting point is the (pre-)given occasion, the simple material necessary for it and not the question of a surprising architectural statement. The connecting element of these works is the methodology, the operation with every-day givens and simple, sometimes misappropriated, materials and superficial industrial materials with the case-specific conditions, such as the required daylight, construction weight, use of standard measurements and standard templates, price/performance relationship of facades, and budgetary limitations. This includes very small objects that are, however, publicly efficient and that sponsor the urban image – for example, a slogan-like recycling center and ornamental bus stops in Landshut that one would rather call architectural actions instead of buildings. And yet, the statements come into being precisely out of the absence of an architectural preoccupation with a sense for reality; they criticize the convention of building from the materials used to the construction method and urbanism. And to make the point, this criticism works with what lies at hand, the ordinary vocabulary: poured concrete panels and prefabricated concrete elements, perforated sheet metal surfaces and grids made of ribbed metal mesh, aluminum panels and prefab elements, acrylic and Corten steel panels, galvanized sheets from the production of air-conditioning channels... The list seems endless, and the value of products of the construction industry is in no way determined. With purely architectural means, sometimes without any specific budgetary restraints, the proof that the conventions of building are generally placed on an artistic level that is much too low is supplied. Even with the most insignificant material and the most simple modern building procedure, complex architectural compositions can be accomplished. This political approach to architecture, stimulating the architectural awareness on the widest possible basis, is maintained even if the use of materials becomes more demanding. The essential instrument is not the bold significance in the sense of Robert Venturi (*1925), and not the opening-up of compact and, therefore, economical spatial cubes but the two- or three-dimensional work with the "publicity-efficient" material component that determines the architecture on the outside. The ornament – whether in a very reduced play of the joints, the sculptural articulation of the facade elements or in the total alienation of historic motives of the 19th century – is one of the possibilities that, in case of a clever plan, does not cost anything but will have a great effect. An otherwise ordinary social housing project in Kempten thus becomes a modern house within an artificial mahogany shell due to the use of plastic material and aluminum. In a surprising manner, Modernism and ornament thus converge, although this has been considered a "crime" for decades ever since Adolf Loos' (1870–1933) dictum, which he presented in 1908 and which was published in 1913.

**Aufstockung Haus Wolf München
Obermenzing 1994**

Ein typischer Flachdach-Bungalow der 60er
Jahre war um ein Geschoß zu erweitern. Nun
trotzt das Haus – metallene Box auf geputz-
tem Sockel – unter hohen, alten Bäumen in
seiner je nach Umgebungslicht mysteriösen,
spiegelnden walzblanken Aluminiumhaut den
postmodernen Verirrungen eines zu Wohl-
stand gekommenen Villenviertels. Schwer
vorstellbar, daß sich dieses Haus einmal auf
das unscheinbare, niedrigere Sockelgeschoß
beschränkt haben sollte. Abgesehen von der
außen angesetzten Treppe respektiert die Aufstockung die alten Gebäudegrenzen, setzt
sich jedoch funktional und konstruktiv in
leichter Holzrahmenbauweise über den bestehenden Grundriß hinweg. Das Obergeschoß
trennt nachhaltig zwischen versteckt vorge-
schaltetem Schlaftrakt und fließenden Über-
gängen im Wohnbereich mit Bibliothek und
Arbeitszimmer. Auf der Garage entstand eine
Dachterrasse. Die neuen Räume profitieren
von wesentlich größeren Fensterflächen,
besonders effektvoll, wenn diese an allen
sechs Außenecken des Neubaus als Festver-
glasung über Eck geführt werden – der Statik
zum Trotz. In der Fassade wiederholt sich das
Motiv in der dreiteiligen Bänderung der über
Eck gebogenen Aluminiumtafeln. Allein aus
dem Spiel der Fugen (vgl. Lagerhalle Kemeter
Eichstätt 1995), der Bezüge zwischen den
Fenstern von Erd- und Obergeschoß sowie
dem Wechsel zwischen außenbündiger Fest-
verglasung und innenbündigen Öffnungsflü-
geln ergibt sich neben der Materialästhetik
von Aluminium, Lärchenholz und Glas die
Qualität des äußeren Erscheinungsbildes.

**Heightening of the Wolf-House
Munich Obermenzing 1994**

A typical flat roof bungalow from the sixties
needed to be expanded by one story. Now, the
house – a metal box on a plastered base –
defies the post-modern nouveau riche aberra-
tions of a villa quarter with its aluminum shell
which, depending on the surrounding light,
seems mysterious and reflective, or flat and
blank. It is hard to imagine that this house
had once been limited to the low and rather
inconspicuous base story. Aside from the
addition of a stairway on the outside, the
heightening respects the old building's limitations. But, with its light, wooden framework
architecture, it overcomes the existing ground
plan both functionally and constructively. The
upper floor is clearly separated into the con-
cealed bedroom tract and the flowing transi-
tions within the living area, library and office
space. On top of the garage, a roof terrace was
created. The new spaces profit from the considerably larger windows – particularly effective if, defying static concerns, they are
designed to go around all six outside corners
of the new structure. The motif is repeated on
the facade in the ternary strip pattern of the
aluminum panels running around the corners.
Aside from the material aesthetics of the aluminum, larch wood and glass, the quality of
the exterior appearance results from the play
of the joints (see also, storage hall Kemeter
Eichstätt 1995), the relationships of the windows on the first and second floor, and the
transition between the fixed glazed surfaces
that are even with the exterior wall plane and
the windows that are even with the interior
wall surface and can be opened.

1

2 3

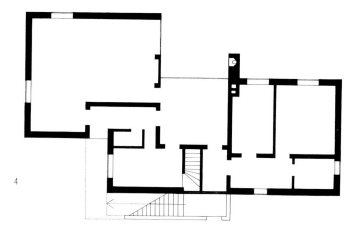

4

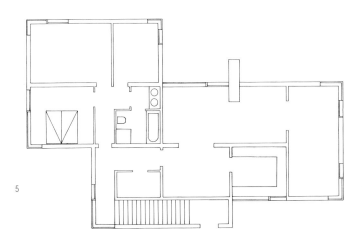

5

7

1. Oberes Treppenpodest
   mit Blick in den Garten.
   Upper stairway landing
   with view of the
   garden.
2, 3. Straßenfront.
   Street facade.
4. Grundriß Bestand.
   Ground plan of existing
   structure.
5. Grundriß Aufstockung.
   Ground plan of
   heightening.

6. Lageplan.
   Site plan.
7. Fassadenausschnitt.
   Facade cut-out.
8. Gebäudeversprung
   vom Wohnraum aus.
   Building recess seen
   from the living room.

6

8

Fachbetrieb für Heizungs-, Lüftungs- und Sanitärtechnik Plauen 1995

In einem Industriegebiet von Plauen, auf einem Hanggrundstück, macht ein Hersteller von Lüftungsanlagen durch eine Architektur auf sich aufmerksam, deren Fassade er selbst produziert. Die Produktion besiedelt damit quasi ihr Produkt. Durch ihre Fassade, nicht durch ihre Form, zielt die Architektur auf die unmittelbare Assoziation zwischen Firmenarchitektur und Firmenprodukt. Da die Materialwahl aus der Funktion heraus nachvollziehbar bleibt, kann dieses Experiment in der Tradition von USM Haller, Wilkhahn, BMW und vor allem Rimowa überzeugen. Im Vordergrund steht nicht der Überraschungseffekt im Sinne Venturis, sondern das konkurrenzlose, auf Ort und Aufgabe bezogene Unikat. Ein Anspruch, der gerade auf der Architekturbühne Industriegebiet leider nach wie vor völlig fehl am Platze scheint. Andererseits werden die Bedingungen des Standorts insofern berücksichtigt, als die Hürde für Bauungenauigkeiten und Ausführungsmängel sehr niedrig liegt. Da derartige Mängel systemimmanenter Bestandteil des Vorbilds wären, bleibt die Darstellung, den Interessen des Generalunternehmers folgend, auch ohne aufwendige Bauleitung dicht am Original. Die Architektur beschränkt sich in diesem Fall, zehn Jahre nach den gebäudegroßen Rillenkoffern in Köln, aber nicht auf das Überdimensionieren eines Klimakanals, sondern entwickelt mit einem weiteren Halbzeug im Sockelbereich, einem begrünten Beton-Steckbausystem für Autobahnböschungen, eine reizvolle, die ungeschliffenen Materialsprachen des Ortes wie der Industrie überwindende Ästhetik.

Technical enterprise for Heating, Ventilation and Sanitary Installations Plauen 1995

Located on sloped property in one of Plauen's industrial areas, a manufacturer of ventilation systems attracts the attention of visitors with an architecture whose facade is directly determined by the commodity produced within. The production site is thus literally resting within its own product. Through the surface appearance of the facade – though not the form itself – the architectural objective is the immediate association between the company's architecture and the company's product. As the choice of material can be understood through the function, this experiment in the tradition of USM Haller, Wilkhahn, BMW and, above all, Rimowa is capable of convincing us. What is in the foreground is not the surprise effect in Venturi's sense, but that unique specimen, without rivals, that references both the location and the task – a claim that, unfortunately, seems to be out of place on the stage of architectural design in the industrial realm. On the other hand, the conditions of the location are considered in so far as the threshold for imprecision in the construction and faults in the realization is very low. As such faults are inherent in the system components of the example, the representation remains close to the original, following the interests of the general contractor and without costly contract management. Ten years after the building-sized "suitcase buildings" for Rimowa (producer of suitcases) in Cologne, in this case, the architecture isn't limited to an oversized dimensioning of an air conditioning channel but develops an attractive aesthetic, overcoming the raw material language of the location and the industry with a prefabricated element in the base area and a modular concrete retaining wall system often used for slopes along highways.

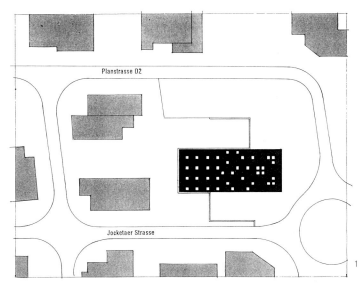

1. Lageplan.
   Site plan.
2-5. Ansichten.
   Elevations.
6-8. Entwurfsstudie/n.
   Design study/studies.

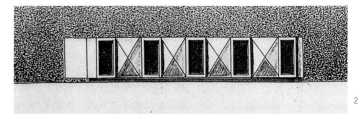

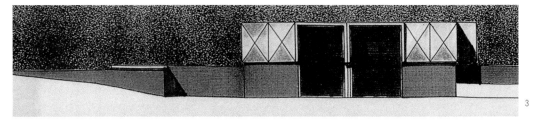

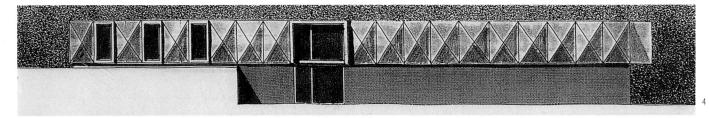

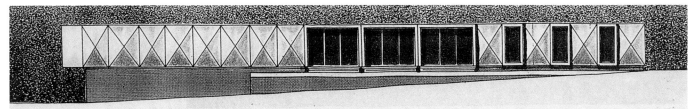

6

7

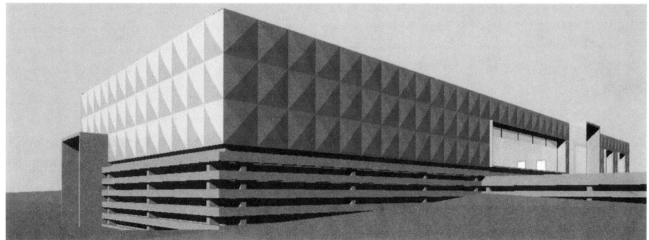

8

Umgestaltung Verlagskantine Callwey München 1995–1996

Ein längsrechteckiger Raum im Untergeschoß eines Verlagshauses der 60er Jahre war in seiner Hauptfunktion zwar beizubehalten, die bislang dank der hochliegenden kleinen Fenster vorhandene Kelleratmosphäre aber aufzuheben. Eine schwierige Aufgabe, war doch außerdem die freie Teilbarkeit des Raumes für Konferenzen, Seminare und Veranstaltungen gefordert und als ein Drittes der Rückbau der Küche zu einem Umschlagplatz für Fertiggerichte. Da die Fensterschlitze mit ihrem prüfenden Blick unter die davor geparkten Autos nicht vergrößert werden konnten, wurden sie kurzerhand hinter opaken, mit Leuchtstoffröhren befeuerten Lichtfeldern verborgen. Nun reichen die Fenster scheinbar von den Heizkörperkonsolen bis zur Decke und übertrumpfen den Ausblick wie die Jahreszeit. Wie bei einem Kastenfenster bleibt die Lüftungsfunktion hinter den milchigen, in Eiche gerahmten Acrylglastafeln erhalten. Die Fensterachsen setzen sich in der Decke mit genuteten Eichenprofilen fort, in die zur optischen Unterteilung des Raumes den Fenstern ähnliche Paravents eingehängt werden können. Quer dazu teilen eingelassene Lampenfelder die Deckenuntersicht. Vom Stabparkett über die Heizkörperverblendungen bis zu den von den Architekten entworfenen Tischen und Stühlen wird die Raumatmosphäre geprägt durch den Einsatz von Eiche, gleichzeitig aber durch den geheimnisvollen weißen Schein der sichtbar aufgeschraubten Acrylglastafeln, die nie ganz eindeutig bekennen, wo sie ihr Licht aufgeschnappt haben.

Redesigned Publishing House Cafeteria Callwey Munich 1995–1996

A long, rectangular space on the basement level of a publishing house built during the '60s was to be preserved with regards to its main function; the basement atmosphere created by the small windows high up on the walls, however, was to be surmounted. This was a difficult task since the space additionally needed to be flexible enough in its use and able to be partitioned into separate spaces for conferences, seminars and events. And the kitchen had to be converted into a center for ready-made-meals, as well. As the window slits with their lovely view of the underbodies of cars parked outside couldn't be enlarged, they were simply hidden behind opaque light surfaces lit with neon tubes. Now the windows appear to stretch from the heater consoles to the ceiling and this far surpasses the vista and the seasons outside. Ventilation behind the milky, oak-framed acrylic panels is maintained, as is the case with a box window. The window axes are continued up on the ceiling with grooved oak profiles into which paravents, similar to the windows, can be inserted for a visual division of the space. Traversing them, recessed light fields separate the under-view of the ceiling. The atmosphere in this space is determined by the use of oak – from the parquet floor to the radiator covers and the tables and chairs that were designed by the architects – but also by the mysterious white glow emanating from the acrylic panels that never completely confess as to where they catch their light from.

1. Grundriß.
   Ground plan.
2. Tagen, Planen und Essen im Untergeschoß.
   Meeting, planning and eating on the lower level.
3. Mobiliar nach Architektenentwürfen.
   Furnishings made according to architects' designs.

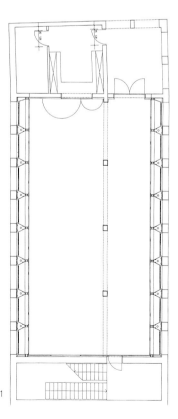

1

2

3

Wertstoff-Sammelstelle Landshut 1996

Wertstoff-Container sind zum Bestandteil des Stadtbildes geworden, eine ästhetische Wertschöpfung findet dabei nicht statt. Da die Container selbst nicht zur Disposition stehen, kann das Ziel nur sein, ihnen einen architektonischen Rahmen zu geben. Am Stadtrand, an einer wichtigen Einfallstraße wird für das Sammeln wie von einer großen Werbetafel aus geworben: ein räumliches Graffito. Die baulichen Mittel für diese Aktion sind äußerst bescheiden. Trafohaus und Bus-Haltepunkt, Fertigprodukte eines Betonwerks, sollten ohnehin entstehen. Dazwischen fand sich Raum für eine überraschende Aktion in derselben Sprache. Sieben Betonscheiben, aus denen mit Hilfe von zwei identischen Aussparungen Buchstaben wurden, sind Signal und Sichtschutz zugleich. Das aber war den Architekten nicht aufrührerisch genug. Passend zum Jahresmotto der Stadt Landshut 1996: «Jahr des Goldes», sorgten sie über Sponsoren für eine goldene Beschichtung und ließen die politische Nachricht «Sammeln ist Gold wert» in der ganzen Stadt kursieren, mit Hilfe goldener Container, goldener Aufkleber und – im Zusammenhang damit – einer Gewinnspiel-Aktion des Lokalsenders wie des Einzelhandels.

Recycling Center Landshut 1996

Recycling containers have become an institution in the urban picture, but an aesthetic product has yet to be discovered. Since the containers themselves are not available, the goal can only be to provide them with an architectural framework. At the edge of the town, on an important access road, recycling is advertised on a large billboard: a spatial graffito. The architectural means for this action are extremely limited. The transformer house and bus stop – the prefabricated products of a concrete factory – had been planned anyway. In between, space was found for a surprising action speaking the same language: seven concrete slabs which, with the help of two identical openings, became letters that are a signal and visual protection at the same time. But this wasn't quite revolutionary enough for the architects. Fitting the annual motto of the town of Landshut in 1996: "Year of Gold", they found sponsorship for a gold coating and distributed the sociopolitical message "Recycling is as good as gold" throughout the town, with golden containers, golden stickers and – in connection with that – a sweepstakes by the local radio station and the retailers.

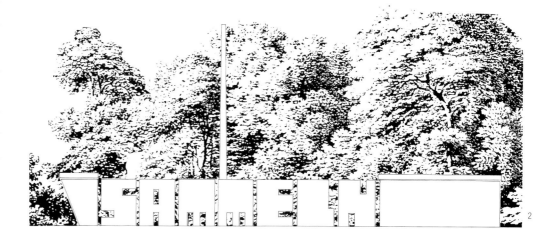

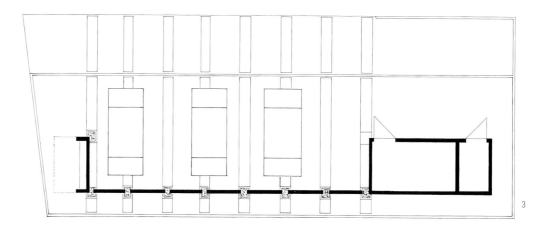

1, 2. Werbefront.
Advertising facade.
3. Grundriß.
Ground plan.

Bus-Haltepunkt Landshut Ländtorplatz 1997

Der Prototyp für ein ebenso stadttypisches wie variables System von Bus-Haltepunkten innerhalb der mittelalterlichen Platzanlage am Rande der Altstadt von Landshut besteht – einschließlich Dach – aus einer 12 mm starken Corten-Stahl-Platte von 8 m Länge und 2,8 m Breite (ca 2,5 Tonnen). Mit dem eingesetzten Laserschneideverfahren ist nach dem Prinzip Scherenschnitt jedes zusammenhängende Muster in einem Arbeitsgang realisierbar. Bedingung für die Funktion als Flächentragwerk ist allein eine den konstruktiven Minimalerfordernissen genügende Massenverteilung des Ornaments. Nach dem Schnitt wurde die Platte in ihre endgültige Form gekantet und mit dem Kran versetzt. Vor Ort wurden lediglich die innenliegenden Glasscheiben montiert. Das einem Vorlagenbuch des 19. Jahrhunderts entnommene Ornament mußte für das computergesteuerte CNC-Schneideverfahren digitalisiert und vektorisiert werden. Der ästhetische Reiz ergibt sich einerseits aus dem erheblich veränderten Maßstab der Corten-Kopie, zum anderen aus dem gewählten fragmentarischen Ausschnitt. Der historische Stadtraum wurde nicht um ein historisches Zitat bereichert, sondern um ein Stück zeitgenössische Architektur – realisiert nach einer historischen Gestaltungsvorlage, möglich aber nur mit modernster Technik. Weitere Unikate sind in Arbeit.

Bus Stop Landshut Ländtorplatz 1997

The prototype for a bus stop system that is as urban as it is variable within the medieval square at the edge of the old town quarter in Landshut consists of a 12 mm thick (including the roof) Corten steel plate 8 meters in length and 2.8 meters in width (approx. 2.5 tons). Following the silhouette principle and due to the laser cutting procedure that was used, every pattern can be realized in a single work procedure. The precondition for the function as an area-covering structural element is a distribution of the mass of the ornament according to the minimum constructive requirements. After cutting, the plate was bent into its final shape and moved with the crane. Only the inside glass panes were mounted in situ. The ornament, taken from a pattern book from the 19th century, had to be digitized and vectored for the CNC-control cutting procedure. The aesthetic charm results from the considerably changed scale of the Corten copy on one hand, and from the selected fragmented cutout, on the other. The historic urban space wasn't enriched with a historic quotation but with a piece of contemporary architecture – realized following a historic design pattern, but made possible only through the use of the most neoteric technologies. Further unique examples are in the works.

1. Grundriß/Schnitt.
   Ground plan/section.
2. Lageplan.
   Site plan.
3,4. Prototyp am
   Ländtorplatz.
   Prototype at
   Ländtorplatz.

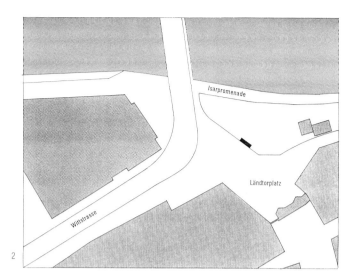

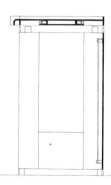

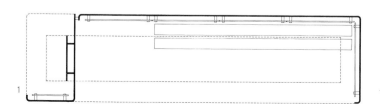

83

Sozialer Wohnungsbau Kempten
1993–1997

Social Housing Kempten
1993–1997

Mitten in einer Siedlung der 60er Jahre am Rande von Kempten, dem Pfarrzentrum gegenüber, komplettiert der Neubau eine lockere Zeilenformation mit Satteldächern zu einem blockartigen Zusammenschluß unterschiedlicher Wohnhaustypen. Der unmittelbare Anschluß an die Nachbarhäuser wurde über große Loggien erreicht. Zwölf öffentlich geförderte 2- bzw. 3-Zimmer-Wohnungen sind konventionell als Zweispänner organisiert, notwendigerweise mit innenliegenden Bädern, in den kleineren Mitteltypen auch mit innenliegenden Küchen. Bemerkenswert ist jedoch die Fassade. Da die gesamte Umgebung des Gebäudes in den 70er Jahren eine zusätzliche Dämmung samt einer Verkleidung aus Faserzementplatten erhielt, mit der üblichen wenig vorteilhaften, weil ästhetisch unkontrollierten Gesamtwirkung, sollten in diesem Fall auf Wunsch des Bauherrn dauerhaftere Schichtstoff-Platten eingesetzt werden. Die Deckschicht dieser Platten, die aus vielen Schichten von mit Melaminharz verpreßten Kraftpapieren bestehen, bilden aus Gründen des UV-Schutzes Dekorpapiere. Das Erscheinungsbild der für den Aufwand einer Druckvorlage frei zu variierenden Oberflächen stieß bislang erst auf wenig gestalterisches Interesse. In diesem Fall wird die Künstlichkeit des Kunststoffs durch das Bildmotiv Mahagoni markant überhöht – kaum zu glauben: eine Standardausführung nach Katalog. Unter weit auskragendem flachen Dach sorgen walzblanke Aluminiumformteile und die sichtbaren Verschraubungen der großen Fassadentafeln im Rahmen ihrer die Geschoßdecken an der Eingangsfront verrätselnden Ornamentik für wechselweise bewegte wie ruhige Ansichten. Auch die rundum streng geordneten bodentiefen Fenster konterkarieren die funktionale Bedeutung des Gebäudes.

At the edge of Kempten, in the middle of a development from the '60s and opposite the parish center, the new building completes a loose row formation with saddle roofs into a block-like conversion of different apartment house types. The immediate connection with the neighboring houses was achieved through loggias. Twelve publicly sponsored 2 and 3 bedroom apartments are organized in a conventional way with two apartments accessed from each landing. It was necessary to place the bathrooms and, in the smaller middle types, the kitchens centrally. What is remarkable, however, is the facade. Since the entire building received an additional layer of insulation during the '70s – the fiber-reinforced concrete slab encasing with the traditionally disadvantageous overall appearance (given the lack of aesthetic control) included – the wish of the client was, in this case, for more durable phenol resin slabs to be used. The top layer of these slabs, consisting of many layers of craft paper compressed with melamine resin, is composed of decorative paper for reasons of UV-protection. The appearance of these surfaces, which can be freely varied if the effort for a printing pattern were made, has in terms of design received little interest in the past. In this case, the artificiality of the plastic material is intentionally enhanced with the motif of the mahogany image; unbelievable, but true: a standard version from the catalog. Beneath the strongly cantilevered roof, blank aluminum form parts and the exposed bolts of the large facade slabs provide us with interchanging moving and calm views within the framework of their ornamentation mystifying the floors on the entrance facade. The strictly structured, floor-to-ceiling windows counteract the functional meaning of the building, as well.

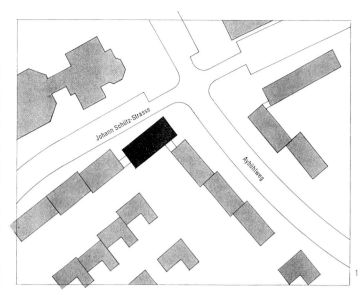

1

1. Lageplan.
   Site plan.
2, 7. Straßenfront.
   Street facade.
3. Grundriß.
   Ground plan.
4. Schnitt.
   Section.
5. Seitenfront.
   Side facade.
6. Bauwich.
   Interstitial space.

2

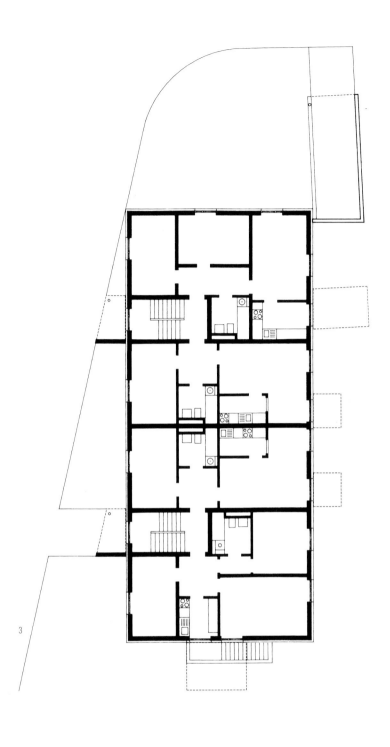

3

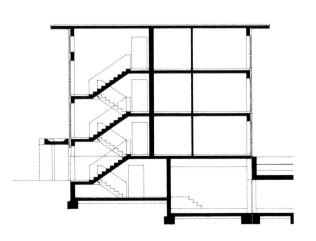

4

5

6

7

85

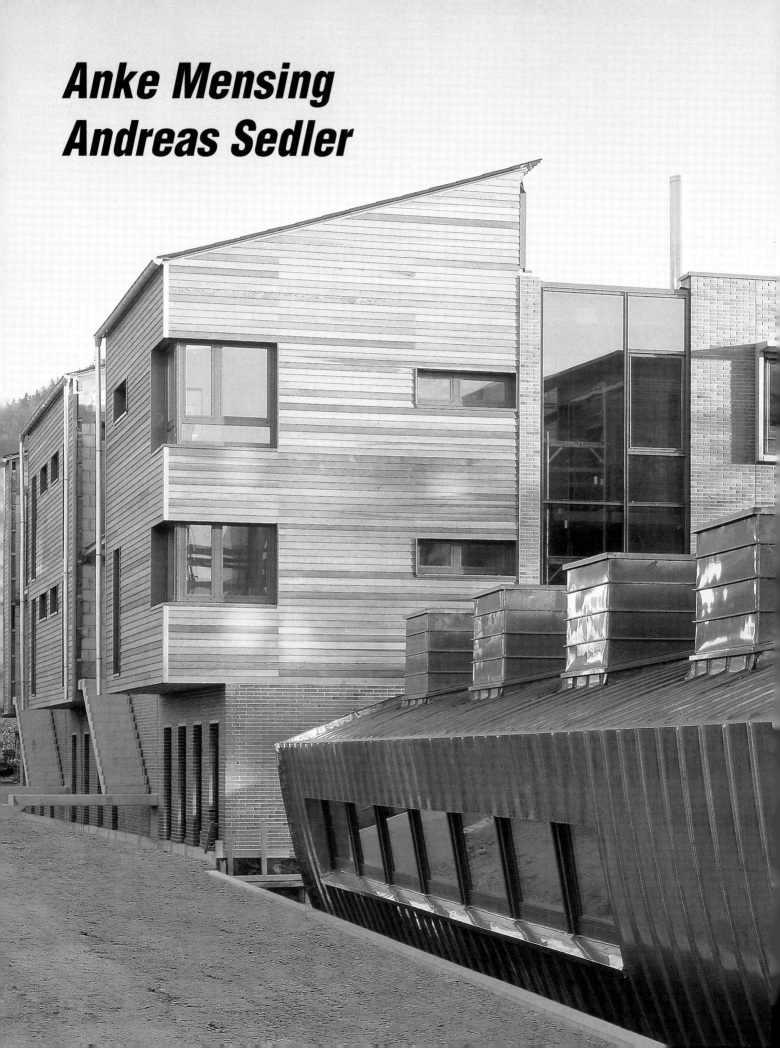

**Anke Mensing
Andreas Sedler**

Raum für Stadt und Kunst

Anke Mensing und Andreas Sedler verstehen ihre Arbeit als Verknüpfung von Objekt, Planung und Städtebau (OPUS) auch künstlerisch. Neben den architektonischen Realisierungen, die immer Stadtreparatur und Altbausubstanz mit einschließen, stehen der Anzahl nach fast gleichrangig Installationen und Objekte. Die Reihe dieser für ernsthafte deutsche Architekten sehr untypischen Experimente reicht vom Frankfurter «Bauwettbewerb» für Architekten und Konditoren 1997 über eine Lichtinstallation anläßlich der Frankfurter «Design Horizonte» 1993, Installationen auf öffentlichen Plätzen in Darmstadt und Utrecht aus dem individuellem Wohnungsmobiliar der Stadtbewohner bis zum Ausstellungspavillon in Form einer begehbaren Litfaßsäule, an der niemand achtlos vorübergehen konnte. Der Übergang zur Architektur ist fließend. Marktstände oder Schirme für ein Freilufttheater als temporäres Dach sind ebenso Einzelobjekt wie Stadt- oder Architekturelement. Als besonders diffiziler Beitrag gehört in diese Reihe, die die Architekten nicht von ihren übrigen Arbeiten separieren, der Entwurf für das Berliner Denkmal der ermordeten Juden in Europa. Interessant ist der Einfluß der künstlerischen, experimentellen und plastischen Arbeit auf die Gebrauchskunst Architektur, zu beobachten an einer umfassenden Stadtreparatur mit Neubauten für Dienstleistung und Verwaltung samt Wohnungen in Seeheim-Jugenheim. Der funktional wie formal abwechslungsreiche Komplex wurde von François Burkhardt im August 1997 in «domus» als Beispiel für die von Vittorio Magnago Lampugnani bereits 1995 gepriesene «Modernität des Dauerhaften» herangezogen – im Verein mit Arbeiten von Mario Botta, Gustav Peichl, David Chipperfield. Das überrascht insofern, als der Beitrag von Opus, aufbauend auf einem dynamischen künstlerisch-individuellen Impetus, keineswegs der formal sehr verhaltenen, nach Konvention und Regelhaftigkeit suchenden Durabilität des steinernen Berlin entspricht. Zwar geht es den Architekten darum, im technisch-funktionalen Sinn des Wortes beständige und dauerhafte Bauwerke zu erstellen. Aber diese Zielsetzung folgt darüber hinaus keineswegs der Gedankenwelt von Lampugnani, dem es um Beständigkeit vor allem im Sinne einer ganz bestimmten stilistischen, klassischen Ausprägung von Einfachheit, Strenge und Askese geht. Insofern sind die Bauten des steinernen Berlin in ihren Ausdrucksformen oftmals viel apodiktischer als der Ruf nach Gewohnheit und Archetypus, nach gelassener Natürlichkeit im Gegensatz zu individualistischer Willkür theoretisch vermuten läßt. Die Projekte von Opus, in ihrer Mittlerposition eher dem Ansatz von Vittorio Gregotti (*1927) zuzurechnen als dem von Mecanoo, suchen formal nicht die stillgestellte Zeit einer bestimmten historischen Bezugsebene. Schon städtebaulich zielt der Ansatz nicht auf Rekonstruktion, sondern versteht Reparatur im Sinne von Analyse und Synthese. Alte Bausubstanz lebt auf im Kontrast zu modernen Ergänzungen, nicht in ihrer anachronistischen Fortführung. Unterschiedliche Funktionen führen zu unterschiedlichen Erscheinungsformen und Materialien. Ohnehin ist Dauerhaftigkeit nicht nur eine Frage der Materialwahl, die die Architekten nicht beschränken wollen, sondern von Situation und Aufgabe abhängig machen. Das wirklich überraschende Ergebnis dieser niederländisch-deutschen Koproduktion ist darum das geschilderte Mißverständnis bzw. die Brücke zwischen zwei Welten: Dauerhaftigkeit und Ideal-Stadt-Plan als architektonischer Stillstand, Dynamik und Labyrinth als architektonische Sensation. Zwischen so unvereinbaren Extremen expressiv die Waage zu halten muß mit Kunst zu tun haben.

Space for city and art

Anke Mensing and Andreas Sedler perceive their work as a combination of object, planning and urbanism (OPUS) and in an artistic sense, as well. Aside from the architectural realizations that always include urban repairs and old building structures, installations and objects are almost of equal importance in terms of numbers. These experiments –very atypical for serious German architects – range from the Frankfurt "building competition" for architects and confectioners 1997 to a light installation at the occasion of the Frankfurt "Design Horizons" 1993 and installations on public squares in Darmstadt and Utrecht made with the individual furnishings of the urban inhabitants, including the exhibition pavilion in the form of an accessible advertisement pillar that nobody could possibly pass without noticing. The transition to architecture is a flowing one. Market booths or umbrellas as temporary roof for an open-air theater are individual objects as much as the urban or architectural element. A very difficult contribution to this series, which the architects don't separate from the rest of their work, is the design for the Berlin holocaust monument. What is interesting is the influence of the artistic, experimental and sculptural work on the practical art of architecture; it can be observed in the extensive urban repair project with new structures for services and administration, including apartments in Seeheim-Jugenheim. The functionally as well as formally well-varied complex was quoted by Francois Burkhardt in August 1997 in "domus" as an example for the "modernity of the durable" that had already been praised by Vittorio Magnago Lampugnani in 1995 – in line with works by Mario Botta, Gustav Peichl, David Chipperfield. This is surprising in as far as the contribution by OPUS, based on a dynamic artistic-individual impetus, in no way corresponds to the formally very withheld durability of the Berlin made of stones, which seeks convention and regularity. The architects' goal is to establish buildings that are, in the technical-functional sense of the word, steady and durable. Yet aside from this, their goal does not at all follow Lampugnani's line of thought, who wants steadiness above all in the sense of a very specific stylistic, classical version of simplicity, strictness and ascetic. In this sense, the buildings of the Berlin made of stone are often much more apodictical in their expressive forms than the call for habit and archetype, for naturalness as opposed to individualistic arbitrariness, might allow one to assume in theory. The projects by OPUS, which in their mediating position can be attributed more to the approach of Vittorio Gregotti (*1927) than that of Mecanoo, formally do not explore the stopped time of a certain historic level of reference. In an urban sense already, the approach does not aim at reconstruction but understands repair in the sense of analysis and synthesis. The old building substance is revived not through its anachronistic continuation but in the contrast with the modern additions. Different functions lead to different forms of appearance and materials. Durability – at any rate – is not just a question of choosing the materials, which the architects do not really want to restrict but rather to make them dependent from the situation and the task. The truly surprising result of this Dutch-German co-production is therefore the aforementioned misunderstanding or the bridge between the two worlds: durability and ideal urban plan as an architectural standstill, dynamic and labyrinth as an architectural sensation. Being able to expressively keep the balance between such incompatible extremes certainly must have something to do with art.

Umnutzung von Tabakscheunen zur Stadtbibliothek Viernheim/Mannheim 1989/1993–1996

Bis in die 20er Jahre wurde in Viernheim großflächig Tabak angebaut. Noch heute belegt in der Innenstadt ein denkmalgeschützter Kranz von zehn ursprünglich fensterlosen Scheunen, notwendig zur Trocknung des Tabaks, die zentrale Bedeutung dieses Wirtschaftszweigs. Mit der Entscheidung, den Blockinnenbereich zur öffentlichen Grünanlage umzugestalten, ergab sich die Chance, die Scheunen trotz ihrer versteckten Position in zweiter Reihe einer kulturellen Nutzung zuzuführen. Drei in einer Nord-Süd-Achse aneinandergereihte, gegeneinander versetzte Tabakscheunen wurden über einen längeren Zeitraum für die Stadtbibliothek (Deutscher Architekturpreis 1991, Anerkennung) und einen Veranstaltungsbereich zu einer Nutzungseinheit zusam-

mengeschlossen. Um den Hallenraum mit den typischen liegenden Dachstühlen nicht zu beeinträchtigen, ist die Verwaltung in einem zur Straße vorstoßenden schmalen Seitenflügel untergebracht. Im Inneren bildet die historische Bausubstanz für die neuen Funktionen lediglich eine Hülle. Ein von den Außenmauern unabhängiges abstraktes Stahlgerüst trägt und ordnet die neu eingefügten Ebenen bis in den offenen Dachraum – ausgehend von den zu quadratischen Vierungen aufgelösten Stützen. In die Vierungstürme wurden einläufige Treppen, ein Bücherlift und Vitrinen eingebaut. Über die Scheunentore und Lüftungsschlitze im bunten Bruchsteinmauerwerk hinaus wurden zusätzlich notwendige Öffnungen auf ein Minimum beschränkt und auf Distanz so verglast, daß die Massivität der historischen Mauern erhalten bleibt. (1. Bauabschnitt: Andreas Sedler im Büro Rittmannsberger u. Kleebank, Möbel: Anke Mensing; 2. Bauabschnitt: OPUS Architekten)

Conversion of Tobacco Barns into Municipal Library Viernheim/Mannheim 1989/1993–1996

Until the '20s, Viernheim was a large-scale tobacco plantation area. Today, a wreath of ten protected landmark barns – originally windowless and essential for drying tobacco – in the center of the town still documents the position of central importance that this industry held. The decision to convert the area inside this block into a public park brought about the opportunity to move the barns into the direction of a cultural utilization, despite their hidden location in the second row. Three tobacco barns lined up in a north-south axis and set off from one another were joined together, over a period of time, into a unit of utilization for the municipal library (German Architectural Award 1991, honorable mention) and as an area for public events. In order to avoid any

corruption of the hall space with the typical flat roof structure, the administrative offices are located in a small side wing projecting towards the street. Inside, the historic structure provides only a shell for the new functions. An abstract steel structure, independent from the outer walls and fixed on supports that are resolved into square crossings, supports and organizes the new levels towering up to the open space beneath the roof. Single-flight stairways, an elevator, and showcases were built into the crossing towers. Aside from the barn gates and ventilation slits, additional openings in the natural stone masonry were kept to a minimum and were glazed in a way that preserved the massiveness of the historic walls which, when viewed from a distance, appear to remain entirely intact. (1st building phase: Andreas Sedler with the office of Rittmannsberger & Kleebank; furnishings: Anke Mensing; 2nd building phase: OPUS Architekten)

1. Obergeschoß und Schnitt.
   Upper floor and section.
2. Bestand.
   Existing structure.
3. Fassade zum Lesehof.
   Facade facing the yard.
4. Lageplan.
   Site plan.
5. Bibliothek auf drei Ebenen.
   Library on three levels.
6. Arbeitsplätze auf der obersten Galerie.
   Work spaces on the upper gallery.
7. Perspektive 2. Bauabschnitt 1996.
   Perspective 2nd building phase 1996.

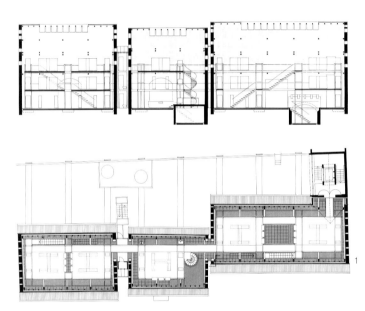

1

2

3

6

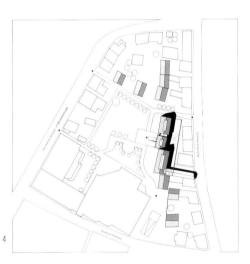

4

5

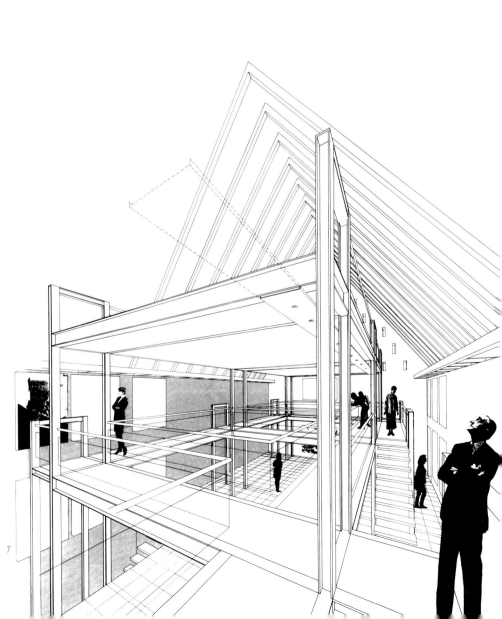

7

Gemeindeverwaltung, Bank und Wohnungen Seeheim-Jugenheim/Darmstadt 1994–1996

Der für deutsche Verhältnisse in seinen Formen und Materialien sehr abwechslungsreiche mehrteilige Komplex stellt sich unterschiedlichen Aufgaben und Bedingungen. Städtebaulich wird die Situation durch das alte Rathaus bestimmt, das langfristig zu erweitern ist, zunächst aber in den gegenüber angemieteten Räumen zusätzliche Flächen gefunden hat. Als Platzbegrenzung des zukünftigen «Rathausforums» betont der Neubau das historische Gebäude in seiner Wirkung als Solitär. Gleichzeitig wird der vorher diffuse Übergang zur kleinteiligen Stadtstruktur zum markanten Blockabschluß, wobei zwischen den unterschiedlichen Dimensionen der Umgebung, vom Hochhaus bis zum Einfamilienhaus, geschickt vermittelt wird. Die Straßenfassade mit dem dreigeschossigen Klinkerbau der Sparkasse, ihrer unter gebogenen kupfergedeckten Leimholzbindern freigestellten Kassenhalle und einem teils verglasten, teils mit geöltem Zedernholz verschalten Treppenturm für die Laubengangbüros und -wohnungen darüber macht das in einer Reihe von giebelständigen Häusern besonders deutlich. Das Rot der südorientierten Platzkante greift über alle unterschiedlichen Funktionen hinweg die Farbgebung des Rathauses in einer Umkehrung auf. Wird dort die graue Putzfassade durch rote Gewände und Gesimse gegliedert, wird hier die rote Wand durch Sichtbeton-Fertigteile über den Fenstern akzentuiert, insbesondere bei den drei durch zweigeschossige Glashallen verketteten Gebäudeköpfen der später variabel zu nutzenden Gemeindeverwaltung. Den Rücken bilden hier hochgesetzte, durch Eingangshöfe strukturierte Maisonette-Wohnungen, die mit ihrem Pultdach im oberen Wohnbereich noch die Südsonne einfangen. Ein allseits belebtes Gebäude ohne Rückseite. (Wettbewerb Rathausforum 1. Preis/mit Gert Maruhn)

Town Administration, Bank and Housing Seeheim-Jugenheim/Darmstadt 1994–1996

For German conditions, the building complex consisting of several sections is quite versatile in its use of form and materials; it confronts the different tasks and conditions, as well. In an urban sense, the situation is determined by the old town hall, which will eventually be extended but for the present has found additional rental space in the building opposite. As a square termination, the new building enhances the historic town hall's effect as a solitary structure. At the same time, the transition to the small-scale town structure that used to be diffuse was turned into a striking block termination that smartly mediates between the range of dimensions in the environment, from the high-rise building to the single-family home. This is especially clarified in a row of gabled houses by the street facade with the Sparkasse's three-story brick building, its free-standing teller hall beneath curved, copper-clad glued-wood girders, and a staircase tower – for the gallery-access offices and the apartments above – that is partially glazed and partially clad with oiled cedar. The red edge of the square ignores all the different functions and returns to the color of the town hall in a reversion. Whereas there the gray plastered facade is structured by red jambs and cornices, the red wall is accentuated here with pieces of fair-faced concrete above the windows, especially in the example of the three building heads connected by two-story glass halls; the heads will later on be used in various ways by the town administration. The rear is formed by maisonette apartments placed high up and structured with entrance yards; with their shed roof, they catch the south sun in the upper living area. This is a building brought to life on all sides, without a back. (Competition, town hall, 1st prize with Gert Maruhn)

1. Kundenhalle.
   Teller hall.
2. Gemeindeverwaltung mit Maisonettewohnungen als Rückgrat.
   Municipal administration with maisonette apartments as a backbone.
3. Obergeschoß.
   Upper floor.
4. Straßenfront mit Kundenhalle und Treppenturm.
   Street facade with teller hall and stairway tower.
5. Lageplan.
   Site plan.
6. Schnitt durch Maisonettewohnungen und Eingangshalle Gemeindeverwaltung.
   Section of maisonette apartments and entrance lobby municipal administration.
7. Schnitt durch Kassenhalle und darüberliegende Wohnungen.
   Section of the teller hall and the apartments above.

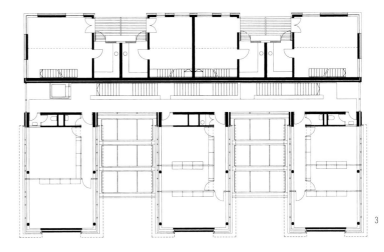

4

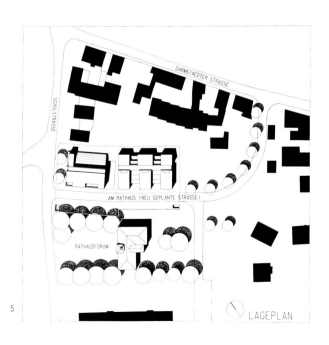

5

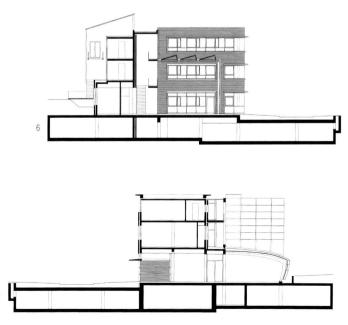

6

7

91

Stadtergänzung und Revitalisierung «Hallesche Höfe» Hall 1997–2000

In Anlehnung an die Situation der Salzstraße im 18. und 19. Jahrhundert, geprägt durch zahlreiche Ausspannhöfe, Gasthäuser, den Packhof und kleine Handwerksbetriebe, soll zwischen Altstadt und Neustadt, im Übergang zwischen Innenstadt und Saaleaue, unter der Zielvorgabe «Hallesche Höfe» kleinteilig und behutsam saniert, ergänzt und revitalisiert werden. Trotz großer Verluste an historischer Bausubstanz ist die typische Hofstruktur zum Teil erkennbar geblieben. Zwischen malerischen Seitenarmen der Saale und in unmittelbarer Nähe zu Universität, Konzerthalle und Rundfunk sollen innerstädtisches Wohnen, ein Kinderladen, kreatives Gewerbe, traditionelles Handwerk, Einzelhandel, Ausstellungs- und Veranstaltungsräume (evtl. ein Kino) sowie Gastronomie und ein Hotel angesiedelt werden. An der Straße wird der Block wieder geschlossen, im Innenbereich durch drei freistehende, schmale Querflügel in vier spezifische, nach vergangenen Vorbildern der Nachbarschaft benannte Einzelhöfe gegliedert: Strohhof, Tucherhof, Kastanienhof und Tannenhof. Der Strohhof im Osten wird für erdgeschossiges Gewerbe ganz überbaut und erst im Obergeschoß zum grünen Innenhof der umliegenden Wohnungen. Zum Flutgraben bleibt die Bebauung offen, das Wegesystem macht die Gesamtanlage in alle Richtungen durchlässig. Die Architektur tritt den Altbauten in einfachen Formen und Materialien eigenständig und modern gegenüber (Klinker-Sichtmauerwerk, holzverkleidete Dachaufbauten im Hof, im Straßenraum zum Teil Putzflächen), sucht aber nach einer Fortschreibung der charakteristischen Merkmale.

City Development and Revitalization "Hallesche Höfe" Hall 1997–2000

Reminiscent of the situation that existed in Salzstrasse during the 18th and 19th centuries, a period characterized by numerous harnessing yards, guest houses, the loading yard and small trade businesses, the goal – approached carefully and in small steps – was to restore, augment and revitalize the area between the old and new parts of the city, in the transition between the inner city and the meadow of the Saale river; the projected goal is to be called "Hallesche Höfe." Despite great losses of historic substance, the typical farmyard structure has remained partially intact and visible. Situated between the picturesque setting of the Saale's tributaries and in the immediate vicinity of the university, concert hall and radio station will be the urban apartments, a children's store, creative crafts businesses, traditional trades, retailers, exhibition and public event spaces (perhaps a movie theater) and various restaurants, and a hotel. At the street, the block is once again closed; on the inside it is structured by three narrow, free-standing transverse wings into four specific farmyards named after former examples located in the neighborhood: Strohhof, Tucherhof, Kastanienhof and Tannenhof. The Strohhof to the east will be completely built over for ground floor businesses and becomes the green inner courtyard for the surrounding apartments only on the upper floor. The development remains open towards the flood channel; the system of pathways provides the whole complex with a permeability in all directions. The architecture faces the old structures with simple forms and materials in an individual and modern way (exposed brick walls, wood-clad roof structures in the yard and some plastered surfaces towards the street); however, it strives for a continuation of the traditional characteristics.

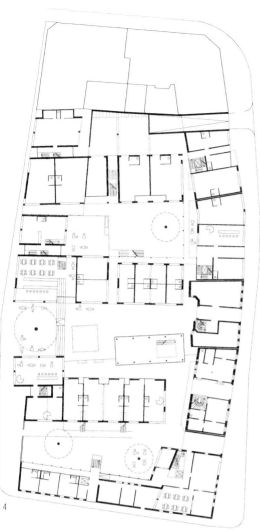

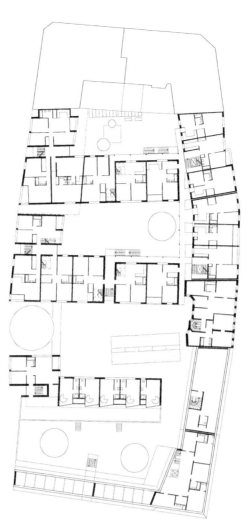

1. Ansicht Mansfelder
   Straße.
   *Elevation Mansfelder
   Strasse.*
2. Ansicht Kastanienhof.
   Elevation Kastanienhof.
3. Perspektive Tucherhof.
   Perspective Tucherhof.
4. Erdgeschoß.
   First floor.
5. Obergeschoß.
   Upper floor.
6,7. Modell.
   Model.

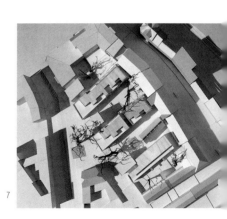

93

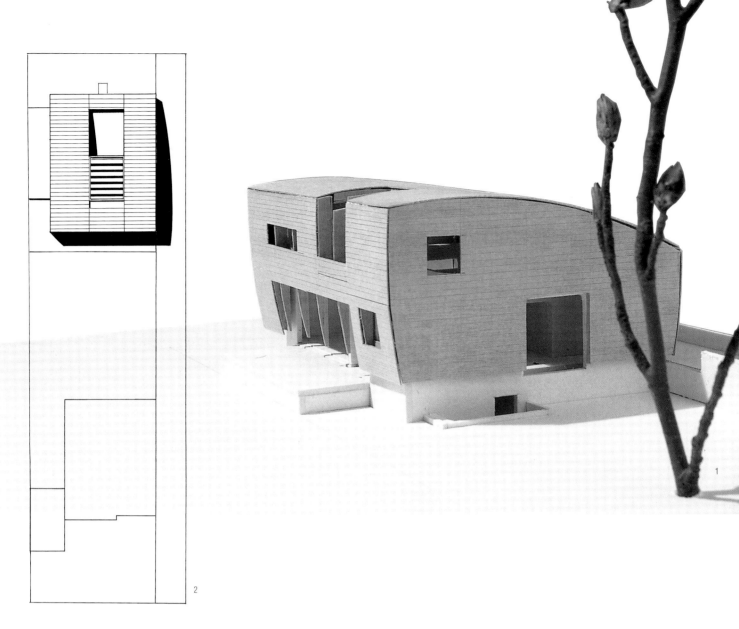

2

Umbau und Aufstockung Wohnhaus H. Griesheim/Darmstadt 1997–1998

Im überhitzten Immobilienmarkt des Rhein-Main-Gebiets gehört die fortgesetzte Teilung von Grundstücken seit langem zum eingeführten städtebaulichen Instrumentarium. Im Gegensatz zu den straßenbegleitenden Einfamilienhäusern einer ruhigen Vorortstraße, war für den in zweiter Reihe errichteten Flachdachbungalow der 70er Jahre nur eingeschossige Bauweise zulässig. Der Wunsch des Bauherrn nach mehr Raum für seine vierköpfige Familie konnte auf dem kleinen Gartengrundstück dennoch nur in Form einer Aufstockung umgesetzt werden. Einerseits war ein zweites Vollgeschoß nicht genehmigungsfähig, andererseits ein gewöhnliches Dachgeschoß weder für den Bauherrn noch für die Architekten vorstellbar. So entstand

die Idee einer über den vorhandenen Altbau gestülpten eigenständigen Form, vergleichbar dem Zufluchtsort von Einsiedlerkrebsen in leeren Schneckengehäusen. Das neu gewonnene Obergeschoß bietet 70 m² Nutzfläche und eine 15 m² große Dachterrasse. Die homogene, hinterlüftete Holzschale – eine ablesbare neue Schicht – deckt die (im Erdgeschoß bereits vorhandene) Klimahülle lediglich ab. Nachträgliche Dämm-Maßnahmen können ebenso integriert werden wie bewegliche Sonnenschutz-Elemente. Die nach Westen geneigte Dachschale wird im Zentrum, vor dem Schlafraum der Eltern durch eine eingeschnittene Dachterrasse bzw. deren Lamellendach durchbrochen. Der Reiz dieser ungewöhnlichen Aufstockung liegt nicht in der Akzentuierung einer Grenze, sondern in einer Neufassung des wenig spektakulären Bestands, die die Symbiose von Alt und Neu dennoch nicht verheimlicht.

Conversion and Heightening H. House Griesheim/Darmstadt 1997–1998

In the overheated real estate market of the Rhine-Main region, the incessant division of properties has long been introduced as an urban instrument. Contrary to the single-family homes along the streets of a quiet suburb, only a single-story architecture was permitted for the flat roofed bungalow erected in the second row during the '70s. The client's desire for more space for his family of four could only be realized on the small garden plot through a heightening of the structure. On the one hand, a full second floor was not permissible; on the other hand, an ordinary attic floor was simply inconceivable to the client and the architects. Thus, the idea of an independent form placed over the existing old structure came into being – comparable to the

refuge hermit crabs seek in the abandoned shells of snails. The new upper floor offers 70 m² of usable area and a 15 m² roof terrace. The homogeneous, ventilated wood shell – a legible new layer – covers only the climate shell (already existing on the first floor) and protects it from UV-radiation. Additional insulation as well as movable sunshade elements can be integrated. The roof shell, pitched towards the west, is interrupted in the center, in front of the parents' bedroom, by a cut-in roof terrace and its lamella roof. The charm of this unusual heightening is not the accentuation of a border, but a new version of the small but spectacular existing structure that does not conceal the symbiosis of old and new.

1,4. Modelle aus
unterschiedlichen
Entwurfsphasen.
*Models from different
design stages.*
2. Lageplan.
Site plan.
3. Isometrie.
Isometric projection.
5. Grundrisse.
Ground plans.
6. Schnitt und Ansichten.
Section and elevations.

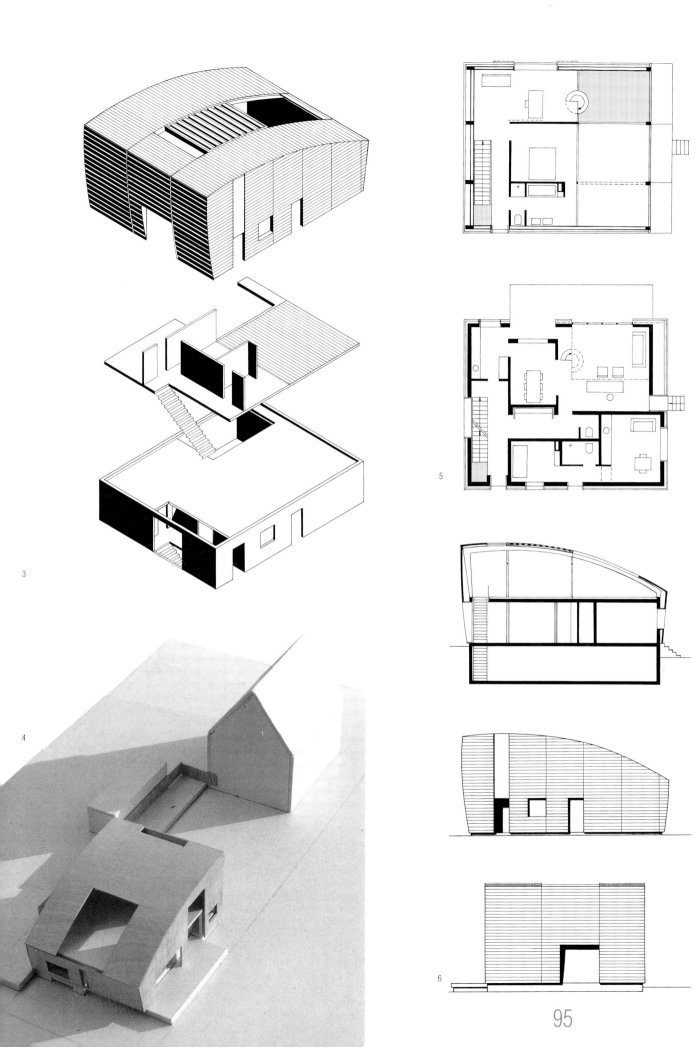

3

4

5

6

Carsten Roth

Büro- und
Ausstellungsgebäude
Otte Ladenbau
Siek/Hamburg
1994–1997.
*Office and exhibition
building Otte Ladenbau
Siek/Hamburg
1994–1997.*

Körper-Sprache

Für Carsten Roth ist Architektur urwüchsiger eigenwilliger Raum, gebaute Form kein Derivat aus Wärmeschutzverordnung, Funktionskatalog und technischen Regelwerken. Dieser künstlerisch-plastische Umgang mit Raum und Licht führt nicht zu Maschinenästhetik oder stromlinienförmigem High-Tech, zu einem Verschwinden der Architektur dank Technik und Umweltbewußtsein, sondern zu einer durch Situation und Aufgabe ausgelösten Körper-Sprache. Technik liefert kein willfähriges synthetisches Bild von «zeitgemäßer» oder «moderner» Architektur, sondern bleibt mit dem Ziel Raum-Architektur nachrangiges Werkzeug. Der Architekt treibt sein Spiel mit ihr, nimmt mit dem Blick auf die Komplexität des Raumerlebens ihre oft genug gescheiterte Wissenschaftlichkeit nicht ernst, schätzt neu eröffnete technische und konstruktive Dimensionen aber als fortschrittliche Raumerzeuger. «Doppelte Fassaden» sind für ihn kein Faktor der Energiebilanz des Gebäudes, sondern sie bilden eine weitere Ebene der städtebaulichen Auseinandersetzung. Aus dem gleichen Grund werden Heizkörper ebenso wie Fenster oder Garagentore mit Vorliebe räumlich eingesetzt und darum im Zweifelsfall «falsch» interpretiert und montiert. Nicht eine einseitig ökonomisch kalkulierte Lastabtragung auf dem kürzesten Weg oder eine ausgefuchste, jenseits ihrer Alltagsbedingungen errechnete Energiebilanz sind von grundsätzlicher, architektonischer Bedeutung, sondern allein die innen wie außen zu erlebende Körperlichkeit der dritten und vierten Dimension. Darin liegt die gesellschaftliche Verpflichtung des Architekten, seine formal zu definierende Verantwortung für Dauerhaftigkeit und Nachhaltigkeit. In Anlehnung an eine von Nietzsche übernommene These Fritz Schumachers (1869–1947) verlangt das einen «Tanz in Ketten». Denn auch beim Einsatz von monolithischem Beton, dem Vordringen der Fassade in den Innenraum oder «destruktiv» weit vor der Außenwand «fliegenden» Fenstern bleiben die Bindungen des Bauens gültig. Das entscheidende Motiv der Architektur ist jedoch der Tanz, die Choreographie des Raumerlebens. Die Ketten behördlicher Auflagen und technischer Grenzen muß der Architekt vergessen machen können. Nicht verwunderlich ist darum, daß dieser Architekt im Umgang mit historischer Bausubstanz, dem prägenden Ausgangspunkt seiner Arbeit, eine große Sensibilität für Eigenheiten und Besonderheiten des Alten an den Tag legt, ohne dieser überkommenen Formkraft bei Umbau, Erweiterung oder Ergänzung die Aktualität und Eigenständigkeit des Neuen zu opfern. Aus beiden Strängen dieses Arbeitsansatzes, dem Nachspüren der konkreten, gebauten Randbedingungen eines Projekts wie dem freien, schöpferischen Ausspielen seines Eigensinns, folgt eine Architektur des Ineinandergreifens, Aufeinanderaufbauens und Schichtens, die mit Andrea Palladio (1508–1580) ebenso das Weiterbauen betreibt – auch eine Form ökologischen Bauens – wie mit Rudolf Schindler (1887–1953) das In-Zweifel-Ziehen einer viel zu glatten und kalten orthodoxen Moderne, die aufgrund ihrer strengen Regularien zwangsläufig in der Sackgasse Internationaler Stil enden mußte. Mit der Poesie architektonischer Raumkunst, die Variation sucht und Wiederholung ausschließt, ist selbst der mit postmodernen Ornamenten notdürftig kaschierte Vulgärfunktionalismus unserer Industrie- und Gewerbegebiete neu zu definieren.

Body language

To Carsten Roth, architecture is an original individual space, and built form is not derived from insulation codes, functional design catalog and technical standards. This artistic-sculptural approach to space and light does not lead to a machine aesthetics or streamlined high-tech solutions, a disappearance of architecture due to technology and environmental awareness, but to a body language initiated by the situation and task. Technology does not deliver an arbitrary synthetic image of "contemporary" or "modern" architecture but remains a second-rank tool with the goal of a spatial architecture. The architect plays his game with technology; he does not take its often-enough failed scientific method seriously with his glance directed to the complexity of the spatial experience, but he does appreciate newly opened technological and constructive dimensions as progressive space producers. "Double-layered facades," to him, are not considered a factor of the energy equilibrium of the building. Rather, they represent another level of urban confrontation. For the same reason, radiators as well as windows or garage gates are used preferably in a spatial way and are therefore, in case of doubt, "falsely" interpreted and mounted. A one-sided, economically calculated amortization with the shortest term or a clever energy balance calculated beyond its every-day conditions are not of primary architectural importance, but only the physicality of the third and fourth dimension that can be experienced inside as much as outside. Herein lies the architect's responsibility towards society, his responsibility for durability and persistence, which must be defined formally. In reference to a thesis by Fritz Schumacher (1869–1947), adapted by Nietzsche, this requires a "dance in chains." Because the limitations of construction remain valid despite the use of monolithic concrete, a facade penetrating into the interior or windows that "destructively fly" far in front of the exterior wall. The decisive motif of the architecture, however, is the dance, the choreography of the spatial experience. The chains of official requirements and technological limitations have to be somehow discarded by the architect. Therefore, it is not surprising that this architect has a great sensibility for the characteristics and special features of the old when dealing with a historic building substance, without sacrificing the actuality and individuality of the new to this outdated formal power in cases of conversions, extensions or additions. From both directions of this work approach – the research of the concrete, preconceived framework conditions of a project and the free creative play of his personal will – follows an architecture of interaction, layering and heightening. With Andrea Palladio (1508-1580) this architecture also promotes a continuation – another form of ecological building. And with Rudolf Schindler (1887–1953) it raises doubts about a much too smooth and cold orthodox Modernism which, due to its strict codex, was forced to end on the dead-end road of the International Style. Even the vulgar functionalism of our industrial areas, which is poorly hidden with post-modern ornamentation, can be redefined with the poetry or architectural space-art that seeks variation and excludes repetition.

97

Ateliergebäude in einem Hinterhof-Ensemble Hamburg Rotherbaum 1992/1995–1996

Im Rahmen des Umbaus der «Autofabrication Hansen» (einer der ersten Stahlbetonskelettbauten aus dem Jahr 1911, heute von der Werbeagentur bis zum Fotografen von Kreativen besetzt) nutzte der Architekt eine Baulücke in der zweigeschossigen Randbebauung des weit verzweigten Hinterhofs zum Bau eines Ateliers für die eigenen Zwecke. In zentraler Lage zwischen Universität, Kongreß-Centrum und Botanischem Garten, aber zwischen einer Vielzahl sehr unterschiedlicher Gewerbe- und Wohnbauten verborgen, stellt der Neubau als Schlußpunkt beider Erschließungsgassen die ursprüngliche Hofsituation wieder her, findet jedoch in der Auseinandersetzung mit der Altbausubstanz zu einem darauf gründenden eigen(willig)en architektonischen Standpunkt. Die angrenzenden Garten-, Brand- und Fassadenmauern werden durch eine über die eigentliche Hoffassade hinausgehende Stahlkonstruktion zu einer neuen skulpturalen Gesamtheit verklammert. Vor den Mauern des südwestlichen Nachbarn begleitet eine Außentreppe, die das Atelier erschließt, ein filigranes Rankgerüst aus Stahlrahmen und -seilen, das vor dem Neubau zur den Hof ästhetisch dominierenden Stahl-/Glasfassade wird, den auch funktional angeschlossenen nordöstlichen Nachbarn durch waghalsige Fassadenübergriffe miteinbezieht, um schließlich eine zweite Eingangssituation zu formulieren. Auf der Suche nach einer neuen, raffiniert ausgeleuchteten Raum-Architektur scheut sich der Architekt nicht, konstruktive und bauphysikalische Konventionen ästhetisch in Frage zu stellen. So wurden zum Beispiel die Garagentore des Erdgeschosses – regelwidrig, aber logisch – so eingebaut, daß sie, wie die Fenster nach außen öffnend, die Plastizität des Baukörpers durch ein Vordach steigern. (BDA Hamburg Architektur Preis 1991–1996)

Studio Building in a Backyard Ensemble Hamburg Rotherbaum 1992/1995–1996

At the time of the conversion of the "Autofabrication Hansen" (one of the first steel skeleton structures, built in 1911, used today by creative people, from advertising agencies to photographers) the architect used an open lot within the two-story edge development surrounding the widely branched-out backyard to build a studio for his own use. Centrally located between the university, the congress center and the botanical gardens, but hidden between a wide variety of industrial and apartment buildings, the new structure reestablishes the original yard situation as the termination of the two access paths. In its confrontation with the old structures, however, it finds its own architectural standpoint based on the latter. The adjoining garden, fire and facade walls are all tied into a new sculptural unity through the use of a steel construction that projects beyond the original front of the yard. In front of the walls of the neighboring building to the southwest, an outside stairway providing access to the studio is accompanied by a filigree trellis of steel framework and cables. In front of the new building, it evolves into a steel and glass facade that aesthetically dominates the yard, integrating the northeastern neighbor, which is adjoined functionally as well through a bold encroachment of the facade, and it terminates in canopies, creating a second entrance. In his search for a new, cleverly lit spatial architecture, the architect does not shy away from questioning, from an aesthetic perspective, constructive and physical conventions. For example, the garage doors of the first floor – against the rules, yet logically – open towards the outside like windows and were installed in a way that, through the use of a canopy, enhances the plasticity of the building volume. (BDA Hamburg architectural award 1991–1996)

1

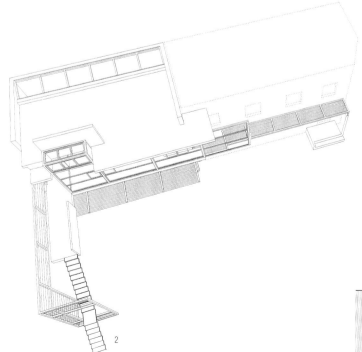

2

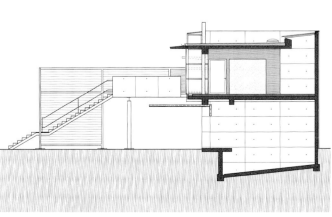

3

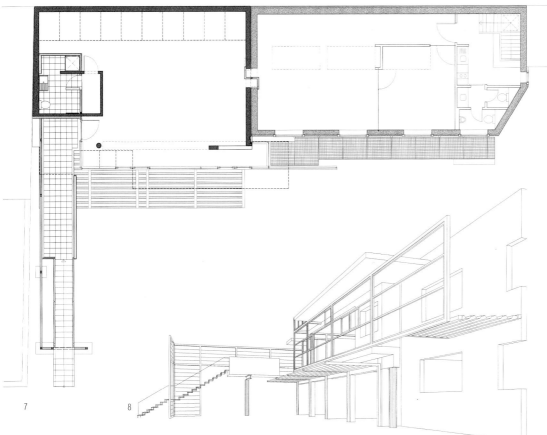

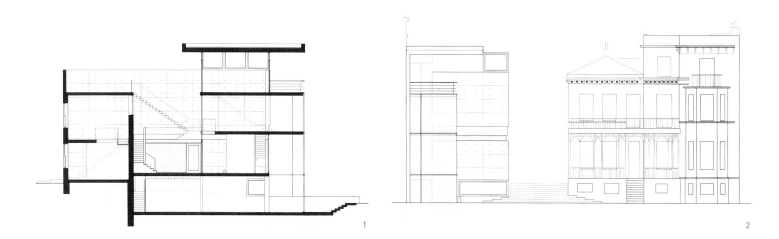

1

2

3

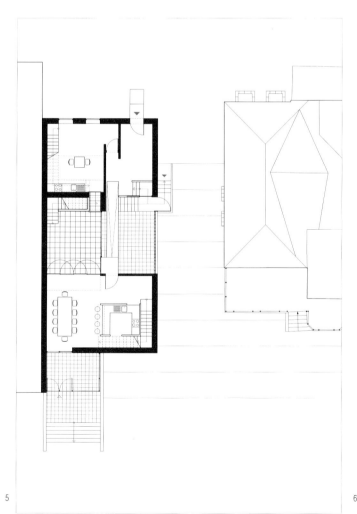

4

1. Längsschnitt.
   Longitudinal section.
2. Ansicht Straßenfront.
   Elevation street facade.
3, 6. Modell.
   Model.
4. Nordansicht.
   Noth elevation.
5. Erdgeschoß.
   First floor.

Villa mit privater Kunstgalerie Hamburg Harvestehude 1994

In der noblen Umgebung von Villen und Konsulaten an der Außenalster war am Harvestehuder Weg auf einem rückwärtig erschlossenen Grundstück, das bei 29 m Breite etwa zur Hälfte mit einer bis an die Grenze reichenden Villa aus dem 19. Jahrhundert besetzt ist, die freie Grundstückshälfte, an die Brandwand einer viergeschossigen Nachbarbebauung anstoßend, für einen Ergänzungsbau vorgesehen. Der leider nicht realisierte programmatische Entwurf beschäftigt sich sehr intensiv mit der modernen Interpretation der historischen Vorgabe. Das neu zu planende, komplementär angelegte Gegenstück zur vorhandenen zweigeschossigen Villa sollte, den Vorlieben des Eigentümers beider Häuser folgend, auf maximal zwei Vollgeschossen ein großes Apartment, eine Einliegerwohnung sowie eine private Kunstgalerie aufnehmen. Mit einer Frontbreite von nur 9 m und unter schwierigen Randbedingungen wie der Forderung, daß der Altbau wie der Garten im Osten nicht einzusehen sein sollten, ist es gelungen, alle drei funktionalen Komponenten des Neubaus sehr individuell zu entwickeln, ohne formal die Gesamtheit aus dem Blick zu verlieren. Zentrales Element ist ein in der Höhe gestaffelter Innenhof, der es beiden Wohneinheiten erlaubt, sich nach Westen zu öffnen. Das introvertierte Apartment wird über eine Brücke durch den Luftraum der Galerie im Souterrain erschlossen. Alle Hofflächen und Dachterrassen sind vom Apartment wie von der Kunstgalerie aus separat zu erreichen. Mit dem Garten ist nur die Galerie verbunden: über einen zweigeschossigen, in Glas gefaßten Luftraum mit vorgelagerter Freitreppe. Weiß durchgefärbter, wegen des alten Baumbestands versiegelter Sichtbeton vermittelt zwischen den benachbarten Putzoberflächen.

Villa with Private Art Gallery Hamburg Harvestehude 1994

In the elegant neighborhood of villas and consulates on the Außenalster River, on a property with a width of 29 m at the rear, half of that occupied by a 19th century villa that extends to the border, an addition at Harvestehuder Weg was planned on the free half of the tract, which also adjoins the fire wall of a four-story neighboring structure. The programmatic design – unfortunately never realized – deals intensely with the modern interpretation of the historic example. The building, to be planned and designed as a complementary counterpart to the existing two-story villa, was to house – according to the wishes of the owners of the two houses – a large apartment, a rental unit and a private art gallery, all on maximum two full floors. With a front width of only 9 m and under difficult framework conditions – for example, the demand that the old building and the garden to the east should be protected from visual intrusions – the attempt to individually develop each of the three functional components of the new structure without formally losing sight of the whole picture was quite successful. The central element is a courtyard with different levels that allow both apartment units to open towards the west. The introverted apartment is accessed via a bridge across the air space of the gallery on the lower floor. All levels of the yard and roof terraces can be accessed separately from the apartment and the art gallery. Only the gallery is connected with the garden through a two-story, glazed air space with an exterior staircase at its front. The white fair-faced concrete, sealed against the old existing trees, mediates between the neighboring plastered surfaces.

5

6

Büro- und Ausstellungsgebäude Otte Ladenbau Siek/Hamburg 1994–1996

Im Gewerbegebiet von Siek, einem kleinen Ort in Autobahnnähe wenige Kilometer östlich von Hamburg, war eine der üblichen schäbigen Fertigungshallen mit angekoppeltem Büroteil im laufenden Betrieb durch einen Neubau für Verwaltung, Planung und Ausstellung aufzuwerten. Zulässig waren zwei Geschosse. Mit dem Ziel einer maximalen Ausnutzung des Grundstücks, auch durch den Nachweis von zehn Stellplätzen wie unter Beibehaltung der Anlieferung mit schweren Sattelzügen entlang der Eingangsfront, entstand – der Baugrenze folgend – in sehr plastischer Ausdrucksweise ein der grundsätzlichen Bedeutung der Augabe angemessenes Statement zur architektonischen wie städtebaulichen Aufarbeitung von Gewerbe- und Industriegebieten. Nach der schon von Palladio angewandten Methode des Weiterbauens, Einfassens und Rahmens vorhandener Bausubstanz verschränken sich Alt und Neu sehr unmittelbar, Fenster an Fenster. Mit ihrem an der Straße vorangestelltem Ausstellungs- und Verwaltungskopf wird die architektonisch nachrangige Basis zu einem zumindest aus ökonomischen Gründen, aber auch aus kultureller Sicht beachtenswerten Dokument einer Bauepoche, die man nicht aus der Welt schaffen kann und soll, deren Fehler aber auf furiose Weise gestalterisch zu beheben sind. Die Kraft der neuen Gewerbe-Architektur, in einem Meer von Belanglosigkeiten zum markanten Vorbild und Schrittmacher zu werden, liegt in ihrem unausweichlichen Realitätsbezug. Architektonisch zielt die eingesetzte Körper-Sprache auf die Einheit aus innenräumlicher und baukörperlicher Brisanz, verdeutlicht in der Variation der Öffnungen und Materialien (wärmedämmender Sichtbeton, vorpatinierte graue Zinkfassade, im Farbton von unpatiertem Kupfer lackierte Aluminiumfassade). Auch die verspringenden Stützen und fragmentarischen Balkenlagen im Eingangsbereich folgen dem Eigensinn der Aufgabe und der Unverwechselbarkeit ihrer Lösung.

Office and Exhibition Building Otte Ladenbau Siek/Hamburg 1994–1996

In the industrial area of Siek, a small town close to the highway situated a few kilometers outside Hamburg, one of the typical shabby production halls with an adjoining office tract was to be evaluated with a new building housing administrative offices, planning offices and exhibition space without the need of stopping production. A two-story structure was permitted under the zoning regulations. With the goal being the maximum use of the property – for example, by installing ten parking spaces and maintaining the deliveries by heavy trucks along the entrance side – along the building border, a statement on the architectural and urban processing of industrial areas was made through a highly sculptural expression while meeting with the fundamental meaning of the task. Old and new immediately interlock, window to window, following the method of extending, framing and integrating an existing structure as applied by Palladio. The architecturally second-rank base structure with its exhibition and administration head placed at the street becomes a remarkable document of a building epoch – not only for economic reasons but from a cultural perspective, as well – that cannot be and shall not be removed from the earth but whose mistakes can be furiously corrected by design. The power of the new industrial architecture to become a striking example and trendsetter in a sea of meaninglessness and mediocrity is based on its unavoidable reference to reality. Architecturally, the body language employed here is directed at the unity of the interior and the constructive explosiveness clarified in the variation of the openings and materials (insulating fair-facade concrete, patinated with grey zinc facade, copper-colored aluminum facade). The set-off supports and fragmentary layers of beams at the entrance area follow the individualism of the task and the unmistakable nature of its solution.

1. Straßenfront mit Zugang.
   Street facade with access.
2. Ausstellungsraum.
   Exhibition space.
3. Seitenfront.
   Side facade.
4. Sichtbeton und Fassade im Detail.
   Details of fair-faced concrete and facade.
5. Obergeschoß.
   Upper floor.
6. Querschnitt.
   Cross section.
7. Ostansicht.
   West elevation.
8. Nordansicht.
   North elevation.

3

4

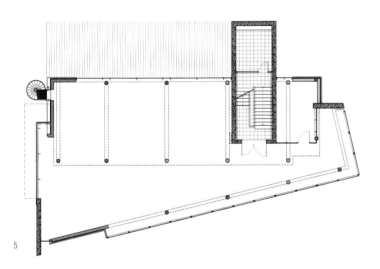

5

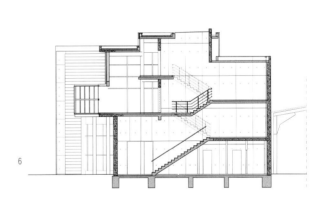

6

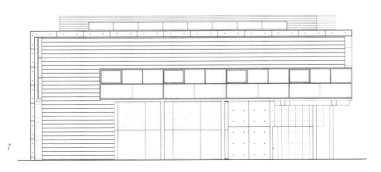

7

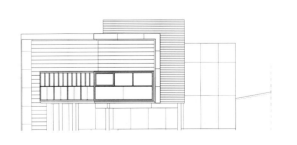

8

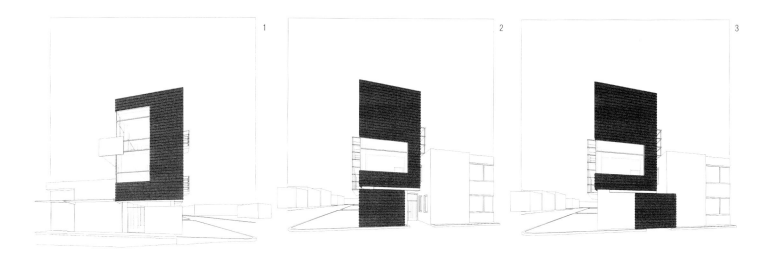

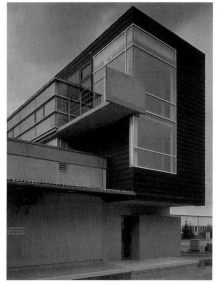

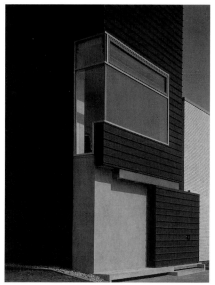

1, 4. Ansicht Norden .
  Elevation north.
2, 5. Zugangsseite, offen.
  Access side, open.
  3. Zugangsseite,
     geschlossen.
     Access side, closed.
  6. 1. Obergeschoß.
     Second floor.
  7. Querschnitt.
     Cross section.
  8. 2. Obergeschoß.
     Third floor.
  9. Isometrie
     Gesamtanlage.
     *Isometric projection of
     complex.*
 10. Straßenfront.
     Street facade.

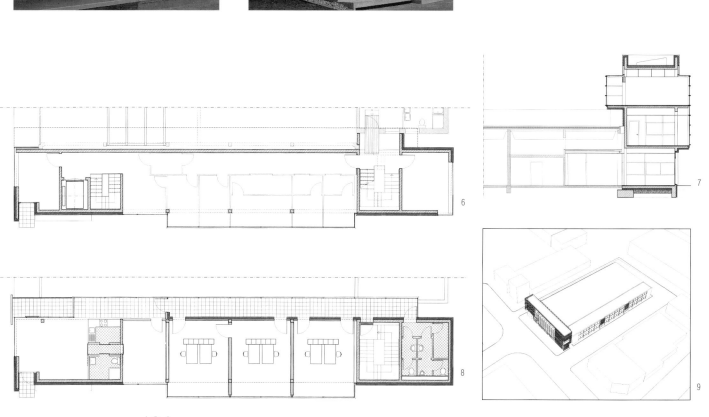

10

Laborgebäude Synopharm
Hamburg Barsbüttel
1994/1997–1998

In einer dem vorangestellten Projekt in Siek vergleichbaren Aufgabenstellung handelt es sich auch in Barsbüttel städtebaulich um Aufwertung und Nachverdichtung eines Gewerbegebiets am östlichen Rand Hamburgs. Entlang der Straße erhielt ein sehr flächenintensiv angelegter, zweigeschossiger Hallenkomplex der 70er Jahre, den sich mehrere Firmen zu Lager- und Verwaltungszwecken teilen, auf einer Bautiefe von nur 5 m beinahe nicht mehr als eine neue «dreidimensionale Fassade». Mit anderen Worten, jeder Stellplatzstreifen unmittelbar am Gebäude taugt in Gewerbe- und Industriegebieten zur architektonischen Umkehr. Das Pharma-Unternehmen nutzt die dreigeschossige, mit einer schwarz eloxierten Zinkfassade ausgestattete Erweiterung funktional zur Abfüllung und Konfektionierung von Wirkstoffen in Kleinstchargen, wobei an die hygienischen Bedingungen von Raumhülle und Bautechnik höchste Anforderungen gestellt werden. Ein Kriterium, das der großen Plastizität des Baukörpers im Grunde zuwiderläuft. Durch wechselnde Auskragungen und Einschnitte, Material-variation, raum- und geschoß-übergreifende Glasflächen gelingt formal auch auf knappster Grundstücksfläche ein sehr dynamischer architektonischer Aufmacher, der sich in den teilweise auch von anderen Firmen bereits neu definierten Straßenraum überaus spannungsvoll einordnet. In den Obergeschossen befinden sich linear angeordnete Einzelbüros, auf der letzten Ebene mit der dank Auskragungen zu beiden Seiten größten Bautiefe außerdem ein Apartment. Bemerkenswert und in der architektonischen Ausdruckskraft überraschend ist wiederum die intensive Verschränkung von Altbestand und Neubau trotz so unterschiedlicher Standards, etwa im Treppenhaus oder im Eingangsbereich mit Schiebewand.

Laboratory Building Synopharm
Hamburg Barsbüttel
1994/1997–1998

In a task similar to the project in Siek, the theme for Barsbüttel is an urban reevaluation and condensation of an industrial area at the eastern periphery of Hamburg. Along the street, a very flatly designed, two-story hall complex from the '70s shared by several companies for storage and administrative purposes received almost nothing more than a new "three-dimensional facade" with a depth of only 5 m. In other words: any parking lot strip directly adjacent to a building can be used for an architectural conversion in an industrial area. The pharmaceutical company uses the three-story extension with black galvanized zinc facade in a highly functional way – for packaging small amounts of active substances – while the highest requirements have been applied to the hygienic conditions of the spatial shell and building technology. This is a criterion that opposes the large plasticity of the building volume. Formally, a very dynamic architectural design succeeds through changing projections and openings, materials and glass surfaces reaching across rooms and floors. It suspensefully integrates into the street space that had already been redefined by other companies in various sections. Single offices are organized longitudinally on the upper floors; on the last level, there is also an apartment, made possible by the fact that the building depth is greatest here due to the projections on either side. What is remarkable and surprising in the expressive architectural power is the intense interlocking of the old and new structures, despite such different standards – for example, in the stairway or the entrance area with sliding doors.

Andreas Scheuring
Claudia Hannibal-Scheuring

Systematik spielerisch

Claudia Hannibal-Scheuring und Andreas Scheuring geben der Sachlichkeit und Kargheit der Moderne eine spielerische Note, die mit anderen Mitteln und Motiven arbeitet als den klassischen, aber auch den dekonstruktivistischen. Ihre Architektur ist gläserner und filigraner angelegt, darum notwendigerweise auch konstruktiver und analytischer formuliert als die weiße Moderne der 20er und 30er Jahre. War Transparenz bei Otto Haesler, Hans und Wassili Luckhardt, Erik Gunnar Asplund oder Mies van der Rohe stets in einen gleichförmigen konstruktiven Rhythmus eingebettet, wird dieser nun überspielt, nicht aufgebrochen wie beim Tanz des Dekonstruktivismus um die Demokratie des Glases. Die experimentelle Freiheit der Konstruktion und ihrer Ausbau-Elemente, wie sie von Günter Behnisch (*1922) seit Beginn der 70er Jahre propagiert wurde, konnte insofern keine Schule begründen, als es nicht gelang, allein daraus konsequent eigenständige Entwicklungen abzuleiten. Dieser das Publikum spaltende Ansatz blieb ein personifiziertes und damit «registriertes» Markenzeichen, kein Beitrag, der sich dem Veränderungsbegehren einer breiten Diskussion stellt oder dem Grundkonsens einer städtebaulichen Ordnung fügt. Das ist die große Stärke dieser Architektur, gleichzeitig aber ihr entscheidender Mangel. Labyrinthische Gebäude verweigern sich dem Labyrinth Stadt. Andreas Scheuring begann sein Studium zwar in Darmstadt mit dem Vorbild Günter Behnisch vor Augen und war an der TU Braunschweig in der Rolle des Oppositionellen, dem das Vordiplom der TH Darmstadt nicht anerkannt wurde, eher geneigt, für den spielerischen Umgang mit allen architektonischen Elementen einzutreten. Aber auch die Architektur dieses Büros distanziert sich schließlich von der barocken Stei-

gerung eines architektonisch gesteuerten Chaos, um Reduktion der Mittel und Elemente, Klarheit und Ökonomie der Konstruktion und städtebauliche Einpassung und Ordnung vorzuziehen – ohne der Freiheit des Raums und seiner kompositionellen Fügung zum Nachteil der Menschen Fesseln anzulegen. Der Kunstgriff liegt darin, nicht alle Regeln vergessen machen zu wollen, sondern die räumliche Besonderheit vor dem Hintergrund einer konstruktiven und einer städtebaulichen Regel darzustellen. Ordnung bleibt notwendiges Grundprinzip, ihre architektonischen und vor allem räumlichen Ziele sind jedoch Kontrast, Variation, Dynamik. Die äußere Erscheinung lebt von einer in mehrere Schichten aufgelösten Fassade, oft mit Glasanteilen zwischen 90 und 100 Prozent, die sich in ihrer instrumentellen Immaterialität eher dem individuellen Umgang mit Licht und Schatten, Einblick und Ausblick verschreibt als einem starren Fassadenbild. Traten beim Therapiezentrum in Bad Lippspringe in freier städtebaulicher Disposition Ordnung und Regel noch etwas stärker in den Hintergrund, gewinnen in den Folgeprojekten, dem eigenen Wohnhaus und der Hochschulbibliothek in Zwickau, Präzision und Reduktion deutlich an Boden. Die Innovationskraft der Architekten läßt sich auch von den Dimensionen einer Fachhochschule oder eines innerstädtischen Einkaufszentrums nicht vereinnahmen. Bedrückend ist jedoch, daß sich dieses für junge Architekten erstaunlich große Ideen- und Erfahrungspotential nach erfolgreichen Wettbewerben bei aller Ökonomie der Mittel nicht immer durchsetzen läßt. So wird das großartige urbane Konzept der Fachhochschule in Heide dank erneuter Sparbeschlüsse wohl leider ohne den integralen Bestandteil der kontemplativen Wasserflächen auskommen müssen, obwohl diese auch als Lichtkanone gedacht sind.

Systematically playful

Claudia Hannibal-Scheuring and Andreas Scheuring provide the factuality and scarcity of Modernism with a playful note, which works with other means and motives than the classical or deconstructive ones. Their architecture is more transparent and filigree, and thus, it is also necessarily more constructively and analytically formulated that the White Modernism of the '20s and '30s. Whereas with Otto Haesler, Hans and Wassili Luckhardt, Erik Gunnar Asplund or Mies van der Rohe transparency was always embedded in a uniform, constructive rhythm, the latter is now being overplayed and not fragmented as it was in the case of Deconstructivism's dance around the democracy of glass. The experimental freedom of construction and its building elements, as was propagated by Günter Behnisch (*1922) since the early '70s, couldn't establish a school since it failed to produce consequentially independent developments. This approach divided the audience and remained a personified and thus "registered" trademark and not a contribution that would confront the need for a change of the broad discussion or submit to the basic consensus of an urban order. This is the greatest strength of this architecture and, at the same time, its decisive fault. Labyrinthian buildings exclude themselves from the urban labyrinths. Andreas Scheuring began his studies in Darmstadt with Günter Behnisch's example before his eyes; at Braunschweig University, he assumed the role of the antagonist, whose pre-diploma from Darmstadt University wasn't recognized, and he rather tended towards defending the playful approach to all architectural elements. But in the end, the architecture of this office also distances itself from the baroque comparison of an architecturally controlled

chaos in order to give preference to the reduction of the means and elements, clarity and economy instead of the construction and urban integration and order – without putting chains onto the freedom of space and its compositional providence to the great disadvantage of all people. The trick is not to forget all the rules but to present the outstanding spatial characteristics against the background of a constructive and an urban rule. Order remains a necessary basic principle; its architectural and especially its spatial goals, however, do contrast and vary, and they are dynamic. The outward appearance lives from a facade – resolved in several layers, often with 90 to 100 percent glass – which in its instrumental immateriality submits to the individual approach to light and shade, insight and outlook, rather than to a rigid facade image. Whereas order and rule were placed more in the background in a free urban disposition in the case of the therapy center in Bad Lippspringe, precision and reduction clearly gain grounds in their subsequent projects – their own house and the university library in Zwickau. The architects' innovative power can neither be restricted by the dimensions of a university for applied science or by an inner-city shopping center. The fact that this incredibly great potential of ideas and experience of these young architects cannot always be realized, despite their success in competitions and their economic use of means, is, however, rather saddening. Thus, the great urban concept of the university in Heide will unfortunately have to do without the integral component of the contemplative water surfaces as a result of recent budgetary decisions – although these were also intended to be a cannon of light.

107

Therapiezentrum Bad Lippspringe
1990–1994

Das Therapiezentrum mit Bewegungsbad und Turnhalle vermeidet jede Assoziation zu herkömmlichen Einrichtungen dieser Art. Am östlichen Ende der kastaniengesäumten Kurpromenade erwartet den Patienten nicht einengendes klinisches Instrumentarium, sondern vor allem ein von allen Beklemmungen befreiender Raum – in der Kreisform besonders intensiv belichtet. Ein wesentliches Moment der Anlage ist der in den auskragenden Dächern und ausgreifenden Gebäudearmen dokumentierte Bezug zur umgebenden Parklandschaft. Um Schwellenängste zu vermeiden, reicht der Einblick vom Eingang bis in den abgesenkten zentralen Innenhof, der ebenso wie der vor dem äußeren Kreisrund abgesenkte Garten eine versteckte Dreigeschossigkeit bewirkt und die

Treppen und Ruhezonen im Zentrum rund um einen Trompetenbaum offen und lichtdurchflutet zusammenschließt. Über 90 Prozent der Gebäudehülle sind verglast. Alle Therapiebereiche schließen sich innen wie außen nur soweit ab wie unbedingt notwendig. Der Badebetrieb des Bewegungsbades wird durch eine Glassteinwand hinter dem Empfang in der Halle erlebbar. Bedruckte Glasscheiben im Wechsel mit verfahrbaren Sonnensegeln und einer zweiten Fassadenschicht aus Stahlrundrohren und Gitterrosten schaffen hier Distanz zum Außenraum. Gleichzeitig entsteht im Zusammenspiel mit runden Oberlichtern aber ein sehr angenehmer Außenbezug. Nicht einmal innerhalb der hohen hygienischen Anforderungen des Inhalationsraums oder in den Fangoräumen des Obergeschosses ist Ausgrenzung oberstes Gebot. (Wettbewerb, 1. Preis; Architekturpreis Vorbildliche Gewerbebauten 1994)

Therapy Center Bad Lippspringe
1990–1994

The therapy center with an exercise pool and gymnasium avoids any association with traditional institutions of its kind. At the eastern end of the spa's chestnut-tree lined promenade, the patients are greeted not by a restricting clinical institution but by a space that brushes aside all apprehensions – this is enhanced especially by the circular shape. An essential element of the complex is its relationship with the surrounding park landscape, expressed in the cantilevered roofs and the projecting arms of the buildings. In order to allay any fears as one crosses the threshold, the view is free from the entrance to the lowered central courtyard which, like the garden lowered before the outer circle, creates a hidden tri-level effect and unites the stairs and rest areas in the center around a Catalpa

Bignonioides in an open and light-flooded way. More than 90 percent of the building's shell is glazed. All therapy areas are closed off on the interior and exterior only to the extent that is absolutely necessary. The bathers in the exercise pool can be detected through to a glass brick wall behind the reception in the lobby. Imprinted glass panes, changing with mobile sun sails, and a second facade layer consisting of round steel pipes and metal grids, create the necessary distancing to the outside space. At the same time, a very comfortable reference to the outside is created through a reference to the round skylights. Exclusion is also not the highest priority even in the high hygienic conditions of the inhalation room or the mud-therapy rooms on the upper floor. (Competition, 1st prize; Architectural Award Exemplary Industrial Buildings 1994)

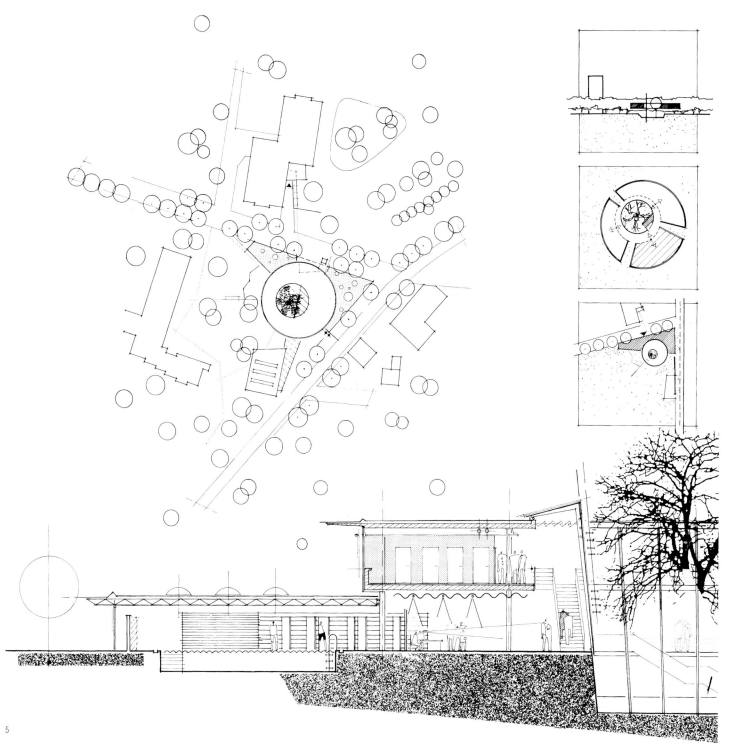

5

1. Gartenseite.
   Garden side.
2. Untergeschoß.
   Basement floor.
3. Obergeschoß.
   Upper floor.
4. Erschliessungshalle
   mit Wartezonen.
   *Access hall with
   waiting areas.*
5. Lageplan mit
   Entwurfskonzept und
   Schnitt.
   *Site plan with design
   concept and section.*
6. Gesamtanlage.
   Complex.

6

1

Wohnhaus Scheuring Köln Klettenberg 1994–1995

Zur Verdichtung ihrer Baustruktur bietet die Stadt Köln potentiellen Bauherren einen Katalog an, der über 4.800 Baulücken nachweist. Seit 1990 sind 1.400 Lücken geschlossen worden und achttausend Wohneinheiten neu entstanden. Zwischen einem Wohnhaus der 30er Jahre und einem Nachtrag der 60er Jahre entstand der in seiner Kargheit schon außen souverän auf die Moderne verweisende Neubau auf einer Distanz von nur 5m. Ein leichter Knick im Straßenverlauf bot Anlaß, leicht aus der geschlossenen Bebauung hervorzutreten. Die raumhoch verglasten Räume beziehen optisch den Straßenraum ein und werden atmosphärisch durch das bewegte Licht einer Birkenallee bestimmt. Auskragende Gitterroste, Außenjalousien und ein zweites Fassadenbild aus den dafür konstruktiv notwendigen Stahlrohren geben der durchschimmernden Holz-/Glas-Fassade Tiefe, Lebendigkeit und «eine bestehend beiläufige Eleganz» (Deutscher Architekturpreis). Im geschickt zwischen Öffentlichkeit und Privatheit vermittelnden Eingangsbereich springt die Fassade auf die Flucht des Nachbarhauses zurück und vermittelt durch die Schattenwirkung Distanz. Die mittig eingestellte, offene, über Dach belichtete Treppe schafft halbgeschossig versetzte Ebenen und auf jeder Etage eine hinter einer Betonscheibe verborgene Funktionsnische mit Installationsschacht. Deckenöffnungen erlauben im Wohnbereich Blickbeziehungen über die gesamte Haustiefe. Der langgestreckte, schmale Garten wird durch einen abgesenkten Hof vor dem Arbeitsraum und zwei Terrassen in der Krone eines alten Ahornbaums ergänzt. (Kölner Architekturpreis 1995, Deutscher Architekturpreis, Anerkennung 1997)

Scheuring House Cologne Klettenberg 1994–1995

For the purpose of condensing its architectural structure, the city of Cologne offered a catalog showing over 4,800 open tracts to potential clients. 1400 gaps have been closed and eight thousand apartments have been created since 1990. Between an apartment house from the '30s and an addition from the '60s, the new structure was erected at a distance of only 5 meters; in its scarcity on the outside, it already hints decisively at Modernism. A slight bend in the street offered the possibility to slightly step out of the closed-up development. The rooms have wall-to-ceiling glazing and visually include the street space; their atmosphere is determined by the moving light of a birch- tree-lined alley. Cantilevered metal grids, exterior blinds and a second facade layer consisting of steel pipes, which are constructively necessary for the blinds, provide the shimmering wood-glass facade with depth, liveliness and "a strikingly casual elegance" (German Architectural Award). The entrance area cleverly mediates between public and private life; here, the facade recedes to the line of the neighboring house and mediates distance due to the effect of the cast shadow. The open staircase is installed centrally and is lit by skylights; it creates different levels set-off in semi-floor height, and on each level, a utility corner with the installation shaft hidden behind a concrete wall panel. In the living area, the openings in the ceilings allow visual references to the entire depth of the house. The long, narrow garden is complemented by a lowered yard in front of the work space and two terraces in the crown of an old maple tree. (Cologne Architectural Award 1995, German Architectural Award, 1997 recognition)

1. Wohnbereich mit Blick in den Garten.
   Living area with view of the garden.
2. Längsschnitt.
   Longitudinal section.
3. Straßenfront.
   Street facade.
4. Eßplatz und Küche.
   Dining area and kitchen.
5. Gartenfront.
   Garden facade.

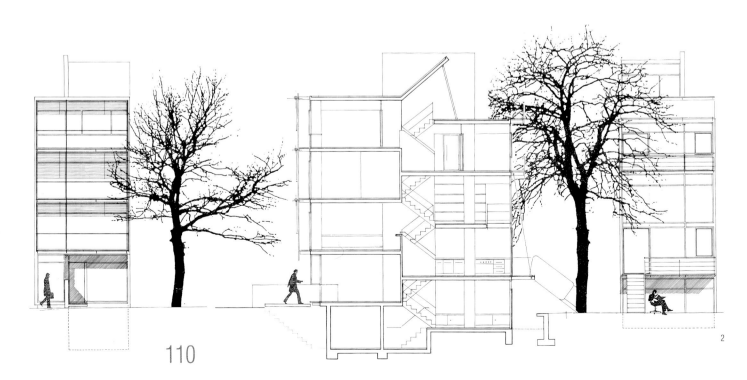

2

3

4

5

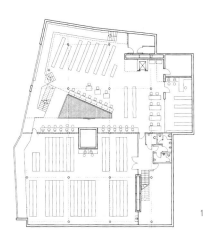

1

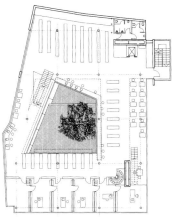

2

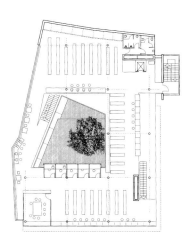

3

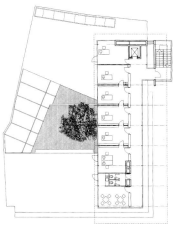

4

5

6

7

Hochschulbibliothek Zwickau 1994–1998

Die Fachhochschule in Zwickau, 1897 als Ingenieurschule für Maschinenbau gegründet, befindet sich heute in einem von der Straße zurückgesetzten Hofgebäude mitten im Stadtzentrum. Dem Kornmarkt vis-à-vis markiert die neue Bibliothek als stadtzugewandter Kopf der Gesamtanlage den Zugang zum Hochschulcampus und öffnet sich, vollständig verglast, dem interessierten Publikum. Die vor dem Eingang durch einen leicht angehobenen kleinen Platz unterbrochene Straßenrandbebauung unterstreicht diese Geste ebenso wie das zu Platz und Straße signalhaft auskragende, schwebende Dach. Dieser Abschluß mit den Räumen der Fachreferenten bindet die einzelnen baukörperlich hervorgehobenen Bereiche der Bibliothek signifikant zusammen. Der Verwaltungstrakt für Fernleihe und Zeitschriften, angeordnet in einem zweigeschossigen Betonrahmen, erlaubt konzentriertes, vor dem Lärm der Straße geschütztes Arbeiten im Zentrum – rund um den bis ins Untergeschoß reichenden, mit einer Robinie bepflanzten Atriumhof. Durch Rundstützen abgefangen, gliedern darunter Arkaden den Straßenraum vor Zeitschriften-Lesesaal und Café am Innenhof. Der zweigeschossige Haupt-Lesesaal bildet sich zum Campus als Ganzglasfassade ab und lockt mit tiefen Einblicken in die Welt der Bücher. Ein vier Geschosse hoher Betonwinkel umfängt das über alle Ebenen reichende, verglaste Treppenhaus. Die Innenräume, bis zu den Möbeln von den Architekten gestaltet, zeigen Sichtbeton, Natursisal und Ahorn natur bzw. schwarz gebeizt. (Wettbewerb, 1. Preis)

University For Applied Science Library Zwickau 1994–1998

The university for applied science in Zwickau, founded in 1897 as a school for mechanical engineering, is today located in a courtyard building set back from the street in the center of the city. Opposite the Kornmarkt, the new library forms the head of the entire complex. It is turned towards the city and marks the access to the university campus, opening up to an enticed audience with its fully glazed facade. The street side development, interrupted by a slightly raised square in front of the entrance, enhances this gesture, as does the floating roof cantilevered towards the square and street. This termination with lecture rooms significantly connects the separate areas of the library that are distinguished with respect to the build volumes and elements. The administrative tract for external orders and magazines is located within a two-story concrete frame and allows for better concentration while working in the center, as it is protected from the street noise – all around the atrium yard with its Robinia and reaching into the basement floor. Supported by round columns, arcades structure the street space beneath, in front of the magazine reading room and café in the courtyard. The two-story main library hall is completely glazed towards the campus and entices with its deep insights into the world of books. A four-story, concrete angle embraces the glazed staircase reaching through all levels. The interior spaces, including the furniture, were designed by the architects and display fair-faced concrete, natural burlap and natural or black-stained maple. (Competition, 1st prize)

1-4. Grundrisse.
    Ground plans.
5. Straßenfront.
    Street facade.
6. Modell Platzfront.
    Model of facade facing square.
7. Platzfront.
    Facade facing square.

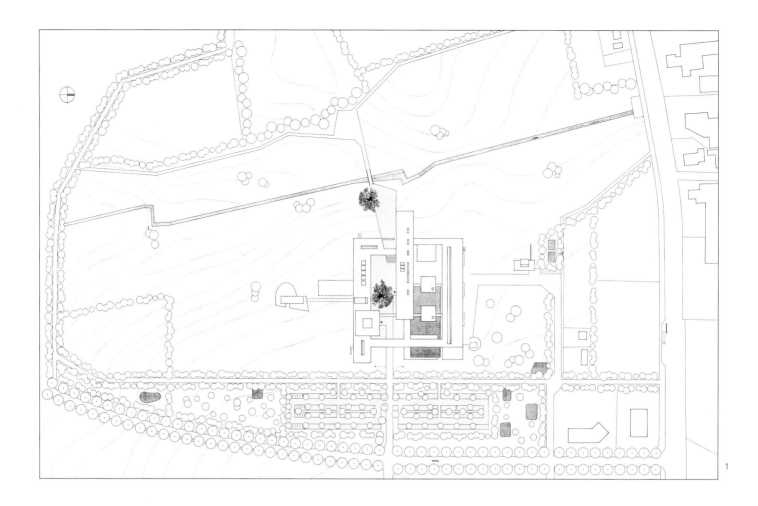

Fachhochschule Westküste Schleswig-Holstein Heide 1994–1999

Der Standort für die neugegründete Fachhochschule befindet sich am östlichen Stadtrand in einer landschaftlich reizvollen Auenlandschaft. Der quadratische, vielfältig erweiterbare Komplex (Mensa, Bibliothek) grenzt sich ähnlich den norddeutschen Landhöfen des 18. und 19. Jahrhunderts markant gegen die freie Landschaft mit ihren Baumreihen und Knicks ab, um seine gebäudebezogenen Freiflächen nach innen zu orientieren – ohne jedoch den Bezug zur Außenwelt aufzugeben. Der Kontrast zwischen der kargen Landschaft und lebendigen, aber künstlich gestalteten Innenhöfen bestimmt den Reiz des städtebaulichen Konzepts ebenso wie dessen komplexe kommunikative Struktur. Der Campus mit einem großen Baum im Zentrum ist als städtischer Platz definiert, von dem aus die Stadt noch im Blick bleibt. Im Gegensatz dazu stehen die Seminargebäude als kontemplative Inseln in der Wasserfläche des Innenhofs. In ihrer Spiegelwirkung steigert die Wasserfläche zugleich den Tageslichteinfall der angrenzenden Büros und Arbeitsräume. Eine dreigeschossige Eingangshalle vermittelt zwischen Campus und Seminarhof. Als beidseitig verglaste Treppenhalle erleichtert sie die Orientierung und erschließt das Dekanat und die zentralen Hörsäle. Durch die Mehrschichtigkeit der äußeren Umfassungswand, die Klinkermauerwerk in Bezug setzt zu Glas, Metall und Beton, wird der absolute Anspruch der Großform relativiert. Windgetriebene Lüftungsrotoren auf dem Dach sorgen im Zusammenhang mit einer Doppelfassade für den Luftaustausch der Hörsäle. (Wettbewerb, 1. Preis)

Westküste University for Applied Science Schleswig-Holstein Heide 1994–1999

The location for the newly founded university is at the eastern edge of town in an attractive meadow landscape. The square, expandable complex (cafeteria, library) strikingly distinguishes itself from the landscape with rows of trees and bends – similar to the country farms in the north of Germany dating from the 18th and 19th centuries – in order to orient its building-related free spaces towards the inside without, however, giving up its relationship with the outside world. The contrast between the landscape and the lively but artificially created inner courtyards determines the charm of the urban concept as well as its complex communicative structure. The campus, with a large tree at its center, is defined as an urban square from where the town can still be seen. Contrary to this, the seminar buildings are placed like contemplative islands in the watery surface of the courtyard. The water with its reflecting surface enhances the daylight entering the adjoining offices and work spaces. A three-story entrance lobby mediates between the campus and the seminary yard. It's a stairway glazed on two sides and it facilitates the orientation and provides access to the dean's office and the central lecture halls. Due to the multiple layers of the exterior enclosing wall, which bring brick into relationship with glass, metal and concrete, the absolute claim of the large-scale form is made relative. Wind-powered ventilation rotors on the roof take care of the air exchange in the lecture halls through a double facade. (Competition, 1st prize)

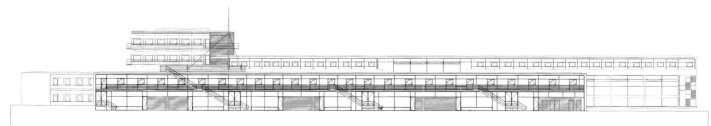

3

4

1. Lageplan.
   Site plan.
2. Querschnitt.
   Cross section.
3, 4. Rohbaustruktur.
   *Rough brickwork
   structure.*
5. Erdgeschoß.
   First floor.
6. Modellausschnitt von
   Süden.
   *Detail model from
   south.*
7. Modellausschnitt von
   Norden.
   *Model detail from
   north.*

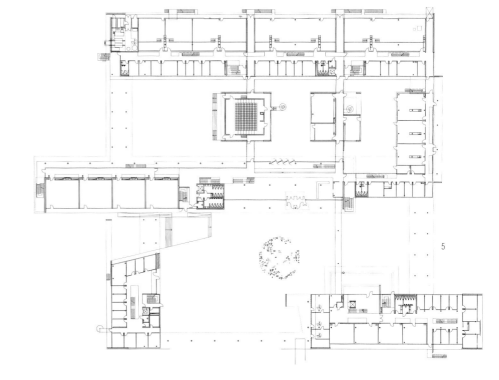

5

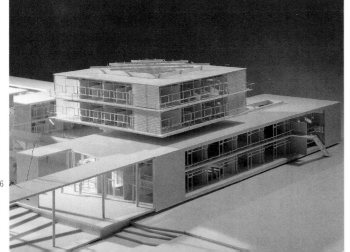

6

7

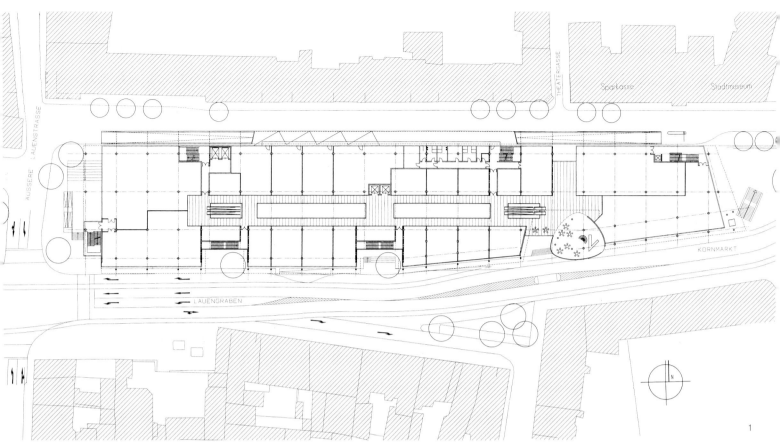

Innerstädtisches Einkaufszentrum Bautzen Kornmarkt 1996–2000

Zentrum des in seinem mittelalterlichen Stadtgrundriß noch heute beeindruckenden Altstadtkerns von Bautzen ist mit Kirche und freistehendem Rathaus der Marktplatz. Der östliche Bereich der Innenstadt – und damit das 250 m lange Grundstück des geplanten Einkaufszentrums – wird durch ost-west-gerichtete Baublöcke und entsprechende Straßen strukturiert, die durch nachgeordnete Nebenstraßen und Blockdurchgänge gekreuzt werden. Von Bedeutung ist, daß der neue Block, markantes Bindeglied zwischen historischer Altstadt und südlicher Innenstadt, auf seiner geschlosseneren Nordseite (Anlieferung, Tiefgaragenzufahrt, verglaste Auffahrten zu den Dachparkplätzen) die historischen Wallanlagen nachzeichnet. Die heute noch vorhandenen historischen Befestigungstürme kennzeichneten dabei die Stadteingänge. Dieses Motiv wird am Lauenturm wie am Kornmarkt, dem westlichen wie östlichen Endpunkt des mehrteiligen Gebäudes, durch platzartige Aufweitungen beibehalten. Das Schließen der Stadtbrache durch eine zweigeschossige, über Dach belichtete Einkaufspassage mit Außenwirkung und vielfältigen Blickbeziehungen in die Stadt folgt dem vorgefundenen städtebaulichen Prinzip des Verengens und Aufweitens in besonderer Weise. Architektonisch läßt sich ahnen, was ein innerstädtisches Einkaufszentrum leisten kann, wenn es nicht ausschließlich nach Renditegesichtspunkten und auf der Basis eines falsch verstandenen Geschichtsbewußtseins zu planen ist. (Wettbewerb, 1. Preis)

Inner-city Shopping Center Bautzen Kornmarkt 1996–2000

The market square with church and the free-standing town hall is in the center of the old town of Bautzen which, with its medieval ground plan, is still quite impressive. The eastern section of the inner city – and thus the 250 meter long property of the planned shopping center – is structured by building blocks orientated east to west, and by the appropriate streets that are intersected by smaller side streets and passageways between the blocks. What is important is that the new block, a striking link between the historic old part of town and the southern inner city, redraws the historic ramparts on its closed-up northern side (deliveries, underground parking access, glazed ramps to the roof parking). The preserved rampart towers originally marked the entrances to the town. This motif is maintained with square-like open spaces at the Lauenturm and Kornmarkt, the western and eastern termination of the building consisting of several parts. Closing the town's fallow land with a two-story, sky-lit shopping mall, which maintains an outdoor effect as well as multiple visual references into the town, follows the existing urban principle of narrowing and expanding in a rather special way. One can sense architecturally what an inner-city shopping center is capable of doing if it is not planned exclusively on the basis of a return on capital and a distorted historical awareness. (Competition, 1st prize)

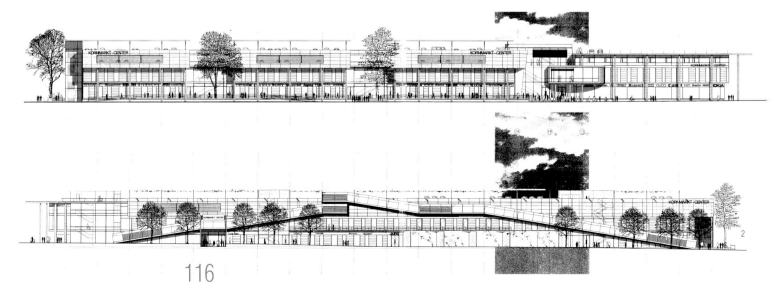

3

1. Obergeschoß.
   Upper floor.
2. Ansicht Straßenseite.
   Elevation street side.
3. Stadtmodell mit
   Wettbewerbsentwurf.
   *Model of the city with
   competition design.*
4. Perspektive
   Einkaufspassage.
   *Perspective shopping
   mall.*

4

Kommunikativer Rationalismus

Hartwig Schneider plädiert mit flachen Dächern, modularen Fassaden, Fenstern in Marschordnung, strengen Fensterbändern, kargem Material, disziplinierter Farbwahl und formellen Erschließungswegen unübersehbar für die Sachlichkeit der klassischen Moderne. Die Konsequenz, die der Architekt dabei an den Tag legt, erinnert an den Aufbruch dieser Formensprache in der Schweiz vor siebzig Jahren, etwa an Bauten von Hans Schmidt (1893–1972), aber auch an die Arbeiten von Michael Alder (*1940). Die Idee des Rationalismus, die heute vor neuem ökologischen und vergleichbarem ökonomischen Hintergrund neu zu interpretieren ist, wird jedoch in ungewohnt kommunikativer Ausprägung aktualisiert. Damit zeigt sich ein Ausweg zwischen der romantisch mißverstandenen, populistischen Postmoderne nur für den eigenen Hausgebrauch und dem grundsätzlichen Unvermögen der orthodoxen Moderne, sich städtebaulich zu integrieren, den eigenen ästhetischen Anspruch ohne Diskriminierung anderer Ansätze zu präsentieren und damit Stadtergänzung und Stadtreparatur erst möglich zu machen. Dank geläuterter Beziehungen zum Bestand entsteht stadträumlich, typologisch und archi-

tektonisch ein dichtes Gefüge von unterschiedlichen Angeboten, Erscheinungsbildern und städtebaulichen Verknüpfungen. Systematische Baustrukturen folgen ihrer typologischen und konstruktiven Logik, lassen diese aber von den besonderen Bedingungen der Landschaft und des Grundstücks scheinbar willkürlich außer Kraft setzen. Harmonie und Variation, die der Architekt sehr rigoros mit Stringenz verbindet, summieren sich nicht zur postmodernen, dekonstruktivistischen oder «kritisch rekonstruierten» historischen Idylle. Auch die Moderne ist nicht als bloßer Stil gefragt, der wie mit einer Zeitmaschine zu (re)kultivieren wäre. Vielmehr geht es um inhaltliche Fortschritte auf mehreren Ebenen, vom Städtebau bis zum Detail. Zeitgemäße Erscheinungsformen im Sinne einer variantenreichen unorthodoxen Moderne bilden dabei lediglich eine weitere, nach wie vor nicht widerstandslos zu diskutierende Ebene der Auseinandersetzung. Neben der stillschweigenden Versuchung, Städtebau stets bei Null zu beginnen, bestand die zweite große Lebenslüge der orthodoxen Moderne darin, funktional Identisches innerhalb ein- und desselben Projekts auch formal ständig zu wiederholen. Diese Berechenbarkeit und Durchschaubarkeit durch Vagheit und

Variation zu ersetzen war schon das Ziel der oppositionellen Moderne eines Rudolf Schindler (1887–1953), Josef Frank (1885–1967) oder Richard Neutra (1892–1970). Mit neuen, vom Gebrauch der Bewohner und der Alterung des Materials mitbestimmten Bildern, die nach der Methode des Verrätselns bei changierenden Fassaden, Materialien und Farbtönen mehr zeigen als den Grundriß dahinter, einer verflochtenen städtebaulichen Organisation und der gezielt einbezogenen wechselhaften baulichen Umgebung steigert sich die Komplexität der Darstellung, variantenreich und geheimnisvoll, bei aller Sparsamkeit und Reduktion scheinbar ins Labyrinthische. Dieser begrenzte, aber wohlüberlegte und konstruktiv wie ökologisch durchdachte formale Reichtum vermeidet bei der Stadtreparatur in Ludwigsburg die menschenverachtende Kälte, vor der postmoderne und neokonservative Kritiker noch in jüngster Zeit warnten, um den Ausstieg aus der Moderne nahezulegen. Schon von Beginn an, vor siebzig Jahren, ordnete Ferdinand Kramer (1898–1985) derartige Anliegen in die Rubrik «reaktionäres Märchen» ein, da Typisierung keineswegs auf jede persönliche Note oder soziales Engagement verzichten müsse.

Communicative rationalism

With flat roofs, modular facades, windows in a lined-up order, strict window strips, scarce materials, disciplined choice of color and formal development Hartwig N. Schneider pleads unmistakably for the factuality of classical Modernism. The consequence, which the architect displays in doing so, reminds us of the emergence of this formal language in Switzerland seventy years ago – for example, in Hans Schmidt's (1893–1972) buildings and the works by Michael Adler (*1940). The idea of Rationalism that today has to be reinterpreted given the new ecological and comparable economic background, however, is actualized in an unusual communicative fashion. This shows a way out of the romantically misunderstood populist Post-Modernism for private use and the basic inability of the orthodox Modernism to integrate in an urban way, to present its own aesthetic claim without discriminating other approaches and thus to enable urban additions and repairs. Due to the purified relations with the existing structures, a dense structure of diverse offerings, appearances and urban connections is created in an urban, typological and architectural sense. Systematic

Sozialer Wohnungsbau
Ludwigsburg,
Stuttgart 1993–1997.
*Social housing
Ludwigsburg,
Stuttgart 1993–1997.*

building structures follow their typological and constructive logic but also allow them loose their power in a seemingly arbitrary way through the specific conditions of the landscape and property. Harmony and variation, rigorously connected with stringency by the architect, do not add up into a post-modern, deconstructivist or "critically reconstructed" historic ideal. Modernism, too, isn't requested as a pure style that would have to be (re)cultivated as with a time-machine. Moreover, the question is contextual progress on several levels, from urbanism to the detail. Contemporary forms of appearance in the sense of a richly varied, unorthodox Modernism only form yet another level of confrontation that still cannot be discussed without resistance. Next to the quiet temptation to always begin urban development at naught, the second big lie of orthodox Modernism was to formally repeat what was functionally identical within one and the same project. Replacing this calculation and transparency with vagueness and variation had already been the goal of the opposition Modernism of a Rudolf Schindler (1887–1953), Josef Frank (1885–1967) or Richard Neutra (1892–1970). With new images co-determined by the use of the inhabitants, and the aging of the materials that show more than the ground plan following the methodology of coding with changing facades, materials and colors, with an interconnected urban organization and the targeted integrated and changing architectural environment, the complexity of the presentation – versatile and secretive – is increased, seemingly, to the point of becoming a kind of labyrinth, despite all attempts at frugality and reduction. In case of the urban repair of Ludwigsburg, this limited yet well-considered and constructively as well as ecologically well-planned formal wealth avoids the inhumane coldness about which post-modern and neo-conservative critics have warned even recently in order to propound the abandonment of Modernism. From the beginning, some seventy years ago, Ferdinand Kramer (1898–1985) placed such approaches into the category "reactionary fairytale," as typification did not have to sacrifice any personal note or social engagement.

Hartwig N. Schneider

Kindergarten Winnenden/Stuttgart 1992–1995

In der von moderner Architektur weit entfernten Rundbogen-Romantik eines Neubaugebiets gibt sich das in Holzlamellen gefaßte Prisma auf den ersten Blick wie die präzise mathematische Formel des Gegengiftes. Die streng geometrische Basis dieser Architektur ist jedoch nicht verbissene Reaktion oder ideologische These, die ausgefallene Form beruht allein auf dem sehr schwierigen und knappen Grundstückszuschnitt, der anderes kaum zuließ. Die beiden nur scheinbar geschlossenen, halbtransparenten Seitenfronten des gleichschenkligen Dreiecks gelten mit einem Winkel von 76° dem wenig attraktiven Ausblick nach Norden wie der im Osten unmittelbar benachbarten Straße. Grund genug, den mathematischen Rohling an seiner in den Garten orientierten Süd-West-Front wie einen Edelstein durch Feinschliff zum Strahlen zu bringen. In reiner Symmetrie wenden sich hinter einer Totalverglasung (EPDM-Profilsystem) vier Gruppenräume der Sonne und einigen unvermeidlich dicht heranrückenden Wohnhäusern zu. Um den architektonischen Kontrast wie die Einblickmöglichkeiten in beiden Richtungen zu mildern, aber auch um die Aufheizung der Innenräume zu kontrollieren, ist der Südseite im Abstand des vorgelagerten Terrassendecks eine zweite Fassade in Gestalt eines Rankgerüstes mit automatisch gesteuerten Sonnensegeln vorangestellt. Der gesamte Bau, eine Komposition aus unbehandelter Douglasie und Glas, moduliert nur zwei Themen: Holz und Licht. Weder die totale Symmetrie noch das enge Materialspektrum stören die Komplexität der in ihrem Gebrauchswert sehr lebendig konzipierten Räume. (Wettbewerb, 1. Preis)

Kindergarten Winnenden/Stuttgart 1992–1995

In the rounded arch romanticism of a new development far removed from modern architecture, the prism enveloped by wood lamella presents itself – at first glance – like the precise mathematical formula of an antidote. The strictly geometric basis of this architecture is, however, not a grim reaction or ideological thesis; the unusual form is based exclusively on the difficult and tight layout of the property, which hardly allowed for anything else. The two seemingly closed, semi-transparent facets of the isosceles triangle with an angle of 76 degrees are turned towards the rather unattractive view to the north and the immediately adjoining street to the east. Reason enough to bring the mathematical blank to a high sheen through fine polishing, like a gem, at its southwest side oriented towards the garden. In pure symmetry, four group-rooms are turned towards the sun and towards several unavoidably close apartment houses behind a complete glazing (EPDM profile system). In order to reduce the architectural contrast and the vistas in both directions, but also to control the heat gain in the interior rooms, a second facade in the form of a trellis with automatically controlled sun blinds is placed in front of the south side at the distance of the projecting terrace deck. The entire building, a composition of untreated Douglas fir and glass, modulates only two themes: wood and light. Neither the total symmetry nor the narrow specter of materials disturb the complexity of the very lively design of the spaces with regard to their utilitarian value. (Competition, 1st prize)

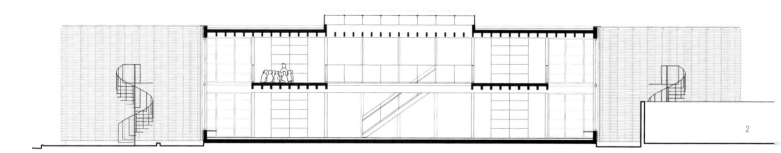

4

1. Galeriezone.
   Gallery zone.
2. Schnitt.
   Section.
3. Glasfassade nach
   Südwesten mit Terrasse
   und Rankgerüst.
   *Glass facade facing
   southwest with terrace
   and steel trellis.*
4. Gartenseite mit
   Rankgerüst.
   *Garden side with steel
   trellis.*
5. Erdgeschoß.
   First floor.
6. Nordostspitze mit
   Eingang, außen.
   *Northeast termination
   with entrance, exterior.*
7. Nordostspitze mit
   Eingang, innen.
   *Northeast termination
   with entrance, interior.*

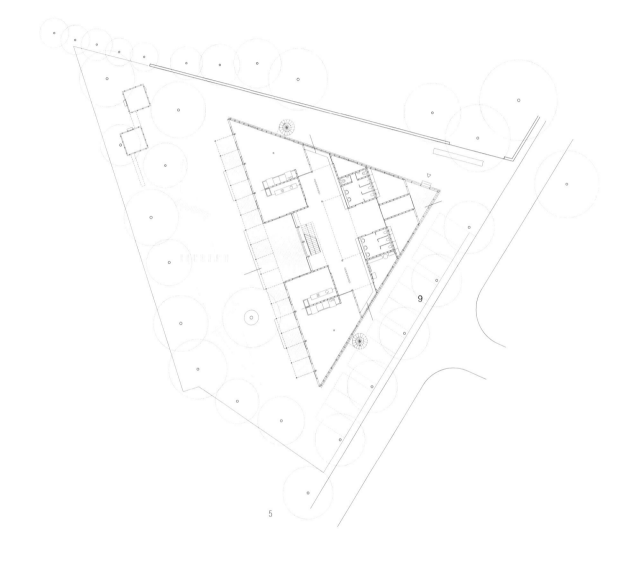

9

5

6

7

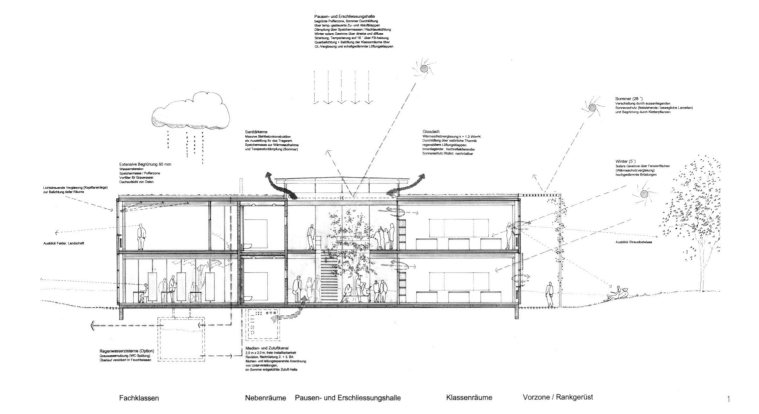

Fachklassen   Nebenräume   Pausen- und Erschliessungshalle   Klassenräume   Vorzone / Rankgerüst

Gymnasium Vaihingen an der Enz/Pforzheim 1995

Der Entwurf schafft eine besondere Identität des Ortes, indem er Gymnasium, Pausenhof und abgesenkte Sporthalle in einer straffen strukturellen Einheit zusammenführt, die den freien Landschaftsraum nur tangiert. Der langgestreckte passagenartig erschlossene Solitär meidet jede Konkurrenz zur umgebenden Landschaft und bezieht als autonomes Raumgefüge Eingangs- und Pausenhof wie verschiedene Terrassen in seine Architektur ein. Weitere Bauabschnitte sind in dieses schlüssige Konzept bereits als Verlängerung nach Osten konsequent integriert. Bis auf Laufbahn und Sportfeld bleibt die unmittelbare Umgebung über alle Ausbaustufen ursprünglich und funktionsfrei: weiträumige Felder und Streuobstwiesen mit weitem Ausblick auf entfernte Hügelketten. Verkehrslärm aus nordwestlicher Richtung wird durch die Position der Sporthalle wie die Ausrichtung aller Stammklassen nach Südosten kompensiert. Der einfache zweigeschossige Baukörper ist in seiner Strenge leicht und luftig als Holzkonstruktion (F 30) entwickelt, im äußeren Erscheinungsbild variiert durch Rankgerüste, den offenen, aber witterungsgeschützten Kreuzungspunkt der externen und internen Erschließungsachse sowie die Ablesbarkeit von Sporthalle und blockweise gruppierten Klassen und Fachräumen. Alle Räume liegen unmittelbar an einer differenzierten, von oben belichteten inneren Pausenhalle, die in ihrem großzügigen, mit dem Außenraum punktuell verbundenen Zuschnitt alle Erschließungsfunktionen übernimmt. Lehrerzimmer, Verwaltung und Bibliothek bilden darin funktional das Zentrum. (Wettbewerb, 1. Preis)

High School Vaihingen on Enz/Pforzheim 1995

The design creates a special identity for the site by uniting the high school, the schoolyard and the lowered gymnasium in a strict structural unity that only tangibly touches the surrounding, free landscape. The long, passage-like solitary structure avoids any competition with the environment and, as an autonomous spatial sequence, includes the entrance and schoolyard as well as various terraces in its architecture. Additional building phases have already been consistently integrated into this logical concept as an extension towards the east. Except for the track and sports field, the immediate surroundings remain original and function-free throughout all building phases: large fields and orchards with a broad view of the distant hills. The traffic noise from the northwest is compensated by the position of the gymnasium and the orientation of all regular classes towards the southeast. The simple two-story building volume is developed as a light and airy wood construction (F 30) in its strictness and varied in its outside appearance by trellises, the open yet weather-protected crossing point of the external and internal development axis, and the readability of the gymnasium, the classrooms and the labs grouped in blocks. All rooms are located directly at a differentiated recess hall lit from above. It fulfills all development functions in its generous layout, at points connected with the outside space. The teachers' room, administration and library functionally form the center. (Competition, 1st prize)

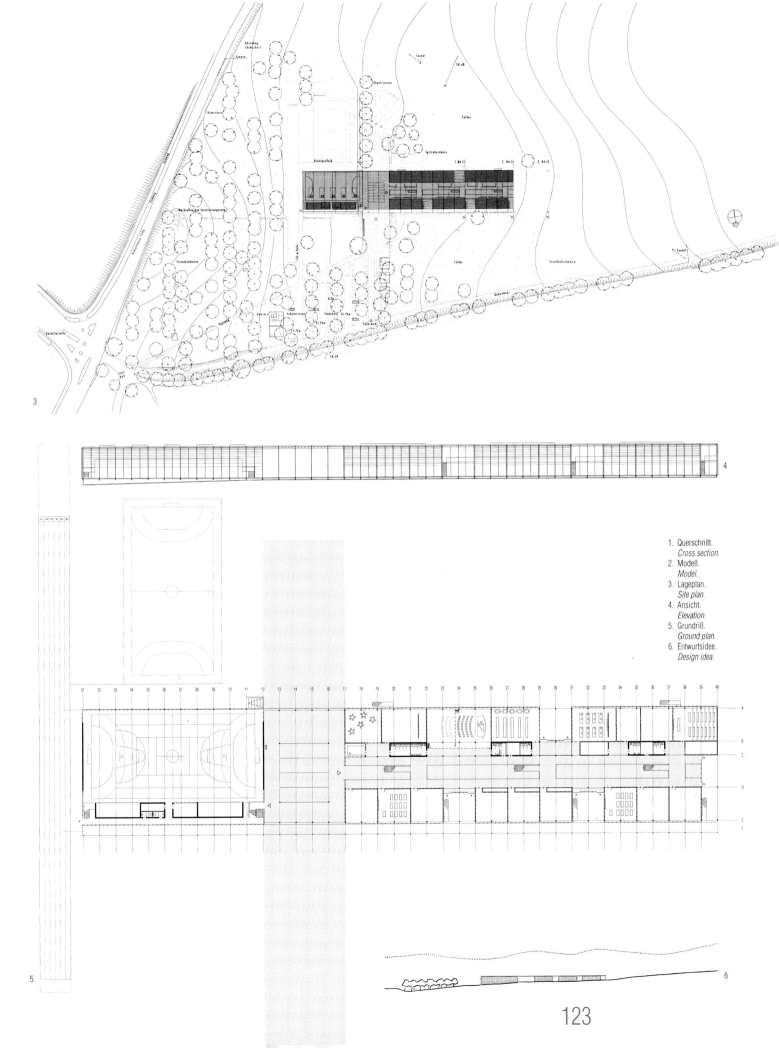

1. Querschnitt.
   Cross section.
2. Modell.
   Model.
3. Lageplan.
   Site plan.
4. Ansicht.
   Elevation.
5. Grundriß.
   Ground plan.
6. Entwurfsidee.
   Design idea.

3

4

5

6

Ausbau des Hauptbahnhofs Stuttgart zum ICE-Durchgangsbahnhof 1997

Der markante Bahnhof von Paul Bonatz, der 1928 einen Vorgängerbau am Schloßplatz ersetzte, wird im Rahmen des Projekts Stuttgart 21 von der Bahn unterirdisch und quer zur bisherigen Trasse angefahren. Daraus resultiert die im Grunde unlösbare Wettbewerbsaufgabe, ICE-Bahnsteige von 400 m Länge in 8 m Tiefe anzulegen, ohne auf die Symbolik und das Tageslicht der Bahnsteighalle zu verzichten, ohne den denkmalgeschützten Altbau (weiter) zu beeinträchtigen, ohne die für den Anschluß der neuen Citylagen wichtige Verbindungsachse der Königstraße aufzugeben. Der von der Jury gelobte, aber nur mit einem Ankauf gewürdigte Entwurf unterscheidet in seiner signifikanten Glaskonstruktion oberhalb der Bahnsteige konsequent zwischen der witterungsgeschützten Bahnsteighalle im Bahnhofsgebäude und einer offenen Stadtloggia mit Glasboden im Park. Die als kinetischer Lichtraum künstlerisch gestaltete Bahnhofshalle schöpft ihre Identität darum im Innen- wie im Außenraum aus der Verknüpfung von Bahnhof, Stadt und Park. Vielleicht waren die angebotenen Freiluftveranstaltungen: Sommerfest, Happening, Love-Parade, Italienische Nacht, Jazz Festival... aber für Stuttgarter Verhältnisse zu keß formuliert, darüberhinaus zu wenig rentabel? Andererseits wäre die Verquickung von Bahnhof und Einkaufszentrum dank Bahnhofs-Loggia einmal nicht die allein gültige geblieben. (Architekten: Team Stuttgart 21: Hartwig N. Schneider, Gabriele Mayer, Jo Frowein, Eduard Schmutz – Wettbewerb, Ankauf)

Expansion of the Stuttgart Main Station into an ICE Through-Station 1997

In the Stuttgart 21 project, the impressive station by Paul Bonatz that replaced a previous structure at Schlossplatz in 1928, is accessed underground by the railroad crosswise to the former route. The result is a basically unsolvable competition task of establishing ICE-platforms with a length of 400m at a depth of 8m without relinquishing the symbolism and the daylight of the platform hall, without (further) influencing the protected historic monument and without doing away with the connecting axis of Königstrasse, which is so important for the integration of the new city locations. The design was praised by the jury yet only honored with a purchase. With its significant glass construction above the platform, it makes a consequential differentiation between the platform hall within the station building that is protected from the elements and the city loggia in the park with its glass floor. The station hall is artistically designed as a kinetic light space and attains its identity through the relationship with the city and the park, inside as well as outside. Perhaps the open-air-events that were offered – summer festival, happening, Love-Parade, Italian night, jazz festival – were too boldly formulated for Stuttgart's habits and, aside from that, perhaps not profitable enough? On the other hand, the station and shopping center would not have remained the only valid combination thanks to the station loggia. (Architects: Team Stuttgart 21: Hartwig N. Schneider, Gabriele Mayer, Jo Frowein, Eduard Schmutz – competition, purchase)

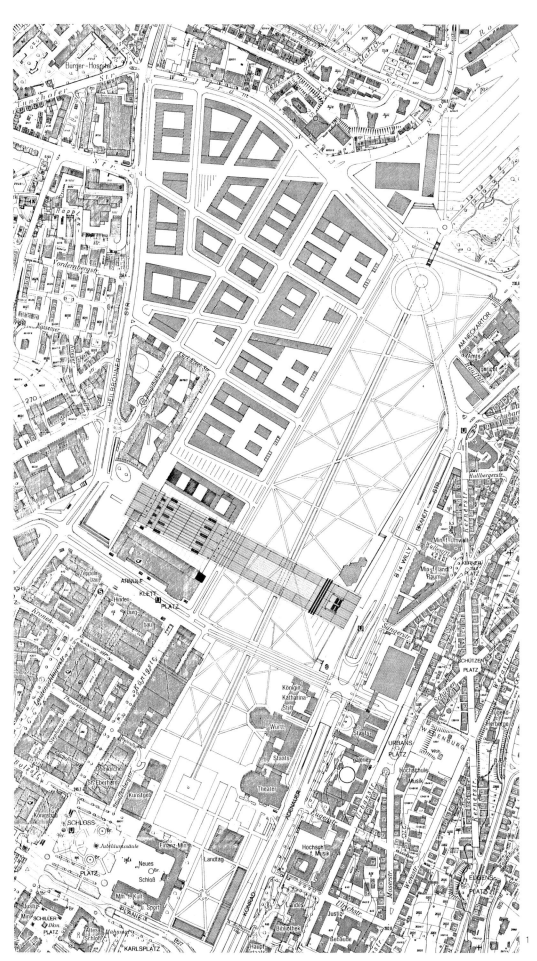

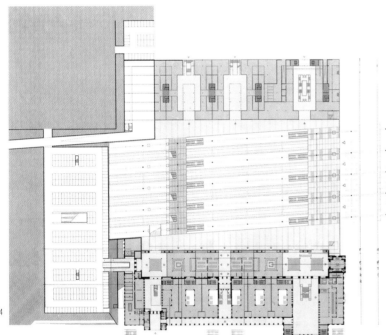

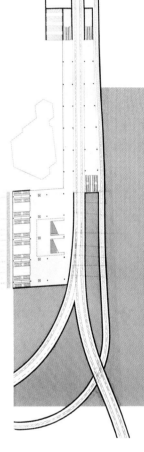

1. Lageplan.
   Site plan.
2. Schnitt Ost-West.
   East-west section.
3. Stadtloggia mit
   Glasboden.
   *City loggia with glass
   floor.*
4. Grundriß.
   Ground plan.
5. Modell.
   Model.

1. Wohnhof nach Süden.
   Living yard facing south.
2. Obergeschoß.
   Upper floor.
3. Ansicht Straßenfront.
   Elevation street facade.
4. Halboffener Hof nach Norden.
   Semi-open yard towards north.
5. Lageplan.
   Site plan.
6. Straßenfront nach Norden mit Tiefgaragenzufahrten.
   Street facade facing north with underground parking accesses.
7. Westfassade.
   West facade.

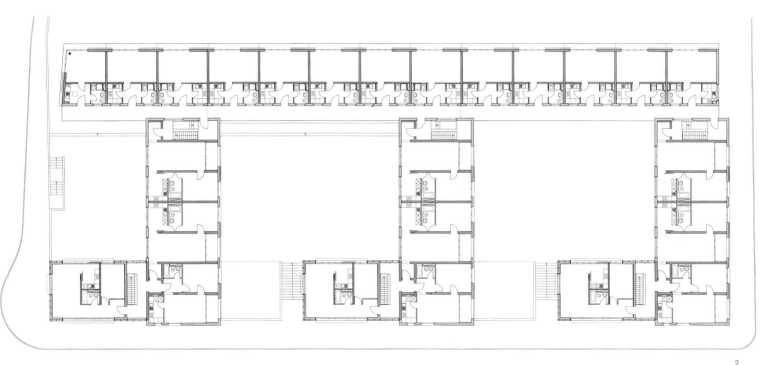

4

5

6

7

Sozialer Wohnungsbau Ludwigsburg/Stuttgart 1993–1997

Nur zwei Straßenblöcke vom Schloßpark entfernt, umgeben von Historie ausstrahlenden «Kaffeemühlen» der 50er Jahre, aber auch von deren postmoderner Übersteigerung, setzt der aus offenen Höfen gebildete, in den Fassaden stark variierte Komplex im Erscheinungsbild grundsätzlich auf die Sachlichkeit der Moderne. Entscheidend ist aber, daß alle Fronten des neuen Quartiers mit ihren Gegenüber kommunizieren. Mit dem schönen Effekt, daß die straßenseitige Öffnung der Höfe jeweils mit einem Altbau als Gegenstück geschlossen wird. Ein 85 m langer, nach Süden orientierter Riegel mit Maisonette-Wohnungen unten und Laubengang-Apartments oben bildet korrespondierend mit der Anschlußbebauung das Rückgrat der Anlage. Nur am Anschlußpunkt der Querriegel sind zwei Maisonettes zugunsten von gedeckten Spielbereichen ausgespart. Die Fassade aus Fenstertüren und fixen wie verfahrbaren türbreiten Holzlamellen-Elementen lebt allein von ihrem Material und den Aktivitäten der Bewohner. Die nach Norden anschließenden Höfe beziehen die gegenüberliegende Bebauung spannungsvoll ein und bieten oberhalb der Tiefgarage bei freier Zugänglichkeit ein hohes Maß an Privatheit, ohne sich individualistischen Übergriffen auszuliefern. Abgesehen von den durch Rasensteine angedeuteten Terrassen der elf Maisonette-Wohnungen sind die wohnungsbezogenen Freiräume auf französische Fenster und in Fensterbändern verborgene Loggien beschränkt. Der Wechsel zwischen dem Beton der Tiefgarage, tiefgrauem durchgefärbten Putz mit bündigen Glasbändern und Holzlamellen-Fassaden mit zurückgesetzten Fenstern und Brise-soleil (Brandschutz) erweckt im Straßenraum den Anschein von Einzelhäusern. (Wettbewerb, 1. Preis)

Social Housing Ludwigsburg Stuttgart 1993–1997

Two blocks away from the castle grounds, surrounded by the historic expressiveness of the "coffee mills" from the '50's, but also by their postmodern exaggeration, the appearance of the complex formed by open yards and strongly varied in the facades places its bets on the factuality of Modernism. What is decisive is that all facades of the new quarter communicate with the houses opposite them. This creates a nice effect: the yard openings toward the street are terminated by an old structure as a counterpart. An almost 100 meter long block oriented towards the south with maisonette apartments on the bottom and access gallery apartments on the top forms the spine of the complex in correspondence with the adjoining development. Two maisonettes are left out only at the point where the intersecting blocks join the structure for the benefit of covered playgrounds. The facade, consisting of glass doors and fixed and movable door-wide wood lamella elements, lives from its material and the inhabitants' activities alone. The yards adjoining to the north include the opposite development in a suspenseful way and offer a high degree of privacy above the parking garage, despite the free accessibility, without turning themselves into individualist attacks. Aside from the terraces – only hinted at with paving stones that allow the grass to grow through – outside the 11 maisonette apartments, the free spaces pertaining to the apartments are limited to French windows and loggias hidden in window strips. The change from the concrete of the parking garage, the deeply gray plaster with level glass strips and wood lamella facades with receding windows and Brise-soleil (fire protection) evokes the impression of separate houses in the street space. (Competition, 1st prize)

Wohn- und Atelierhaus
Hamburg Ottensen
1995–1997.
*Apartment and studio
house Hamburg
Ottensen 1995–1997.*

Ingrid Spengler
Frido Wiescholek

Ökonomisch expressiv

Ingrid Spengler und Frido Wiescholek suchen das funktionale und technische Experiment ebenso wie einen architektonischen Fortschritt, der die Ziele der Moderne zu Beginn des Jahrhunderts noch nachvollziehbar macht, ohne damit die Durchsetzungskraft einer zeitgemäßen, technisch begründeten Formensprache in der notwendigen Auseinandersetzung mit den volkstümlichen Kulissen der Postmoderne zu mindern. Architektur darf nicht Konservatismus dekorieren. Gegensätze sind durch Symmetrie oder Harmonie nicht aufzulösen. Die Lust an der Störung, die auch einmal die Arbeiten von Johann Eisele (*1948) und Nicolas Fritz (*1948) vorantrieb, ist jedoch durch Disziplin auf den Punkt zu bringen. Diese Zielsetzung illustriert nicht zuletzt die formale und ökonomische Konsequenz des im Rahmen des Stern-Wettbewerbs «Mein Wunschhaus» entwickelten Typenhauses. Ohne Rücksicht auf das tradierte Bild des Einfamilienhauses sucht dieses schlüssige Modell eines Stadtbausteins in der Redefinition von Organisation und Struktur vor allem die urbane Verknüpfung und größtmögliche Flexibilität über die Standardbedürfnisse einer Familie mit zwei Kindern hinaus. Drei Ebenen mit integriertem Freiraum und Stellplatz sorgen für ökonomische Grundstücksverhältnisse. Die Architektur unter flachem Dach leugnet dieses Grundanliegen nicht und zeigt eine kultivierte, bewohnerorientierte Moderne alias Funktionalismus in der Tradition der Typenhäuser von Le Corbusier, wobei die Annäherung an die Produktionsbedingungen einer modernen Elementbauweise architektonisch keine geringe Hürde ist. Mit Blick auf die Durchsetzbarkeit am Markt hängt viel davon ab, wie feinsinnig die Systematik der Fertigung überspielt werden kann, wie eng die ästhetischen Entscheidungen der Architekten (Fassadenmaterial, Fensterformate...) im Baukasten des Herstellers angelegt werden. Letztlich besteht jedoch die Gefahr, daß die entscheidenden Größen – Kalkulation und «Angstzuschlag» – von der erwarteten bzw. befürchteten Verkaufsauflage beeinflußt werden. Besonders weitreichende, innovative Haustypen scheitern dann an den Baukosten, obwohl sie städtebaulich und funktional ökonomischer kaum sein können. Die Hartnäckigkeit der Architekten liegt darin, diese grundlegende Argumentation nicht hinter formalen Extravaganzen zu verbergen, die in diesem engen Kostenrahmen nur aufgesetzt sein könnten. Architektur spiegelt hier, mit einer gewissen Rigidität und Unnachgiebigkeit, weniger sachlich als expressiv im Interesse der Stadt und ihrer Bewohner ihre Entstehungsbedingungen. Die soziale Verantwortung der Architekten äußert sich nicht in einer formal einheitlich lesbaren Opposition, sondern argumentiert in jedem einzelnen Fall anhand spezifischer Bedingungen. Da sich das Problembewußtsein der Gesellschaft für die soziale Brisanz von Architektur und Städtebau in Deutschland, belegt durch die wohlbekannten Obsessionen der «Häuslebauer», über Jahrzehnte keineswegs dramatisch gewandelt hat, geht es darum, diesen Markt zu bedienen oder vielmehr nicht zu bedienen. Übrig bleibt die Arbeit mit aufgeklärten «Randgruppen» oder der Versuch, Aufklärungsarbeit selbst zu leisten – als Architekt und damit unter dem Verdacht, eigenen Interessen nachzugehen. Anders als ihre niederländischen Kollegen anläßlich der Erasmus-Brücke in Rotterdam sind deutsche Parlamentarier noch nicht dafür ausgezeichnet worden, «der Kunst Vorrang vor allen finanziellen Zwängen eingeräumt» zu haben. Die Überzeugungskraft der Architektur wird dann wirksam, wenn die Rahmenbedingungen dies zulassen. So illustriert vorerst das Wohn- und Atelierhaus in Hamburg Ottensen unter schwierigsten innerstädtischen Grundstückbedingungen das architektonische Potential des geschilderten Typenhauses.

Economically expressive

Ingrid Spengler and Frido Wiescholek are searching the functional and technological experiment as much as an architectural progress that makes the goals of Modernism in the beginning of the century still understandable without reducing the stance of a contemporary, technologically based form language in the necessary confrontation with the traditional backdrops of Post-Modernism. Architecture must not decorate conservatism. Opposites can't be resolved through symmetry or harmony. The pleasure in disturbance that once advanced the works by Johann Eisele (*1948) and Nicolas Fritz (*1948) can, however, be brought to the point through discipline. This goal reveals both the formal and the economic consequences of the prefabricated type house developed for the Stern-magazine competition "My dream house." Without considering the traditional image of the single-family-home, this definitive model for an urban module is striving, above all, for both the urban connection and the greatest possible flexibility, going well beyond the standard requirements of a family with two children in the redefinition of organization and structure. Three levels with an integrated outdoor space and carport provide the economic property conditions. The architecture beneath a flat roof does not deny this basic concern and shows a cultivated Modernism (a.k.a. Functionalism) oriented towards the inhabitants in the tradition of Le Corbusier's type houses; the architectural approach to the production of a modern modular building style is not a small hurdle. In terms of positioning it on the market, a lot depends on how subtly the systematics of the production can be overplayed, and how closely the aesthetic decisions of the architects (facade material, window formats...) can be met with in the producer's modular box. In the end, there is the danger that the decisive factors – calculation and "extra cost for fear" – are influenced by the expected or feared sales edition. Comprehensive and innovative house types then fail due to the building cost, although they could hardly be more economical in an urban and functional way. The architects' stubbornness doesn't hide this argumentation behind formal extravagances that could only be pretentious given the tight budget. Here, architecture reflects its conditions of creation with a certain rigidity and inflexibility, less factually than expressively in the interest of the city and its inhabitants. The architects' social responsibility isn't expressed in a formally uniform and readable opposition but arguments on the basis of specific conditions in every single case. As society's awareness of the social problem of architecture and urban development in Germany has hardly changed through the decades and is clearly shown in the well-known obsessions of the homemakers, the point is to serve this market or, rather, not serve it. What remains is the work with enlightened "fringe groups" or the attempt to do this enlightening work by themselves – as architects and, thus, under the suspicion that they are following their own interests. Contrary to their Dutch colleagues, who were for the Erasmus bridge in Rotterdam, the German parliamentarians have not yet been awarded for having "given art a preference over all financial restrictions." Architecture's convincing power becomes effective only if the framework conditions allow for this to happen. Thus, the apartment and studio house in Hamburg Ottensen, for now, illustrates the architectural potential of the mentioned prefabricated type house under the most difficult inner-city property conditions.

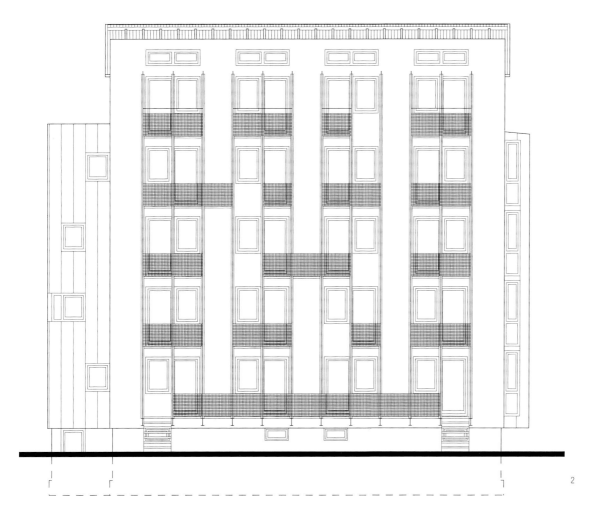

1. Gebäudefront zur
   Sibeliusstraße.
   *Building facade facing
   Sibeliusstrasse.*
2. Südansicht Einzelge-
   bäude.
   *South elevation
   separate buildings.*
3. Gartenseite mit
   Rankgerüsten.
   *Garden side with
   trellises.*
4. Erdgeschoß
   Zweispänner.
   *First floor dwelling
   units.*
5. Lageplan.
   Site plan.
6. Südansicht Gesamtan-
   lage.
   *South elevation
   complex.*

3

Standardisierter Sozialer Wohnungsbau Hamburg Bahrenfeld 1993–1996

Ein Thema dieser Nachverdichtung einer Sechziger-Jahre-Siedlung ist ein Beherbergungsfall, der längst in Vergessenheit geraten ist: zwei (Aussiedler-) Familien in einer Wohnung (im Grundriß ablesbar nur am vermeintlich luxuriösen zweiten WC). Dazu kam wegen problematischer Gründungsverhältnisse auf unterirdischen Salzstöcken die Notwendigkeit einer Pfahlgründung und separater Einzelbaukörper. Dennoch werden konventionelles Erscheinungsbild und alltägliche Qualität eines sozialen Wohnungsbaus, der heute vor allem im Fall von Substandards zum Modellvorhaben wird, mit architektonischen Mitteln überwunden. Die sieben Wohnhäuser mit 82 Wohnungen stoßen auf eine Ebene der Rezeption vor, die angesichts des Budgets und der Kleinserie für standardisiertes Bauen untypisch ist. Der Kunstgriff besteht darin, die Häuser bis in die einzelne Wohnung hinein innerhalb des begrenzten «Spielraums» von standardisierten Fensterformaten und Stahlbauteilen dennoch und überdeutlich zu individualisieren. Nicht zuletzt das bewohnbare Rankgerüst mit seiner Variation des Themas Balkon garantiert ein signifikantes Erscheinungsbild und läßt Raum für Spuren der Bewohner. Dazu tritt eine von Haus zu Haus zwischen Ocker, Braunrot und Graublau markant wechselnde Farbgebung. Abgesehen von der zeitlich befristeten Überbelegung erreichen besonders die Zweispänner im Wechselspiel von drei etwa gleichgroßen Individualräumen mit einer als Allraum fungierenden, separat belichteten Eßdiele eine hohe Nutzungsqualität.

Standardized Social Housing Hamburg Bahrenfeld 1993–1996

One theme of this condensation of a development from the sixties is an example of a type of housing that has long been forgotten: two (immigrant) families in a single apartment (this can be detected in the layout only because of the supposed luxury of a second bathroom). Additionally, the existence of subterranean salt mines on the site necessitated the use of a post-and-beam construction and separate building volumes. However, the conventional appearance and every-day quality of social housing – which nowadays has become a model for lower standards – are overcome through the use of architectural means. The seven houses with 82 apartments enter a level of reception that is unusual considering the limited budget and the relatively small production series that is atypical for a standardized construction of this kind. The real trick here is to very clearly individualize the houses and apartments – within and despite the limited room for play allowed by the standardized window formats and steel components. Not least, the inhabitable steel trellis with its variation on the terrace theme guarantees a significant appearance and leaves space for the personal traces of its inhabitants. Additionally, the coloration of the different houses strikingly varies from ochre to a brownish red and grayish blue. Setting aside consideration of the temporary overcrowding, the apartments, stretching across two structures with the interplay of three individual rooms of approximately the same size and a separately lit dining area functioning as a common space, have an especially high quality of utilization.

4

5

6

Wohn- und Atelierhaus Hamburg Ottensen 1995–1997

Ein Bauplatz, den es erst zu schaffen galt (durch Ankauf des über den Garten optisch verbundenen Altbaus) und ein eigenwilliger, aus den Abstandsflächen und Belichtungsmöglichkeiten gewonnener Baukörper, der kaum zu fotografieren ist. Dennoch – oder gerade deswegen? – ist das Resultat nicht Ausnutzungsarithmetik, sondern spannungsvolle Architektur. Vor dem Hintergrund des bunt gemischten Gründerzeitviertels zeigt sich der moderne prismatische Baukörper nicht als Eindringling, sondern wertet noch in dieser Enge die Gesamtsituation auf. Wie ein Monitor auf seinem Sockel scheinen Apartment und Hauptwohnung auf dem Atelier beweglich gelagert zu sein und beschränken sich seitlich auf reduzierte Betriebsöffnungen. Mit einer großzügigen Glasfassade gilt der bevorzugte Ausblick der mächtigen Kastanie im Süden. So läßt der um die Spindeltreppe gezogene, angeschnittene Schiffsbug mit Schornstein, Ausguck, Brücke und Sonnendeck auch in die anschließende Hofsituation noch die Südsonne einfallen. Das Stück Himmel, das den rückwärtigen Häusern dennoch genommen wurde, findet sich in der tiefblauen Farbgebung des Wohnturms wieder, während der Maschinenraum darunter – mit Garage, Technik und luftigem, in den Gartenhof orientierten Atelier – in seiner stabileren Fassade aus Torfbrandklinkern fast zum Bestand zu gehören scheint. Überraschender als die günstige Energiebilanz ist die enge Verknüpfung aller Bereiche mit großzügigen Freiräumen.

Apartment and Studio House Hamburg Ottensen 1995–1997

A building site that first had to be created (by purchasing the old structure, visually connected through the garden), and an unconventional building volume created out of the margin surfaces and lighting possibilities, a volume that is almost impossible to photograph. Despite this (or perhaps because of this) the result is not simply a mathematical computation of optimum utilization but exciting architecture, as well. With the background of the colorfully mixed "Gründerzeit" quarter dating from the years of rapid industrial expansion in Germany, the modern prismatic building volume does not present itself as an intruder but instead raises the value, even within this confined setting, of the overall location. Like a monitor on its base, the apartment and main living space seem to be placed on top of the studio as though they are movable, and they limit themselves along the sides to reduced service openings. With a generous glass facade, the preferred view is directed towards the majestic chestnut three to the south. Thus, the dissevered ship bow with chimney, overlook, bridge and sun-deck wrapping around the spiral staircase allows sunlight to enter into the adjoining yard. The section of sky that was taken away from the houses in back can be reencountered in the dark blue color of the living tower. The machine room beneath the tower – with garage, technical installations and the airy studio oriented towards the garden – almost seems to be part of the existing structure in its more stable and robust burnt-peat brick facade. More surprising than the low energy use is the tight connection of all areas with generous open spaces.

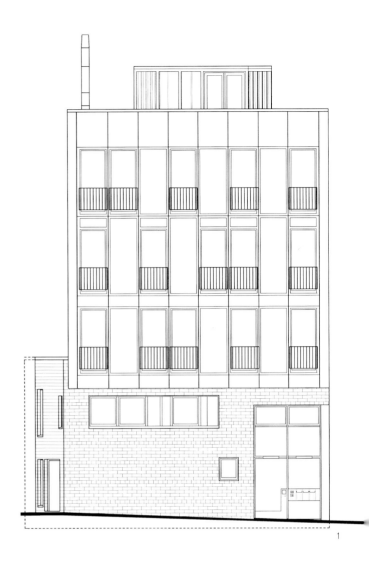

1

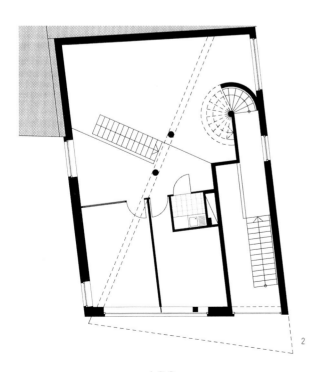

2

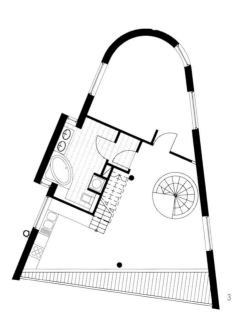

3

1. Südansicht.
   South elevation.
2. Erdgeschoß.
   First floor.
3. Obergeschoß.
   Upper floor.
4. Seitenfront mit Garagenzufahrt.
   Side facade with garage access.
5. Nördliche Gebäudespitze.
   Northern building termination.
6. Modell.
   Model.

4

5

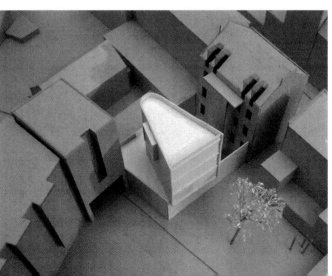

6

Wohnen und Arbeiten im Straßen-bahndepot Hamburg Eppendorf 1997

Das heute als Busdepot genutzte Industrie-areal bietet in bester Stadtlage alle Vorausset-zungen für eine spektakuläre Umnutzung und urbane Verdichtung auf insgesamt 50.000 m² Grundstücksfläche. Die Backsteinhallen aus den zwanziger Jahren erreichen 6,80 m in der Höhe, 80 m in der Länge und als Doppelhalle 40 m in der Breite. Innerhalb einer Symbiose aus Werkstätten, Ateliers, Büros, Geschäften und Restaurants möchte die Stadt ca. 500 Wohnungen und einen Stadtteilpark realisiert sehen. Ziel des Entwurfs ist darum nicht ein musealer, restaurativer Stillstand, sondern die zielgerichtete Steuerung eines Veränderungs-prozesses, der das Ensemble langfristig zum Mittelpunkt eines lebendigen großstädtischen Quartiers macht. Die Abgeschlossenheit der Anlage wird konsequent aufgehoben – auch durch Abbruch maroder Bausubstanz. Dadurch wird die alte Struktur vielfach erst sichtbar und erlebbar, ergänzende Neubauten geben der historischen Substanz in der archi-tektonischen Auseinandersetzung neues Gewicht, der Komplex öffnet sich über Park-anlagen und Passagen den Passanten. Dem Motto «Wohnen über den Dächern» ver-pflichtet, durchdringen weithin sichtbar zwölf gläserne, viergeschossige Punkthäuser mit ihren Aufständerungen und Erschließungs-kernen die begrünten Dächer der großen Hal-len. In Abhängigkeit von Lichteinfall und Funktionszusammenhang werden unter den Dächern die Funktionen Arbeit, Kultur und Freizeit als «Haus im Haus» eingestellt, ergänzt durch Passagen und platzartige Auf-weitungen, die den vorhandenen Oberlicht-bändern folgen.

Living and Working in the Tram Depot Hamburg Eppendorf 1997

The industrial area that is used today as a bus depot is in an excellent location in the city and offers all the preconditions for a spectacular reutilization and urban condensation on the 50,000 square meter property. The brick halls from the twenties reach a height of 6.80 meters, are 80 meters in length and, as double halls, have a width of 40 meters. Within the symbiosis of workshops, studios, offices, stores and restaurants, the city also wants to realize approximately 500 apartments, as well as a new park for the quarter. The goal of the design, therefore, is not a static, museum-like restoration but the targeted objective of a process of change that in time will make the ensemble the center of a lively urban quarter. The exclusivity of the complex is consequen-tially removed, not least by the tearing down of the old and dilapidated building substance. Through this, the old structure can now be seen and experienced for the first time, and additional new structures provide the historic building substance with a new significance in the architectural confrontation – the complex opens up to the pedestrians via parks and pas-sages. Devoted to the motto "living above the rooftops" twelve glassed-in, four-story-high point buildings, with post and beam structures and development cores, can be seen from afar and are interspersed among the planted, gar-den-like rooftops of the large halls. Depending on the angle of the light and their functional context, the functions work. Culture and leisure are installed beneath the rooftops – a "house within the house," complemented by passageways and piazza-like openings that follow the existing strips of skylights.

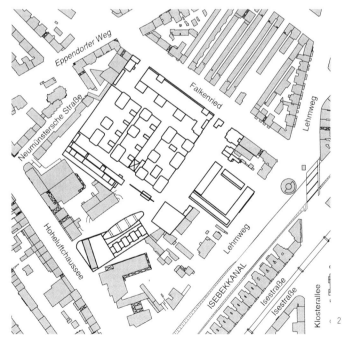

1. Fotomontage Luftaufnahme. *Photo montage aerial view.*
2. Lageplan. *Site plan.*
3. Fotomontage Hallennutzung. *Photo montage hall utilization.*
4, 5. Schnitt Gesamtanlage. *Section complex.*

3

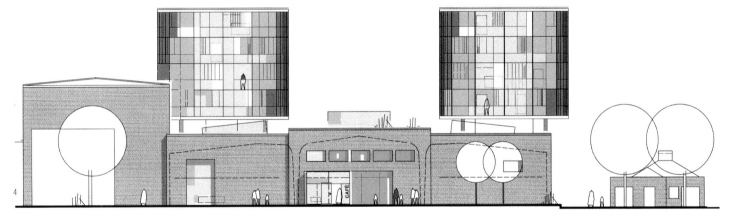

4

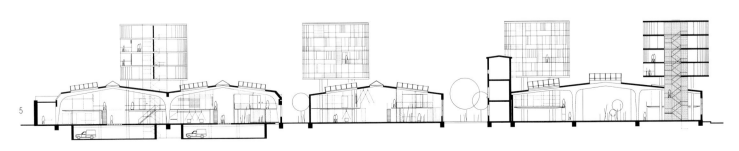

5

1. Perspektive
   Reihenbebauung von
   Süden.
   *Perspective row
   development from
   south.*
2. Perspektive
   Reihenbebauung von
   Norden.
   *Perspective row
   development from
   north.*
3. Nutzungs- und
   Ausbauvarianten.
   *Versions of utilization
   and interiors.*
4. Ansichten.
   Views.

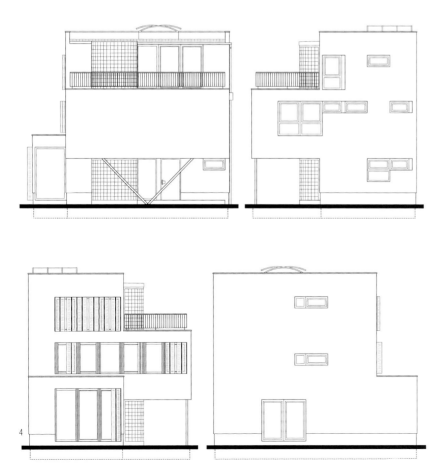

Typenhaus (Aktion «Wunschhaus» des Stern) 1996–1998

Die Illustrierte Stern befragte ihre Leser und setzte das Ergebnis in einem Wunschhaus-Wettbewerb unter Architekten um. Wohnwunsch Nr. 1 ist das Einfamilienhaus: «pfiffig, ökologisch, bezahlbar, freistehend und praktisch». Aus der neuen Phalanx von Fertighausherstellern und Architekten bricht dieses Typenhaus dennoch aus. Anders als beim Wettbewerbsgewinner, der zwei Häuser zum Preis von einem aufbot, steckt der Kern der Entwurfsidee – bis hin zu Spindeltreppe und über Dach belichteten Galerien – in der Addierbarkeit und Stadttauglichkeit des schon darum unkonventionellen Modells, nicht zuletzt auch in einer denkbar geringen Grundstücksgröße. Das mit seinen Anforderungen wachsende, letztlich dreigeschossige variabel nutzbare Haus bietet neben geschützten Freiräumen dank Erschließung und Zuschnitt einen Nutzungsspielraum, der vom Einsteigerhaus für junge Familien bis zum Mehrgenerationenhaus reicht – Stellplatz inklusive. Extensiv begrünte, flach geneigte Dächer, Glassteine im Treppenturm und großformatige Fassadenplatten aus Aluminium, Glas, Stahl, Holz oder Verbundwerkstoffen versprechen ein neues Fertighaus-Image – zumindest in den edleren Varianten oberhalb der klassischen (Dämm-) Putzvariante. Bleibt die Frage nach der Gestaltungshoheit in der Reihe. Die ersten Exemplare sollen in Hamburg realisiert werden. (Wettbewerb, 3. Preis)

Standard House ("Dream House" campaign of Stern magazine) 1996–1998

Stern magazine polled its readers and realized the result in a dream-house competition involving several architects. The wished-for type of domicile that received highest ranking is the single-family home – "smart, ecological, affordable, free-standing and practical." This standard prefabricated house, which was awarded third prize, does, however, break out of the new phalanx of prefabricated house producers and architects. As opposed to the winner of the competition, who offered two houses for the price of one, the core principle of this design concept – not excluding the spiral staircase and floor cut-out – lies in this model's expandability and its compatibility with the city. Because of this fact and, not least, also because of its utilization of rather small property lots, it is already rather unconventional. The house grows according to the demands of the inhabitants and can ultimately be expanded to a height of three stories. Aside from the protected free spaces, several different possibilities for utilization are offered that result directly from the development and layout, ranging from a starter home for young families to a home with room for several generations of family members. A carport can also be included. Extensively planted gently sloping roofs, glass bricks in the stairway tower, and large-scale facade panels made of aluminum, glass, steel, wood or composite materials promise a new image of the prefabricated house– at least in the more sophisticated versions. What remains is a question about the integrity of the design when applied to a row of these structures.

Zvonko Turkali

Bürogebäude zur
Nachverdichtung eines
Gewerbegebiets Hanau
1995–1996.
*Office building for the
condensation of an
industrial area Hanau
1995–1996.*

Integrierte Strukturen

Zvonko Turkali läßt die Ästhetik seiner Bauten aus deren Struktur folgen. Ohne nach der Methode High-Tech auf eine Sensation im Sinne technologischer Futurisierung abzuzielen, wird eine außen und innen nachgewiesene Konstruktion zum Maßregler der architektonischen Erscheinung. Damit sind nicht die clusterförmig vernetzten, räumlichen Strukturen des Strukturalismus angesprochen, die sich angesichts typologisch unschärfer oder strukturell eindimensionaler, nur oberflächlich differenzierbarer Bauaufgaben jenseits von Bürohaus, Schule und Wohnungsbau auf eine Formensprache nach strukturalistischen Motiven reduzieren, wenn das architektonische Gesamtgebilde nicht mehr anschaulich auf eine elementare Hierarchie von räumlichen Grundbausteinen zurückzuführen ist. Ohnehin provoziert eine von innen nach außen entwickelte Gebäudeorganisation in ihrer «labyrinthischen Klarheit» (Aldo van Eyck, *1918) den großen Nachteil der städtebaulichen Unschärfe an ihren Rändern. Auch hier deutet die Distanz zur künstlerischen Originalität des Architekten auf eine Architektur hin, die die Kunst der langen Gültigkeit und Dauer jeder voreiligen modischen oder auch archaischen Symbolik vorzieht. Es geht dem Architekten «nur» um linear entwickelte Baukörper und ihre anschauliche konstruktive Fügung. Eine neue Modernität, offen für die Bedingungen der Aufgabe und des Ortes, die fortbaut und Stille zuläßt, um aufmerksamer zu werden und fähig, genau zu sehen: zwischen den Dingen. Dieses klassische Prinzip führt trotz der für modernes Bauen notwendigen Unterscheidung von Skelett und Außenhaut zu einer so klaren «Struktursprache», daß man bei aller Abgrenzung zum Strukturalismus als Stil dem methodischen Grundansatz nach (Langue et Parole) von einer linearen, städtebaulich eingebundenen Variante sprechen könnte. Wenn Konstruieren das logische und konsequente Zusammenfügen bezeichnet, dann muß dieser Vorgang für das Auge des Betrachters auch umkehrbar sein. Der architektonische Blick ist zunächst ein analytischer, der die strukturalen Verhältnisse ergründen will. Die architektonische Komposition wird aufgelöst, zerlegt und dechiffriert. Das macht den Code der Architektur nachvollziehbar und anschaulich. Diese Kunst des Fügens und Differenzierens als Ausdruck eines Konstruktionsgedankens ist ein wesentliches Grundprinzip baulicher Schönheit. Nach Julius Posener tritt darin ein entscheidender Beitrag der Mathematik zur Architektur zutage: «Sie ist ein Ordner; sie beschränkt das Walten des Gefühls und macht den Bau ‹absolut›.» Das andere Grundprinzip von Bauten ist danach, daß sie, da sie dem Leben dienen, epischen Charakter haben: «Sie dienen und stellen gleichzeitig dar». Nimmt man die These von Herman Hertzberger (*1932) hinzu: «Entwerfen kann nichts anderes sein als fortbauen auf dem Darunterliegenden und es sozusagen verbauen», zeigt sich, wie tief eine auf Anschaulichkeit gründende Einfachheit von Konstruktion und Form reichen kann. Die große Stärke dieser Struktursprache liegt darin, daß sie selbst an städtebaulich schwierigen Standorten und im unmittelbaren Zusammenhang mit Altbausubstanz die Gegebenheiten bauend aufgreift und weiterführt, ohne ihren konstruktiven Rhythmus und formalen Anspruch aufzugeben. Bei einem Bürohaus im Gewerbegebiet von Hanau, zur Zeit von der Telekom genutzt, war einer der Grundsteine die Autowaschhalle des benachbarten Autohändlers.

Integrated structures

The aesthetics of Zvonko Turkali's buildings results from their structure. Without aiming at sensation in the sense of a technological futurization following the method of High-Tech, a construction visible outside as well as inside becomes the measuring rod of the architectural appearance. This doesn't refer to the networked, cluster-shaped spatial structures of Structuralism that are reduced to a formal language following structural motifs – considering the typologically unclear or structurally one-dimensional, superficially differentiable building tasks beyond office building, school and apartment building – if the architectural overall creation can no longer be clearly understood and led back to an elementary hierarchy of spatial basic building elements. In any event, a structural organization developed from the inside out provokes – in its "labyrinthine clarity" (Aldo van Eyck, *1918) – the great disadvantage of the urban ambiguity at its edges. Here, too, the distance to the artistic originality of the architect points to an architecture that prefers art to the validity or endurance of any hurried fashionable or archaic symbolism. The architect "only" cares about linearly developed building volumes and their understandable constructive organization. A new modernity that is open to the conditions of the task and location, that continues to build and allows for silence in order to become more attentive and capable of seeing clearly: between things. This classical principle, despite the distinction between skeleton and outside shell necessary for modern architecture, leads to such a clear "structural language" that, although differentiated from Structuralism as a style, the methodological principle (Langue et Parole) could allow one to speak of a linear, urban integrated version. If constructing describes the logical and consequential joining together, then this process has to be reversible for the observer's eye. The architectural glance is at first an analytical one that strives to explore the structural circumstances. The architectural composition is dissolved, taken apart and deciphered. In this way the architectural code becomes understandable and tangible. The art of joining and differentiating as an expression of a constructive thought is an essential principle of architectural beauty. According to Julius Posener, a decisive contribution of mathematics to architecture is therein exposed: "It is an organizer; it limits the rule of emotions and makes the building 'absolute'." The other basic principle of buildings then, since they serve life, is that they have an epic character: "They serve and, at the same time, represent." If one adds Herman Hertzberger's (*1932) thesis: "Designing can't be anything other than a continuation of building upon what's beneath and, in a sense, a building over," we see how deeply a simplicity of construction and form based on clarity can reach. The great strength of this structural language is that, even in difficult urban sites and in direct connection with old building substance, it takes up the given situation and continues it without giving up its constructive rhythm and formal claim. In the case of an office building in Hanau's industrial area, currently occupied by Telekom, one of the central elements was the car wash of the neighboring car dealership.

139

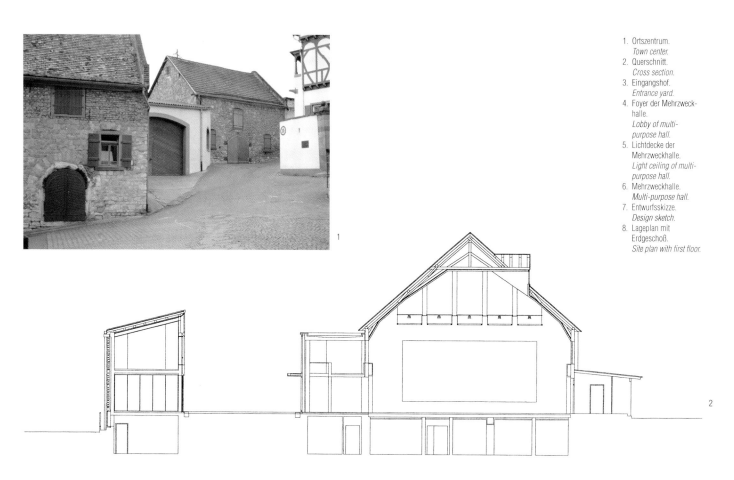

1. Ortszentrum.
   Town center.
2. Querschnitt.
   Cross section.
3. Eingangshof.
   Entrance yard.
4. Foyer der Mehrzweck-
   halle.
   *Lobby of multi-
   purpose hall.*
5. Lichtdecke der
   Mehrzweckhalle.
   *Light ceiling of multi-
   purpose hall.*
6. Mehrzweckhalle.
   Multi-purpose hall.
7. Entwurfsskizze.
   Design sketch.
8. Lageplan mit
   Erdgeschoß.
   Site plan with first floor.

1

2

3

4

5

6

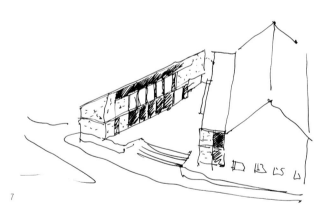

7

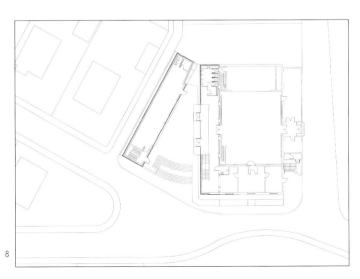

8

Umbau und Erweiterung Bürgerhaus Guntersblum 1991–1995

In der kleinen Gemeinde Guntersblum 25 km südlich von Mainz, im Ortskern geprägt durch Bauernhöfe in Bruchsteinmauerwerk und Fachwerkhäuser, war eine Turnhalle aus dem Jahr 1929 zum Bürgerhaus umzuplanen und um ein Foyer, eine Bibliothek sowie Versammlungsräume zu erweitern. Mit einem weit geöffneten, über die gesamte westliche Gebäudelänge breit angelegten Foyer und einem ähnlich schmal geschnittenen separaten Bau, der vom Untergeschoß abgesehen ausschließlich nach Südosten orientiert ist, gelingt eine für das Ortsbild entscheidende, städtebauliche Neuordnung. Der nach Süden orientierte, architektonisch markant gefaßte Vorplatz gibt der Gesamtanlage eine eigenständige, der Symbolik des sich Versammelns gewidmete Identität. Als Sonderfunktion wurde die Bibliothek im Obergeschoß des neuen Flügels unter einem Pultdach untergebracht. Mit dem variablen Versammlungsraum auf der einen und Foyer und Mehrzweckhalle auf der anderen Seite entwickelt sich der Freiraum im Zusammenspiel der Hauptfunktionen zu einem wesentlichen Bindeglied. Architektonisch wird trotz des modernen Instrumentariums – Skelettbau, Sichtbeton, Metallfenster, Blechdach – eine Brücke geschlagen zum historischen Ortsbild. Auf sehr feinsinnige Art und Weise gelingt es im Rahmen der konstruktiv begründeten Rationalität sogar, die Lebendigkeit im Erscheinungsbild einzufangen, die klare Baustrukturen, zu denen auch Bauernhöfe gehören, erst nach langen und wechselvollen Perioden des Gebrauchs aufweisen. (Gutachterwettbewerb, 1. Preis/mit H. Bechler)

Conversion and Extension Community Center Guntersblum 1991–1995

In the center of the small community of Guntersblum, 25 km south of Mainz, characterized by natural stone masonry farms and framework houses, a gymnasium built in 1929 was to be converted into a community center and extended with a lobby, a library and meeting rooms. The spacious lobby stretching along the entire western front of the building, and a similarly narrow, separate building oriented exclusively towards the southeast except for the basement floor, succeed in creating a decisive urban reorientation for the layout of the town. The forecourt, oriented towards the south and enclosed in an architecturally striking way, provides the complex with an independent identity devoted to the symbolism of gatherings. The library was placed on the upper floor of the new wing beneath a shed roof as a special utility. With the variable-use meeting room on one side and the lobby and a multi-purpose hall on the other, the free space becomes an essential link in the context of the interaction of the main functions. Architecturally – despite the modern implementation of a skeleton construction, fair-faced concrete, metal windows and metal sheet roof – a bridge to the old town center is being created. In a very subtle and clever way, and within the framework of the constructive rationality, the liveliness is mirrored in the exterior appearance; clear building structures, farms among them, will usually show this only after a long and transformational period of use. (Expert competition, 1st prize with H. Bechler)

141

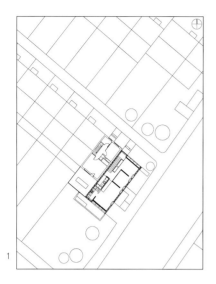

1

2

3

Aufstockung Wohnhaus Bromig
Frankfurt 1994–1996

Am Endpunkt einer Reihenhauszeile sollte ein eingeschossiger Anbau aus den 50er Jahren umgeplant und aufgestockt werden. Auf kleinster Fläche entstand so neben der Garage die Praxis eines Sportmediziners und darüber, synonym zu den anschließenden Reihenhäusern erdgeschossig erschlossen, eine raffiniert geschnittene 3-Zimmer-Wohnung mit einem doppelt erschlossenen gefangenen Raum im Zentrum. Konsequent getrennt liegen Erschließung und Serviceräume, Ankleide und Einbauschränke an der Brandwand. Oberhalb der Zugangstreppe findet sich gut versteckt der Abstellraum. Grundsätzlich erlauben raumhohe Schiebetüren fließende Raumfolgen ebenso wie separate Einzelräume. Durch großzügige Öffnungen im Dach (Wohnraum, Bad) und bodentiefe Fenster wird die geringe Grundfläche der Wohnung nochmals optisch überspielt – insbesondere an den Schmalseiten, wo zum Garten und zur ruhigen Erschließungsseite raumhohe französische Fenster mit Außenjalousien angeordnet wurden. Die Zwischenwände des Wohnbereichs, nichttragend und frei von Sanitär-Installationen, sind variabel. Konstruktiv war die Aufstockung nur als leichte, in diesem Fall vorfabrizierte Holzkonstruktion möglich. Formal hebt sich die in ihrer konstruktiven Ordnung ebenso plastisch wie rational anmutende Ergänzung, im Erdgeschoß mit einem orangeroten Putz, im Obergeschoß mit einer graublau lasierten Holzfassade ausgestattet, vom Altbestand ab und führt den nur vermeintlich modernen Habitus der Reihenhäuser zurück zu seinen Ursprüngen.

Heightening Bromig Apartment House
Frankfurt 1994–1996

A one-story extension from the '50s at the end of a row of houses was to be redesigned and heightened. On a very small surface next to the garage, the office of a sports doctor was created, and above it, with the access through the ground floor analogous to the adjoining row houses, a cleverly laid out 3-bedroom apartment with a closed-in room in the center, accessible from two sides. Intentionally separated, the access, the service rooms, the dressing room and the built-in-closets are all located at along fire wall. Generally, the floor-to-ceiling sliding doors allow for flowing room sequences as well as for separate rooms. Generous openings in the roof (living space, bathroom) along with the floor-to-ceiling windows visually overcome the small ground plan of the apartment – especially along the narrow sides where, towards the garden and the quiet access front, floor-to-ceiling French windows with outside blinds have been arranged. The interstitial walls of the living space are variable since they are non-supporting and contain no sanitary installations. Constructively, the heightening was possible in this case only in the form of a light, prefabricated wood structure. Formally, the addition that is sculptural as well as rational in its constructive organization distinguishes itself from the old section with an orange-red layer of plaster on the ground floor and a blue-stained wood facade on the upper floor, and it guides the only seemingly modern personality among all the row houses back to its origins.

4

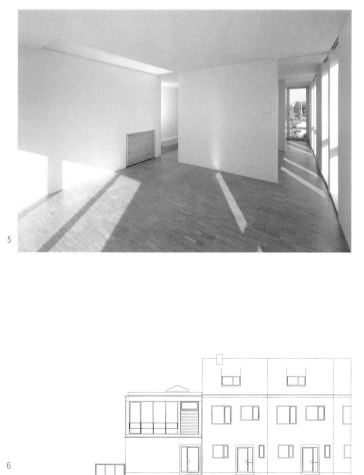

5

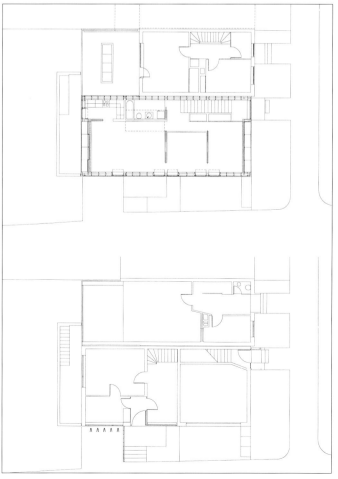

6

7

143

1. Ansicht Südfassade.
   Elevation south facade.
2. Bestand.
   Existing situation.
3. Nordansicht
   Kundenpavillon.
   *North elevation
   customer pavilion.*
4. Erdgeschoß.
   First floor.
5. Lageplan.
   Site plan.
6. Entwurfsskizze.
   Design sketch.
7. Blick von Osten mit
   Mitarbeiter-Eingang.
   *View from the east with
   employees' entrance.*

2

1

3

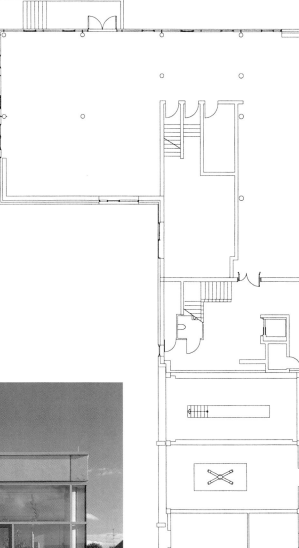

4

144

Bürogebäude zur Nachverdichtung eines Gewerbegebiets Hanau 1995–1996

Neben der Erweiterung bestehender Gewerbebauten in der Horizontalen steht typologisch die Verdichtung der Gewerbezonen durch vertikales Weiterbauen. Auf diesem Weg entstand in Hanau ein streng rationales Bürohaus, das eine Autowaschhalle architektonisch ungeschehen macht – nicht durch Abriß, sondern durch nachhaltige Integration frei nach dem Motto: Bürohaus der Telekom verschlingt schäbige Waschhalle (darum das angehobene Erdgeschoß bzw. der markante Sockel). Nur die beiden Tore des Altbaus sind noch zu sehen. Entscheidender als die markante gestalterische Bereinigung mit einfachsten Mitteln im Rhythmus eines Betonskeletts ist jedoch der räumliche Gewinn. Zum einen für den Bauherrn, der Teile des Parkplatzes seines angrenzenden Autohauses nutzbringender einsetzt und dabei den eigenen Betrieb räumlich abschließt und akzentuiert, zum anderen für die weitere Nachbarschaft, die ihren Standort nun auf markante Art und Weise architektonisch benennen kann. Die modulare Ordnung der Sichtbetonelemente wird durch rote Ziegelfelder, glasfaserarmierte Betonlamellen-Elemente und kontrastierende Glasflächen ebenso in Spannung versetzt wie durch eine individuelle, ortsbezogene städtebauliche Komposition aus Kundenpavillon, Bürotrakt und Zugangsbauwerk. Die Urbanisierung extra muros, darf, gerade weil sie nur in kleinen Schritten erfolgen kann, nicht unterschätzt werden. Je stärker sich gewerbefremde Nutzungen durchsetzen, desto eher wird aus dem besonderen ein weitgehend normales, ein durchmischtes und vielfältiges Stück Stadt.

Office Building for Condensation of an Industrial Area Hanau 1995–1996

Typologically, the condensation of the industrial areas through vertical extension stands next to the horizontal extension. In this way, a strictly rational office building was established in Hanau. It architecturally erases a carwash structure – not through demolition but through a distinct integration following the motto: Telekom office building devours shabby carwash (which explains the raised ground floor level and the striking base). Only the two gates of the old structure remain visible. The spatial gain is, however, much more decisive than the striking design, "cleaning up" the scene with the simplest of means in the rhythm of a concrete skeleton. On one hand, this is true for the client, who uses parts of the parking lot of his adjoining car dealership in a more efficient way and, at the same time, spatially terminates and accentuates his own business; on the other hand, it is also true for the other neighbors, who now can architecturally describe their location in a impressive way. The modular structure of the fair-faced concrete elements enters into a suspenseful relationship with red brick surfaces, fiberglass reinforced concrete lamella elements and contrasting glass surfaces, as well as through an individual urban composition consisting of the client pavilion, office tract and access structure relating to the location. The urbanization extra muros should not be underestimated, especially since it could be realized only in small steps. The more unconventional utilizations are established, the more the special turns into a normal, mixed and multiple part of a city.

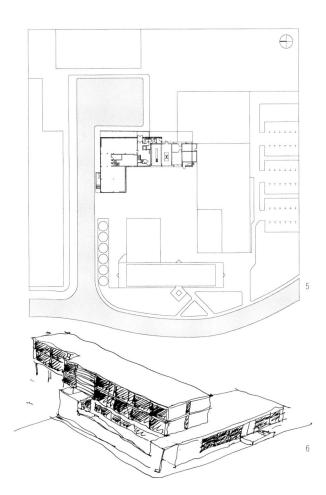

5

6

7

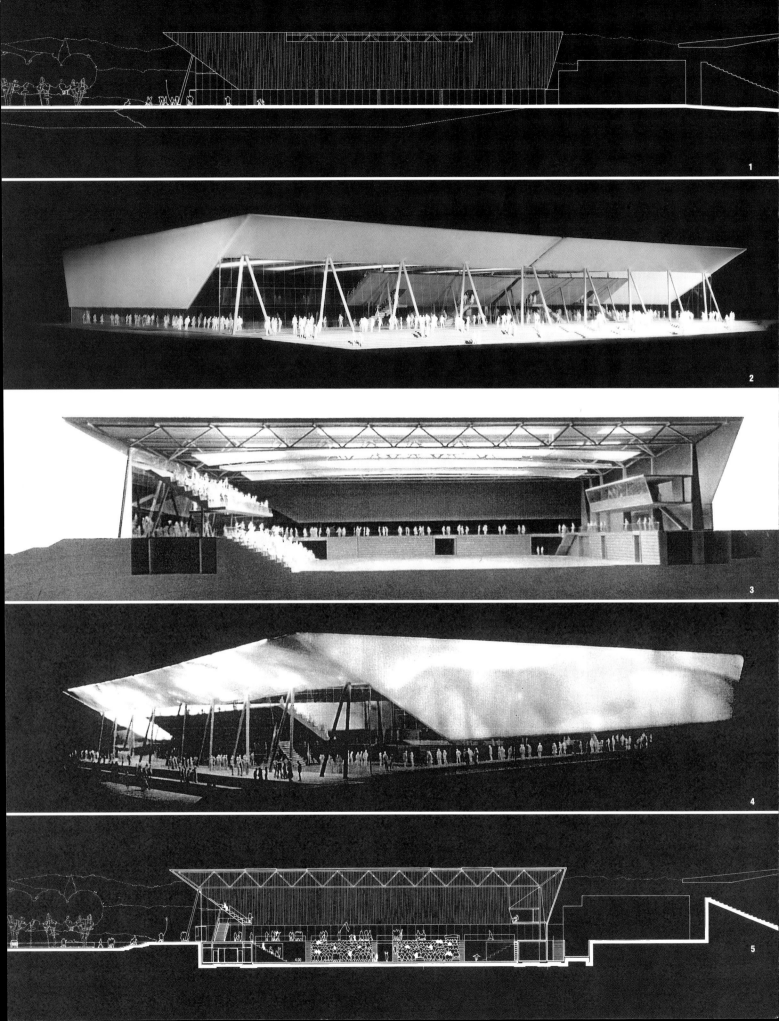

1

2

3

4

5

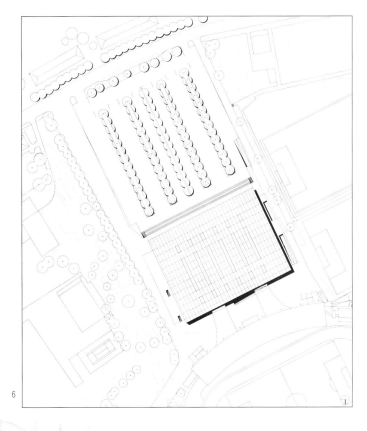

6

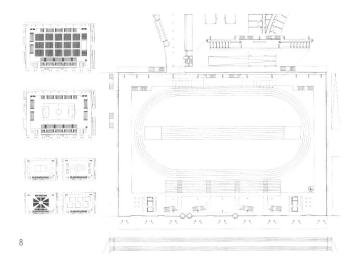

7

8

Sport- und Veranstaltungshalle Linz/Österreich 1997

Das in seiner Begrüßungsgeste signifikante Gebäude präsentiert sich dem Besucher als öffentlicher Ort. Dank einer Fassade aus mattiertem Industrieglas vor farbigen Leuchtstofflampen entsteht nachts ein farbig durchleuchteter schwebender Körper. Gedacht als festlicher Rahmen für Konzerte und Ausstellungen ebenso wie als robuster Austragungsort für sportliche Wettkämpfe vom Boxkampf über Fußballspiele bis zur Leichtathletik zeigt sich im Grundriß ein neutrales Rechteck, das auf der Nordseite an ein großes Stadion angrenzt, dem auf der stadtzugewandten Südseite jedoch ein großer, durch Baumreihen strukturierter (Park-) Platz vorgelagert ist. Mit der Vorgabe, die Spielfeldebene des Vorgängerbaus mit allen Ergänzungsflächen zu erhalten, um die Grundfläche nur auf den Schmalseiten zu erweitern, war der Standort festgelegt. Auf der weit geöffneten repräsentativen Zugangsseite entwickelt sich die Dynamik des Großraums im Zusammenspiel von Konstruktion und Baukörper wie durch ein Zurückschlagen der Verhüllung öffentlich. Durch das Anheben der Tribünen im Eingangsbereich erhält der Besucher tiefen Einblick in das Geschehen. Dieses Motiv, bei der kleineren Ballsporthalle in Frankfurt Höchst bereits realisiert, wird unterstützt durch umlaufende Glasbänder und das Auflösen der Auflager für die im Abstand von 12 m angeordneten Dreigurtbinder in zwei Pendelstützen. Entscheidend für das weite atmosphärische Spektrum innen ist eine Lichtinszenierung, die mit verglasten Dachflächen, in Glas und Tragwerk integrierten Spiegel- und Ausblendrastern und textilen Lichtdeckenelementen oberhalb des Spielfelds komplex zu steuern ist. (Wettbewerb, 2. Preis)

Sports and Events Hall Linz/Austria 1997

The building presents itself as a public place with its significant welcoming gesture. Due to a facade comprised of matted industrial glass in front of colored neon lights, at night a colorfully lit and floating volume comes into being. Conceived as a festive framework for concerts and exhibitions as well as a robust site for sports competitions ranging from boxing to soccer and light athletics, the ground plan is a neutral rectangle adjoining a large stadium on its north side; at the south side facing the city, a large (parking) lot structured by rows of trees is situated in front of the building. The precondition for preserving the playing field level of the old structure with all extension areas in order to extend the basic surface only along the narrow sides predetermined the site. On the wide open, representative access side, the dynamics of the large space develops publicly in the interaction of construction and building volume as if through a lifting of the veil. Because the grandstands are raised in the entrance area, the visitor gets a deep insight into events. This motif, already realized in the smaller sports hall in Frankfurt Höchst, is enhanced by surrounding glass strips and the resolution of the bearings for the three-boom joists arranged at a distance of 12 meters into two rocker columns. What is decisive for the creation of an extensive atmospheric spectrum is a lighting production that can be elaborately controlled – glazed roof surfaces, mirror and fade-out grids integrated into the glass and supporting structure, and with lightweight textile ceiling elements above the field. (Competition, 2nd prize)

147

Bernd Albers

Bernd Albers
Oranienplatz 4
D–10999 Berlin

Biographie

1957	in Coesfeld/Westfalen geboren;
1980–1987	Architekturstudium an der TU Berlin, Diplom bei Peter Lehrecke und Otto Steidle;
1984–1987	freie Mitarbeit im Büro Hans Kollhoff/Berlin;
1987–1994	Lehrtätigkeit an der ETH Zürich, Oberassistent von Hans Kollhoff;
1989	Gastdozent an der Internationalen Sommerakademie «Architektur im Ruhrgebiet» (IBA Emscher Park);
1990	Gastdozent an der Internationalen Sommerakademie für Architektur in Karlsruhe;
1995	Gastprofessur an der 7. Internationalen Sommerakademie «Architettura e Città» in Neapel;
seit 1996	Gastprofessur an der FH Potsdam;
1988–1993	Architekturbüro in Zürich;
seit 1989	Architekturbüro in Berlin;
1996–1998	Zusammenarbeit mit Dieter Hoffmann-Axthelm beim Gutachten «Planwerk Innenstadt Berlin»;
1994–1998	wichtige Realisierungen: Wohn- und Geschäftshäuser in der Wasserstadt Spandau, Berlin

Biography

1957	born in Coesfeld/Westfalen;
1980–1987	architectural studies at TU Berlin, degree with Peter Lehrecke and Otto Steidle;
1984–1987	freelance cooperation in the office of Hans Kollhoff/Berlin;
1987–1994	teacher at ETH Zurich, head assistant to Hans Kollhoff;
1989	guest lecturer at the International Summer Academy «Architektur im Ruhrgebiet» (IBA Emscher Park);
1990	guest lecturer at the International Summer Academy for architecture in Karlsruhe;
1995	guest lecturer at the 7th International Summer Academy «Architettura e Città» in Naples;
since 1996	guest professor at the University for Applied Science in Potsdam;
1988–1993	architectural office in Zurich;
since 1989	architectural office in Berlin;
1996–1998	cooperation with Dieter Hoffmann-Axthelm for the expert opinion on «Planwerk Innenstadt Berlin»;
1994–1998	important realizations: apartment and office buildings in Wasserstadt Spandau, Berlin

Mitarbeiter seit 1990 (Auswahl) / Collaborators since 1990 (selection)

Armin Behles, Florian Matzger, Tobias Nöfer, Sigi Stucky, Salomon Schindler, Alexander Wagner, Hannes Werner

Bibliographie (Auswahl) / Bibliography (selection)

Eigene Texte / texts: Living 2/1993; Arch+ 118/1993; Archis 3/1994; Thies Schröder: Berlin – Berlin, Berlin 1995; Domus 793/1997; Senatsverwaltung für Stadtentwicklung, Umweltschutz und Technologie (Hrsg. / ed.): Planwerk Innenstadt Berlin – Ein erster Entwurf, Berlin 1997

Projektpublikationen / project publications: Domus 708/1989; Casabella 557/1989; Faces 19/1991; Casabella 595/1992; Archis 7/1993; Werk, Bauen + Wohnen 11/1993; Archis 3/1994; Lotus 80/1994; Stadtbauwelt 48/1996; DIE ZEIT 28.11.1996; Neue Berliner Stadtquartiere, Katalog Architekturmuseum / catalog architectural museum Frankfurt 1996; Houses for Sale, Katalog Galerie / catalog gallery Sophia Ungers Köln 1997; Topos 19/1997; Domus 793/1997; Berliner Zeitung 15. 4. 1998

Ausstellungen / Exhibitions

Berlin 1+1=1, Aedes Berlin 1990; Bernd Albers Stadt-Körper, Architektur-Forum Zürich 1992; Application & Implication, Centre National d'Art Contemporain Grenoble 1993; Berlin – Entwerfen im Kontext, Prag / Prague 1994; Triennale Mailand / Milan Triennial 1995; Architectura et Cita, Neapel / Naples 1996; Neue Berliner Stadtquartiere, Architekturmuseum / architectural museum Frankfurt/M. 1996

Werkauswahl / Selected works

Moabiter Werder, Berlin 1991;
Stadtteil / urban quarter Pulvermühle (1. Preisgruppe / award group), Berlin 1992;
Gewerbe- und Wohnblock / commercial and apartment block Rotaprint (2. Preis / prize), Berlin 1994;
Wohn- und Geschäftshaus / apartment and commercial building, Berlin 1994–1998;
Wohn-, Büro- und Geschäftshaus / apartment, office and commercial building, Berlin 1994–1998;
Investitionsbank / investment bank (2. Preis / prize), Berlin 1994;
Neustadt Biesdorf (1. Preis / prize), Berlin 1994;
Galerie / gallery Bob van Orsouw, Zürich 1996;
Landeszentralbank (2. Preis / prize), Chemnitz 1996;
Turmhaus und Bahnarkaden / tower house and railway arcades Stuttgarter Platz (1. Preis / prize), Berlin 1996;
S-Bahnhof / tram station Teltow (1. Preis / prize), Berlin 1996;
Villa Marienburg, Köln / Cologne 1996;
Planwerk Innenstadt, Berlin 1996/97;
Hauptbahnhof / main station Stuttgart 21 (Ankauf / purchase), Stuttgart 1997;
Museum der bildenden Künste / museum for fine arts (7. Rang / rank), Leipzig 1997;
Wohnquartier Bauausstellung Pankow/ housing quarter architectural exposition Pankow (3. Preis / prize), Berlin 1997-1999.

Markus Allmann
Amandus Sattler
Ludwig Wappner

Allmann Sattler Wappner Architekten
Bothmerstraße 14
D-80634 München

Biographien

Markus Allmann

1959	in Ludwigshafen geboren;
1979–1986	Architekturstudium an der TU München, Diplom bei Friedrich Kurrent;
1983	Auslandspraktikum und freie Mitarbeit in den Büros Douine und Prunis/Avignon, Favre und Guth/Genf;
1986/87	Mitarbeit im Büro Betrix und Consolascio/Zürich;
1987–1993	Architekturbüro Allmann und Sattler in München;
seit 1993	Architekturbüro Allmann Sattler Wappner in München;
1993	Kunstförderpreis der Stadt München;
1997	Deutscher Architekturpreis für das Schulzentrum in Flöha bei Chemnitz;
	wichtige Realisierungen: Gymnasium Flöha 1992–1996; Wertstoffhof, München

1995–1997; Herz Jesu Kirche, München 1996–1999

Amandus Sattler
1957   in Marktredwitz/Bayern geboren;
1979–1985   Architekturstudium an der TU München, Diplom bei Thomas Schmid;
1982   Gründung der Studiengemeinschaft «Sprengwerk» für Kunst und Architektur in München;
1985/86   selbständige Tätigkeit, u.a. kostensparende Bausysteme in Holzrahmenbauweise;
1987–1993   Architekturbüro Allmann und Sattler in München;
seit 1993   Architekturbüro Allmann Sattler Wappner in München;
1993   Kunstförderpreis der Stadt München;
1997   Deutscher Architekturpreis für das Schulzentrum in Flöha bei Chemnitz;
     wichtige Realisierungen: Gymnasium Flöha 1992–1996; Wertstoffhof, München 1995–1997; Herz Jesu Kirche, München 1996–1999

Ludwig Wappner
1957   in Hösbach/Bayern geboren;
1979–1985   Architekturtudium an der TU München, Diplom bei Thomas Schmid;
1982   Gründung der Studiengemeinschaft «Sprengwerk» für Kunst und Architektur in München;
1985–1989   Mitarbeit im Büro Schmidt-Schicketanz und Partner in München;
1987–1993   Arbeitsgemeinschaft MAP/München mit Allmann und Sattler/München;
1989–1993   Lehrtätigkeit an der TU München, Assistent von Bernhard Winkler am Lehrstuhl für Gebäudelehre und Entwerfen;
seit 1993   Architekturbüro Allmann Sattler Wappner in München;
1993   Kunstförderpreis der Stadt München;
1997   Deutscher Architekturpreis für das Schulzentrum in Flöha bei Chemnitz;
     wichtige Realisierungen: Gymnasium Flöha 1992–1996; Wertstoffhof, München 1995–1997; Herz Jesu Kirche, München 1996–1999

Biographies

Markus Allmann
1959   born in Ludwigshafen;
1979–1986   architectural studies at TU Munich, degree with Friedrich Kurrent;
1983   practical semester abroad and freelance cooperation with the Douine and Prunis/Avignon, Favre and Guth/Geneva;
1986/87   cooperation in the office Betrix and Consolascio/Zurich;
1987–1993   architectural office Allmann and Sattler in Munich;
since 1993   architectural office Allmann Sattler Wappner in Munich;
1993   art sponsoring award of the city of Munich;
1997   German Architectural Award for the school center in Flöha/Chemnitz;
     important realizations: Flöha high school 1992–1996; recycling center, Munich 1995–1997; Herz Jesu Church, Munich 1996–1999

Amandus Sattler
1957   born in Marktredwitz/Bayern;
1979–1985   architectural studies at TU Munich, degree with Thomas Schmid;
1982   foundation of the study community «Sprengwerk» for art and architecture in Munich;
1985/86   freelance work, among others, cost-efficient wood framework building systems;
1987–1993   architectural office Allmann und Sattler in Munich;
since 1993   architectural office Allmann Sattler Wappner in Munich;
1993   art sponsoring award of the city of Munich;
1997   German architectural award for the school center in Flöha/Chemnitz;
     important realizations: Flöha high school 1992–1996; recycling center, Munich 1995–1997; Herz Jesu Church, Munich 1996–1999

Ludwig Wappner
1957   born in Hösbach/Bayern;
1979–1985   architectural studies at TU Munich, degree with Thomas Schmid;
1982   foundation of the study community «Sprengwerk» for art and architecture in Munich;
1985–1989   collaboration in the office Schmidt-Schicketanz und Partner in Munich;
1987–1993   work community MAP/Munich with Allmann und Sattler/Munich;
1989–1993   teacher at TU Munich, assistant to Bernhard Winkler at the chair for building and design;
since 1993   architectural office Allmann Sattler Wappner in Munich;
1993   art sponsor award of the city of Munich;
1997   German architectural award for the school center in Flöha/Chemnitz;
     important realizations: Flöha high school 1992–1996; recycling center, Munich 1995–1997; Herz Jesu Church, Munich 1996–1999

Mitarbeiter / Collaborators

Christiane Abel, Detlef Böwing, Katharina Duer, Karin Hengher, Robert Klein, Robinson Pourroy, Susanne Rath, Olga Ritter, Jan Schabert

Bibliographie (Auswahl) / Bibliography (selection)

Bauwelt 16/1996; Bauwelt 20/1996; AIT 6/1996; Baumeister 5/1996; DBZ Deutsche Bauzeitschrift 6/1996; Süddeutsche Zeitung 17.4./14.6./8.8.1996; Neue Zürcher Zeitung 2.5.1997; Detail 1/1998; Glasforum 1/1998; Bauwelt 15/1998

Ausstellungen / Exhibitions

10 Projekte / 10 projects 1991–1994, Architekturgalerie München / Munich 1994

Auszeichnungen / Awards

Kunstförderpreis der Stadt München 1993; Architekturpreis (lobende Anerkennung) des Neuen Sächsischen Kunstvereins 1994; Architekturpreis Beton (lobende Erwähnung) 1997; Deutscher Architekturpreis 1997; Gestaltungspreis der Wüstenrotstiftung 1998

Werkauswahl / Selected works

Stadtbad / municipal pool Schöneberg (2. Preis / prize), Berlin 1991
Schwimm- und Sporthalle / pool and gymnasium Olympia 2000 (Ankauf / Sonderpreis / purchase / special award), Berlin 1992
Gymnasium mit Dreifachturnhalle / high school with triple-use gymnasium (1. Preis / prize), Flöha/Chemnitz 1992–1996
Bürogebäude / office building Donnersberger Brücke (2. Preis / prize), München/Munich 1992
Grundschule und Sporthalle / primary school and sports hall (Ankauf / purchase), Samerberg 1993
Gymnasium / high school (Ankauf / purchase), Freising 1994
Städtisches / municipal Museum Simeonstift (Ankauf / purchase), Trier 1994
Haus Feix / Feix House, Bad Wörishofen 1995–1996
Wertstoffhof / recycling center Lerchenau, München / Munich 1995–1997
Herz Jesu Kirche / Church (1. Preis / prize), München / Munich 1996–1999
Theater am Hirschgarten (2. Preis / prize), Erfurt 1996
Hochschule für Film und Fernsehen / university for film and television, Babelsberg 1996
Labor- und Bürogebäude / laboratory and office building Bärlocher, München / Munich 1996
Landtag Thüringen / representative offices of Thuringia, Erfurt 1996
Friedhof / cemetery Riem (3. Preis / prize), München / Munich 1997
Hauptverwaltung / main administration Bayerische Rückversicherung (1. Preis / prize), München / Munich 1997

Georg Augustin
Ute Frank

Augustin und Frank Architekten
Schlesische Straße 29-30
D-10997 Berlin

Biographien

Georg Augustin
1951   in Schaffhausen geboren;
1971–1973   Studium des Bauingenieurwesens an der TH Karlsruhe;
1973–1979   Architekturstudium an der TU Berlin, Diplom bei Declan Kennedy;
1979–1986   Mitarbeit im Büro Hinrich und Inken Baller/Berlin und im Büro Bangert-Jansen-Scholz-Schultes/Berlin; freie Mitarbeit im Ingenieurbüro Gerhard Pichler;
seit 1986   Architekturbüro Augustin und Frank in Berlin;
1986–1990   Lehrtätigkeit an der TU Berlin, Assistent von Andreas Reidemeister und Bernd Jansen am Fachgebiet Baukonstruktion und Entwerfen;

1989	Gründung der Architektengruppe «Hundekopf» mit mehreren Ausstellungen 1990/91;
1997	Beteiligung an der 3. Internationalen Architekturbiennale in Sao Paulo mit einem Sozialen Wohnungsbau in Berlin-Tegel;
seit 1997	Gastprofessur an der TU Berlin, Fachgebiet Entwerfen, Baukonstruktion und Baupraxis;
	wichtige Realisierungen: Haus Scherer, Berlin 1992–1993 / 98; Sozialer Wohnungsbau Lichtenberg, Berlin 1992–1997; Sozialer Wohnungsbau Tegel, Berlin 1993–1996; Büro- und Geschäftshaus Karlshorst, Berlin 1995–1998; Kindertagesstätte Spandau, Berlin 1996–1998

Ute Frank

1952	in Landau geboren;
1969–1975	Architekturstudium an der TH Karlsruhe;
1975–1979	Studium der Architektur und Baugeschichte an der TU Berlin, Diplom bei Declan Kennedy und Goerd Peschken;
1979–1986	Wissenschaftliche Arbeiten zur Architektur- und Stadtbaugeschichte: «casa uguale famiglia?», Biennale Venedig 1982; «Terrainspekulation und U-Bahn-Bau» (Exerzierfeld der Moderne – Industriekultur in Berlin im 19. Jahrhundert, München 1984); «Städtebau in Berlin» in Zusammenarbeit mit Goerd Peschken;
1979–1986	Mitarbeit in verschiedenen Berliner Büros, u.a. bei Werner Düttmann und im Rahmen der IBA Berlin bei Hardt-Waltherr Hämer, Pilotprojekt der Behutsamen Stadterneuerung;
seit 1986	Architekturbüro Augustin und Frank in Berlin;
1989–1990	Lehrtätigkeit an der TU Berlin, Lehrauftrag «Übergänge Berlin – West-Ost-Berlin» am Institut für Stadt- und Regionalplanung;
1997	Beteiligung an der 3. Internationalen Architekturbiennale in Sao Paulo mit einem Sozialen Wohnungsbau in Berlin-Tegel;
	wichtige Realisierungen: Haus Scherer, Berlin 1992–1993/98; Sozialer Wohnungsbau Lichtenberg, Berlin 1992–1997; Sozialer Wohnungsbau Tegel, Berlin 1993–1996; Büro- und Geschäftshaus Karlshorst, Berlin 1995–1998; Kindertagesstätte Spandau, Berlin 1996–1998

Biographies

Georg Augustin

1951	born in Schaffhausen;
1971–1973	studies of building engineering at TH Karlsruhe;
1973–1979	architectural studies at TU Berlin, degree with Declan Kennedy;
1979–1986	collaboration in the office Hinrich and Inken Baller/Berlin and in the office Bangert-Jansen-Scholz-Schultes/Berlin; freelance collaboration in the engineering office Gerhard Pichler;
since 1986	architectural office Augustin and Frank in Berlin;
1986–1990	teacher at TU Berlin, assistant to Andreas Reidemeister and Bernd Jansen at the faculty construction and design;
1989	foundation of the architectural group «Hundekopf» with several exhibitions 1990/91;
1997	participation at the 3rd International Architecture Biennial in Sao Paulo with a social housing project in Berlin-Tegel;
since 1997	guest professor at TU Berlin, faculty design, construction and architectural practice;
	important realizations: Scherer House, Berlin 1992–1993/98; social housing Lichtenberg, Berlin 1992–1997; social housing Tegel, Berlin 1993–1996; office and commercial building Karlshorst, Berlin 1995–1998; day care center Spandau, Berlin 1996–1998

Ute Frank

1952	born in Landau;
1969–1975	architectural studies at TH Karlsruhe;
1975–1979	architectural studies and architectural history at TU Berlin, degree with Declan Kennedy and Goerd Peschken;
1979–1986	scientific work on architectural and urban history: «casa uguale famiglia?», Venice Biennial 1982; «Terrainspekulation und U-Bahn-Bau» (Exerzierfeld der Moderne – Industriekultur in Berlin im 19. Jahrhundert, Munich 1984); «Städtebau in Berlin» in cooperation with Goerd Peschken;
1979–1986	cooperation in different Berlin offices, e.g., with Werner Düttmann and for the IBA Berlin with Hardt-Waltherr Hämer, pilot project for a careful urban renewal;
since 1986	architectural office Augustin and Frank in Berlin;
1989–1990	teacher at TU Berlin, teaching assignment «Übergänge Berlin – West-Ost-Berlin» at the Institute for Urban and Regional Planning;
1997	participation at the 3rd International Architectural Biennial in Sao Paulo with a social housing in Berlin-Tegel;
	important realizations: Scherer House, Berlin 1992–1993/98; social housing Lichtenberg, Berlin 1992–1997; social housing Tegel, Berlin 1993–1996; office and commercial building Karlshorst, Berlin 1995–1998; day care center Spandau, Berlin 1996–1998

Mitarbeiter seit 1992 / Collaborators since 1992

Peter Begon, Christa Beck, Nils Buschmann, Bernard Cherix, Anne Claude, Ségolène Demerliac, Laurent Fesselet, Andreas Glücker, Ursula Hartig, Anja Hoffmann, Petra Hoffmann, Martin Janekovic, Daniel Kahala, Sabine Kuhn, Christian Moczala, Hedwige Murer, Rainer Scherwey, Susanne Schnorrbusch, Peter Schupp, Armin Teufel

Bibliographie (Auswahl) / Bibliography (selection)

Bauwelt 29/1997; Der Tagesspiegel 14.9.1997; Foyer 3/1997; Kataloge zu den genannten Ausstellungen / catalogs for the mentioned exhibitions; Architektur Aktuell 3/1998; Bauwelt 19/1998; Bauwelt 20/1998

Ausstellungen / Exhibitions

Die Spree vom Treptower Park bis zum Tiergarten, Galerie Aedes Berlin 1990; Wohnungsbau für die Hauptstadt Berlin, Aedes Architekturforum 1990; Wohn- und Geschäftshaus an der Paulsborner Straße, Aedes Architekturforum 1991; Berlin Heute, Berlinische Galerie im Martin Gropius Bau 1991; Lichtenberger Linie, Lichtenberg plant und baut 1991–1994, Bezirksamt Berlin Lichtenberg 1994; 3. Internationale Architekturbiennale / 3. international architectural biennial Sao Paulo 1997

Werkauswahl / Selected works

Städtebauliche Konzeption / urban conception Spreeraum Stralau – Johannisthal, Berlin 1990
Stadtentwicklung und -ergänzung / urban development and addition Quartier 108, Berlin 1990
Wohn- und Geschäftshaus / apartment and commercial building Grunewald, Berlin 1990 (in Planung / planned)
Wohnungsbau / apartment building Kreuzberg (2. Preis / prize), Berlin 1991
Kindertagesstätte / day care center Kreuzberg (2. Preis / prize), Berlin 1991 (in Planung / planned)
Aufstockung Haus Scherer / heightening Scherer House, Berlin 1992–1993/98
Sporthalle / sports hall Schöneberg, Berlin 1992 (in Planung / planned)
Grundschule / primary school Spandau (3. Preis / prize), Berlin 1992
Sozialer Wohnungsbau / social housing Lichtenberg (1. Preis / prize), Berlin 1992–1997
Hotel Ramada Köpenick (3. Preis / prize), Berlin 1993
Sozialer Wohnungsbau / social housing Tegel, Berlin 1993–1996
Büro- und Geschäftshaus / office and commercial building Karlshorst, Berlin 1995–1998
Kindertagesstätte / day care center Spandau (1. Preis / prize), Berlin 1996–1998
Landesvertretung Rheinland-Pfalz / representative offices Rhineland-Palatinate (5. Preis / prize), Berlin 1997
Physikalisches Institut Humboldt Universität (1. Preis/prize), Berlin 1997/98

Peter Cheret
Jelena Bozic

Cheret und Bozic Architekten
Nägelestraße 7
D-70597 Stuttgart

Biographien

Peter Cheret

1953	in Lörrach geboren;
1976–1980	Architekturstudium und Diplom an der FH Konstanz;
1980–1982	Architekturstudium an der Universität Stuttgart;
1980–1988	Mitarbeit im Büro W. Lauber, Haas und Hermann/Stuttgart und im Büro Günter Hermann/Stuttgart;

1988–1990 Bürogemeinschaft mit Joachim Englert;
1988–1993 Lehrtätigkeit an der Universität Stuttgart, «Einführung in das Entwerfen» bei Boris Podrecca am Institut für Innenraumgestaltung;
seit 1993 Architekturbüro Cheret und Bozic in Stuttgart;
1993/94 Lehrstuhlvertretung an der FH Trier;
1993/94 Architekturpreise für mehrere Bauten der Internationalen Gartenbauausstellung IGA 1993 in Stuttgart und des Zoologischen Gartens Wilhelma in Stuttgart;
seit 1994 Professur an der Universität Stuttgart, Institut für Baukonstruktion, Lehrstuhl 1 für Baukonstruktion und Entwerfen;
wichtige Realisierungen: Erweiterung Wilhelma, Stuttgart 1988–1993; Kulturzentrum Giengen 1991–1995; Landespavillon Baden-Württemberg 1992–1993 (transloziert und umgenutzt); Pavillon «Grüne Universität» 1993 (demontiert und eingelagert); Deutsches Landwirtschaftsmuseum, Stuttgart 1994; Katholisches Gemeindezentrum, Heilbronn 1994–1997; Kindergarten Reutlingen 1995–1996

Jelena Bozic
1959 in Slavonski Samac/ehem. Jugoslawien geboren;
1969 Umsiedlung nach Deutschland;
1980–1987 Architekturstudium an der Universität Stuttgart, Diplom bei Klaus Humpert;
1984/85 Gaststudium bei Dolf Schnebli an der ETH Zürich;
1987–1993 Mitarbeit im Büro Lederer Ragnarsdóttir/Stuttgart und im Büro Cheret/Stuttgart;
1989/90 und
1993/94 Lehrtätigkeit an der Universität Stuttgart, «Einführen in das Entwerfen» bei Boris Podrecca am Institut für Innenraumgestaltung;
seit 1993 Architekturbüro Cheret und Bozic in Stuttgart;
1993/94 Architekturpreise für mehrere Bauten der Internationalen Gartenbauausstellung IGA 1993 in Stuttgart und des Zoologischen Gartens Wilhelma in Stuttgart;
wichtige Realisierungen: Erweiterung Wilhelma, Stuttgart 1988–1993; Kulturzentrum Giengen 1991–1995; Landespavillon Baden-Württemberg 1992–1993 (transloziert und umgenutzt); Pavillon «Grüne Universität» 1993 (demontiert und eingelagert); Deutsches Landwirtschaftsmuseum, Stuttgart 1994; Katholisches Gemeindezentrum, Heilbronn 1994–1997; Kindergarten Reutlingen 1995–1996

Biographies

Peter Cheret
1953 born in Lörrach;
1976–1980 architectural studies and degree at the FH Konstanz;
1980–1982 architectural studies at Stuttgart university;
1980–1988 collaboration in the offices W. Lauber, Haas and Hermann/Stuttgart and Günter Hermann/Stuttgart;
1988–1990 office community with Joachim Englert;
1988–1993 teacher at Stuttgart University, «Introduction to Design» with Boris Podrecca at the Institute for Interior Design;
since 1993 architectural office Cheret and Bozic in Stuttgart;
1993/94 adjunct professor at FH Trier;
1993/94 architectural awards for several buildings of the International Garden Expo IGA 1993 in Stuttgart and the zoological garden Wilhelma in Stuttgart;
since 1994 professor at Stuttgart University, Institute for Architectural Construction, Professorship for construction and design;
important realizations: extension Wilhelma, Stuttgart 1988–1993; cultural center Giengen 1991–1995; pavilion for Baden-Württemberg 1992–1993 (relocated and reutilized); pavilion «Green University» 1993 (dismantled and stored); German Agricultural Museum, Stuttgart 1994; catholic community center, Heilbronn 1994–1997; kindergarten Reutlingen 1995–1996

Jelena Bozic
1959 born in Slavonski Samac/formerly Yugoslavia;
1969 emigration to Germany;
1980–1987 architectural studies at Stuttgart University, degree with Klaus Humpert;
1984/85 guest studies with Dolf Schnebli at ETH Zurich;
1987–1993 collaboration in the offices Lederer Ragnarsdóttir/Stuttgart and Cheret/Stuttgart;
1989/90 and
1993/94 teacher at Stuttgart University, «Introduction to Design» with Boris Podrecca at the Institute for Interior Design;
since 1993 architectural office Cheret and Bozic in Stuttgart;
1993/94 architectural awards for several buildings of the International Garden Expo IGA 1993 in Stuttgart and the zoological garden Wilhelma in Stuttgart;
important realizations: extension Wilhelma, Stuttgart 1988–1993; cultural center Giengen 1991–1995; pavilion for Baden-Württemberg 1992–1993 (relocated and reutilized); pavilion «Green University» 1993 (dismantled and stored); German Agricultural Museum, Stuttgart 1994; catholic community center, Heilbronn 1994–1997; kindergarten Reutlingen 1995–1996

Mitarbeiter seit 1988 / Collaborators since 1988

Anna Blaschke, Anja Braun, Pascal Dworak, Iris Ettel, Cordula Feinauer, Hermann Gaenslen, Monika Geißler, Florian Heim, Adrian Hochstrasser, Dorothee Hoffmann, Hanna von der Kall,

Ralf Kohfeld, Anne Mössle, Anke Nierhaus, Sven Seiffert, Sabine Süs, Michael Zeuner

Bibliographie (Auswahl) / Bibliography (selection)

Bauwelt 21/1993; Arch+ 118/1993; Bauhandwerk 11/1993; db Deutsche Bauzeitung 2/1994; db Deutsche Bauzeitung 4/1995; db Deutsche Bauzeitung 7/1995; Bauwelt 8/1996

Auszeichnungen / Awards

BDA Auszeichnung guter Bauten 1993; Auszeichnung Beispielhaftes Bauen der Achitektenkammer Baden-Württemberg 1994; Holzbaupreis Baden-Württemberg 1994 (zweifach / twice); Auszeichnung Beispielhaftes Bauen der Achitektenkammer Baden-Württemberg 1997

Werkauswahl / Selected works

Erweiterung / extension Wilhelma Bad Cannstadt (2. Preis / prize), Stuttgart 1988–1993
Kunsthalle (Ankauf / purchase), Heilbronn 1989
Wohnhaus / apartment house Bohlingen 1990–1992
Kulturzentrum / cultural center (1. Preis / prize), Giengen 1991–1995
Landespavillon Gartenbauausstellung / pavilion gardening and landscape exposition IGA (1.Preis / prize), Stuttgart 1993
Pavillon Grüne Universität / Green University pavilion IGA, Stuttgart 1993
Deutsches Landwirtschaftsmuseum / German agricultural museum Hohenheim, Stuttgart 1994
Ausstellungspavillon Windkraftwerk / exhibition pavilion wind power plant, Heroldstatt 1994
Katholisches Gemeindezentrum / catholic community center (1. Preis / prize), Heilbronn 1994–1997
Kindergarten, Reutlingen 1995–1996
Brücke über das Nesenbachtal / bridge across Nesenbach valley (1. Preis / prize mit / with Rittich und Bornscheuer), Stuttgart 1995–1999
Schulungszentrum / educational center Brügman (1. Preis / prize), Papenburg 1995
Gärtnerisches Betriebsgebäude / commercial building for a gardening shop, Stuttgart 1996
Altarraum-Gestaltung Katholisches Gemeindezentrum / altar design Catholic community center (1. Preis / prize), Heilbronn 1996
Naturparkverwaltung und Museum / natural preserve administration and museum Märkische Schweiz, Buckow 1997

Hansjörg Göritz

Studio Göritz
Jordanstraße 7
D-30173 Hannover

Biographie

1959 in Hannover geboren, Vater Maurer;
1979 Abitur/1980 Gesellenbrief des Maurerhandwerks und Meisterschule;
1981–1985 Selbststudium der Architektur;
1982 Studienreisen in Italien und Griechenland;
1984/85 Stipendiat an der Architectural Association in London;
1985 Reisen zu Bauten von Lubetkin, Aalto und Le Corbusier;
seit 1986 «Studio Göritz» in Hannover;
1989–1991 Mitarbeit im Büro Bangert-Jansen-Scholz-Schultes/Berlin;
1991 Studien zum Werk von Kahn, Ando und Barragan;

1994 Deubau-Preisträger und weitere Auszeichnungen für die Arbeiten «Steinräume»;
seit 1995 Gastlehrer an der FH Hildesheim;
1996 Förderungspreis Baukunst der Akademie der Künste Berlin;
wichtige Realisierungen: Haus «Trennemoor» Kirchhorst, Hannover 1990–1992;
Büro- und Ausstellungsgebäude, Hildesheim 1990–1993; Haus Horstkotte
Ahlem, Hannover 1991–1993; Wohnungsbau Bemerode, Hannover 1993–1996;
S-Bahn Station Nordstadt (Expo 2000), Hannover 1996–1997

Biography

1959 born in Hannover, father was a mason;
1979 bacchaleaureat/1980 Gesellenbrief des Maurerhandwerks und Meisterschule;
1981–1985 autodidactic architectural studies;
1982 travels to Italy and Greece;
1984/85 stipendium at the AA in London;
1985 travels to buildings by Lubetkin, Aalto and Le Corbusier;
since 1986 architectural office in Hannover;
1989–1991 collaboration in the office Bangert-Jansen-Scholz-Schultes/Berlin;
1991 studies on the oeuvre of Kahn, Ando and Barragan;
1994 Deubau award winner and additional awards for his «Steinräume»;
since 1995 guest teacher at FH Hildesheim;
1996 sponsoring award for architecture of the Academy of Fine Arts Berlin;
important realizations: "Trennemoor" House Kirchhorst, Hannover 1990–1992;
office and exhibition building, Hildesheim 1990–1993; Horstkotte House Ahlem,
Hannover 1991–1993; apartment building Bemerode, Hannover 1993–1996;
tram station Nordstadt (Expo 2000), Hannover 1996–1997

Mitarbeiter seit 1986 (Auswahl) / Collaborators since 1986 (selection)

Frauke Brockhausen, Jürgen Büscher, Peter Haslinger, Andreas Kleinschmidt, Gordon Kisser,
Michael Schröder, Ina Wäßerling

Bibliographie (Auswahl) / Bibliography (selection)

Eigene Texte / texts: Deutsches Architektenblatt 12/1994; AIT 1–2/1995; AIT Forum 7–8/1995;
AIT 1–2/1996; Jahrbuch Architektur und Licht 1997 und 1998
Projektpublikationen / project publications: das bauzentrum 1/1994; Frankfurter Allgemeine Zeitung 22.3.1994; Deutsches Architektenblatt 5/1994; Neue Zürcher Zeitung 1.7.1994; architektur
+ wohnen 4/1994; AIT 9/1994; Centrum Jahrbuch Architektur und Stadt 1994; db deutsche bauzeitung 7/1995; Arkitekten 29/1996; Bauwelt 33/1997; Berliner Zeitung 5.11.1997; Baukultur
11/1997; Baumeister 11/1997; Architektur Aktuell 12/1997; Häuser 3/1998

Ausstellungen / Exhibitions

Von Laves bis morgen, Orangerie Hannover Herrenhausen 1988; Konzepte für Dresden, Hochschule für Bildende Künste Dresden 1990; Ideen-Orte-Entwürfe/40 Jahre Architektur und Städtebau in der Bundesrepublik Deutschland (Bundesbauministerium), Messehaus am Markt Leipzig
1990; Designed in Germany, World Design Expo Mexico City 1991; Renaissance der Bahnhöfe –
Die Stadt im 21. Jahrhundert, Zitelle Venedig/Architekturbiennale / Venice architectural biennial
1996

Auszeichnungen / Awards

Commendation Royal Institute of British Architects 1985; Auszeichnung Ziegel im Wirtschafts-
bau 1992; Deubau-Preis 1994; Architekturpreis Ziegel 1994; BDA-Preis Niedersachsen 1994;
Förderungspreis Baukunst Akademie der Künste Berlin 1996; Erich-Schelling-Preis 1998 (Nomi-
nierung/nomination)

Werkauswahl / Selected works

«Steinräume»
«Steinhaus im Holzhaus» Haus «Trennemoor» / "Trennemoor" House Kirchhorst, Hannover
1990–1992
«Steinerne Wand» Ausstellung und Verwaltung / exhibition and administration Klimmt,
Hildesheim 1990–1993
«Halle im Steinernen Block» Haus Horstkotte / Horstkotte House Ahlem, Hannover 1991–1993
«Langes Dormitorium» Wohnungsbau / housing Bemerode, Hannover 1993–1996
«hortus conclusus» Haus / House Hemmingen, Hannover 1993/94
«insula» Sozialwohnungen / social housing Block 46, Hannover 1993
«Zellen im Quader im Steinkreis» Haus / House, Hannover 1994
«palaestra» Sportanlage / sports complex MTV Treubund, Lüneburg 1995/96
«Einraumhaus» Seelhorster Garten Bemerode, Hannover 1996
«pluteus et turris» Lichtensteinisches Landesmuseum (2. Preis / prize), Vaduz
«Archen»
«Regenwaldhaus» Herrenhausen (4. Preis / prize), Hannover 1995
«Deutscher Pavillon» Expo 2000 (5. Rang / rank), Hannover 1997
«Horti Conclusi»
«Roemer-Pelizaes-Museum» (Ankauf / purchase), Hildesheim 1990
«hortus conclusus» Zentralkrankenhaus / central hospital (1. Preis / prize), Bremen 1992
«iuventum» Jugendzentrum / youth center, Oldenburg 1995

«New Loft System» LBS Zentrale Bemerode (4. Rang / rank), Hannover 1997
«Transparente Substanz – Substantielle Transparenz»
«Haus mit Glassteinlaterne» Zahnarztpraxis / dentist's office, Hannover 1987–1989
«arcus aus Glasblöcken» S-Bahn Stationen / tram stations Expo 2000 (1. Rang / rank)
Hannover 1995
«Linie aus Steinblöcken» S-Bahn Außenbezirke / tram outskirts Expo 2000, Hannover 1995
«Körper aus Glasblöcken» S-Bahn Station / tram station Nordstadt, Hannover 1996–1997

Andreas Hild
Tillmann Kaltwasser

Hild & Kaltwasser Architekten
Nikolaistraße 2
D-80802 München

Biographien

Andreas Hild
1961 in Hamburg geboren;
1983–1985 Architekturstudium an der TU München;
1985–1988 Architekturstudium an der ETH Zürich bei Fabio Reinhart;
1988 Diplom an der TU München bei Rudolf Wienands;
1988 Europan–Preisträger;
1988 «Denkmal oder Denkmodell», Staatliche Kunsthalle Berlin;
1988 «Analoge Architektur», Wanderausstellung: u.a. Architekturforum Zürich,
Architekturmuseum Frankfurt;
1989 «Modes de vie, architecture de logement», Centre Pompidou Paris;
1990 «Ökologischer Wohnungs- und Städtebau», Bauhaus Dessau;
1991–1996 Lehrtätigkeit an der TU München, Assistent von Rudolf Wienands am
Lehrstuhl für Grundlagen der Darstellung und Gestaltung;
seit 1992 Architekturbüro Hild und Kaltwasser in München;
1993 Bayerischer Wohnungsbaupreis (Besondere Anerkennung), Bauherrenpreis
des BDA und Ortsbildpreis Oberallgäu für Sozialen Wohnungsbau in Immenstadt;
1993 «Münchner Schule», Akademie der schönen Künste München;
1995 Innovationspreis Holzfenster, «Münchner Förderpreis für Architektur»
(Nominierung), Installation Haus Bonnin Eichstätt;
1996 BDA Preis Bayern (Anerkennung) für eine Aufstockung in München, Euro-
Belgian Award für eine Aufstockung in Eichstätt;
seit 1996 Vertretungsprofessur an der Universität Kaiserslautern, Lehrstuhl für Entwerfen,
Gestaltung und Baukonstruktion;
1997 Architekturpreis Beton (Anerkennung) für eine Lagerhalle in Eichstätt;
wichtige Realisierungen: Sozialer Wohnungsbau, Kempten 1993–1997;
Aufstockung Haus Wolf, München 1994; Farbenlager Kemeter, Eichstätt
1994–1995; Aufstockung Haus Bonnin, Eichstätt 1995; Verlagskantine, München
1995–1996; Wertstoff-Sammelstelle, Landshut 1996; Bus-Haltepunkt, Landshut
1997; Kleines Theater, Landshut 1997–1988

Tillmann Kaltwasser
1959 in München geboren;
1980–1987 Architekturstudium an der TU München, Diplom bei Rudolf Wienands;
1987–1992 Mitarbeit im Büro Wienands und Partner/München;

seit 1992   Architekturbüro Hild und Kaltwasser in München;
1993   Bayerischer Wohnungsbaupreis (Besondere Anerkennung), Bauherrenpreis
des BDA und Ortsbildpreis Oberallgäu für Sozialen Wohnungsbau in Immenstadt;
1993   «Münchner Schule», Akademie der schönen Künste München;
1995   Innovationspreis Holzfenster, «Münchner Förderpreis für Architektur»
(Nominierung), Installation Haus Bonnin Eichstätt;
1996   BDA Preis Bayern (Anerkennung) für eine Aufstockung in München, Euro-Belgian
Award für eine Aufstockung in Eichstätt;
1997   Architekturpreis Beton (Anerkennung) für eine Lagerhalle in Eichstätt;
wichtige Realisierungen: Sozialer Wohnungsbau, Kempten 1993–1997;
Aufstockung Haus Wolf, München 1994; Farbenlager Kemeter, Eichstätt
1994–1995; Aufstockung Haus Bonnin, Eichstätt 1995; Verlagskantine, München
1995–1996; Wertstoff-Sammelstelle, Landshut 1996; Bus-Haltepunkt, Landshut
1997; Kleines Theater, Landshut 1997–1988

Biographies

Andreas Hild
1961   born in Hamburg;
1983–1985   architectural studies at TU Munich;
1985–1988   architectural studies at ETH Zurich with Fabio Reinhart;
1988   degree at TU Munich with Rudolf Wienands;
1988   Europan award winner;
1988   "Denkmal oder Denkmodell", Staatliche Kunsthalle Berlin;
1988   "Analoge Architektur", traveling exhibition, among others Architekturforum
Zurich, architectural museum Frankfurt;
1989   "Modes de vie, architecture de logement", Centre Pompidou Paris;
1990   "Ökologischer Wohnungs- und Städtebau", Bauhaus Dessau;
1991–1996   teacher at TU Munich, assistant to Rudolf Wienands at the chair for
principles of presentation and design;
since 1992   architectural office Hild und Kaltwasser in Munich;
1993   Bavarian housing award (special recognition), clients award of BDA and
local image award Upper Allgäu for social housing in Immenstadt;
1993   "Münchner Schule", academy for fine arts Munich;
1995   innovation award wooden windows, "Münchner Förderpreis für Architektur"
(nomination), installation Bonnin House Eichstätt;
1996   BDA award Bavaria (recognition) for a heightening in Munich, Euro-Belgian
Award for a heightening in Eichstätt;
since 1996   substitute professor at Kaiserslautern University, chair for design and building
construction;
1997   German concrete award (recognition) for a storage hall in Eichstätt;
important realizations: social housing, Kempten 1993–1997; heightening Wolf
House, Munich 1994; paint storage Kemeter, Eichstätt 1994–1995; heightening
Bonnin House, Eichstätt 1995; publishing house cafeteria, Munich 1995–1996;
recycling center, Landshut 1996; bus stop, Landshut 1997; Kleines Theater,
Landshut 1997–1998.

Tillmann Kaltwasser
1959   born in Munich;
1980–1987   architectural studies at TU Munich, degree with Rudolf Wienands;
1987–1992   collaboration in the office Wienands und Partner/Munich;
since 1992   architectural office Hild und Kaltwasser in Munich;
1993   Bavarian housing award (special recognition), clients award of BDA and
local image award Upper Allgäu for social housing in Immenstadt;
1993   "Münchner Schule", academy of fine arts Munich;
1995   innovation award wooden windows, "Münchner Förderpreis für Architektur"
(nomination), installation Bonnin House Eichstätt;
1996   BDA award Bavaria (recognition) for a heightening in Munich, Euro-Belgian Award
for a heightening in Eichstätt;
1997   German concrete award (recognition) for a storage hall in Eichstätt;
important realizations: social housing, Kempten 1993–1997; heightening
Wolf House, Munich 1994; paint storage Kemeter, Eichstätt 1994–1995;
heightening Bonnin House, Eichstätt 1995; publishing house cafeteria, Munich
1995–1996; recycling center, Landshut 1996; bus stop, Landshut 1997; Kleines
Theater, Landshut 1997–1998.

Mitarbeiter seit 1994 (Auswahl) / Collaborators since 1994 (selection)

Margerita Martin-Huescar, Dionys Ottl, Michael Rosenstein, Walter Stefan, Thomas Talhofer

Bibliographie (Auswahl) / Bibliography (selection)

Eigene Texte / texts: Baumeister 5/1995; Centrum Jahrbuch Architektur und Stadt 1996; Deutsches Architektenblatt 4/1997; Baumeister 8/1997
Projektpublikationen / project publications: Bauwelt 28–29/1993; Bauwelt 37/1995; Baumeister 6/1995; Arquitectura Viva 45/1995; Baumeister 10/1995; Bauwelt 39/1996; Centrum Jahrbuch Architektur und Stadt 1996; domus 776/1996; DAM Jahrbuch 1996; DAM Jahrbuch 1997; db Deutsche Bauzeitung 4/1998; Baumeister 7/1998

Ausstellungen / Exhibitions

Denkmal oder Denkmodell, Staatliche Kunsthalle Berlin 1988; Modes de vie, architecture de logement, Centre Pompidou Paris 1989; Ökologischer Wohnungs- und Städtebau, Bauhaus Dessau 1990; Münchner Schule, Akademie der schönen Künste München / academy of fine arts Munich 1993; Münchner Förderpreis für Architektur / Munich sponsoring award for architecture, Künstlerwerkstatt München 1995; Aufstockung Haus Bonnin / heightening Bonnin House, Installation Eichstätt 1995

Auszeichnungen / Awards

Bayerischer Wohnungsbaupreis (Besondere Anerkennung / special recognition) 1993; Bauherrenpreis des BDA 1993; Innovationspreis Holzfenster 1995; BDA-Preis Bayern (Anerkennung / recognition) 1996; Euro Belgian Award; Das Goldene Haus; Architekturpreis Beton (Anerkennung / recognition) 1997

Werkauswahl / Selected works

Hotel in der Altstadt, Eichstätt 1994
Quartier Wasserstadt Spandau / quarter, Berlin 1994
Aufstockung Haus Wolf / heightening Wolf House, München/Munich 1994
12 Sozialwohnungen / social housing apartments, Immenstadt 1993
Sozialer Wohnungsbau / social housing Kempten 1993–1997
Farbenlager / paint storage Kemeter, Eichstätt 1994–1995
Fachbetrieb für Sanitärtechnik / company for sanitary technology, Plauen 1995
Aufstockung Haus Bonnin / heightening Bonnin House, Eichstätt 1995
Wohnbebauung / housing development, Ingolstadt 1995
Wohnanlage / apartment complex, Landshut 1995
Terrassen-Wohnanlage / terrace apartment complex Altdorf, Landshut 1995
Umgestaltung Verlagskantine / redesign publishing house cafeteria Callwey, München / Munich 1995–1996
Stuhl und Tisch / chair and table Modell Callwey 1996
Betriebswohnungen / company housing, TU Weihenstephan, Dürnast 1996
Wertstoff-Sammelstelle / recycling center Landshut 1996
Bar und Wohngebäude / bar and apartment building, Eichstätt 1997
Kleines Theater, Landshut 1997–1998
Bus-Haltepunkt / bus stop Ländtorplatz, Landshut 1997
Einfamilienhaus / single-family home, Rudelzhausen 1997–1999

Anke Mensing
Andreas Sedler

Opus Architekten
Objekt Planung und Städtebau
Heidelberger Straße 96
D-64285 Darmstadt

Biographien

Anke Mensing
1963   in Amsterdam geboren;
1982–1987   Studium «Architectonische Vormgeving» an der Gerrit Rietveld Akademie
Amsterdam;

1986	Mitarbeit im Büro Haus-Rucker-Co/Düsseldorf und Peter Wilson/London;
1987	Mitarbeit bei OPERA three dimensional design/Den Bosch;
1988/89	Stipendiatin der «Stichting Fonds vor Beeldende Kunsten, Vormgeving en Bouwkunst»;
1988	Mitarbeit im Büro Eisele und Fritz/Darmstadt;
seit 1989	mit Andreas Sedler Architekturbüro OPUS – Objekt Planung und Städtebau in Darmstadt;
1989–1997	Kunst-Objekte und Installationen in Darmstadt, Utrecht, Offenbach, Frankfurt;
1993	Joseph Maria Olbrich Plakette für die Umnutzung einer Turnhalle in Viernheim und den Ausstellungspavillon «Alltag in der Stadt» in Darmstadt;
1994	«Kunstaanmoedigingsprijs Amstelveen voor Architetuur» (Nominierung);
1997–1998	Gastprofessur an der Staatlichen Akademie der Bildenden Künste in Stuttgart, Fachbereich Architektur; wichtige Realisierungen: Stadtbibliothek Viernheim 1993–1996; Mehrzweckhalle Viernheim 1991–1992; Gemeindeverwaltung, Bank und Wohnungen in Seeheim-Jugenheim 1994–1996

Andreas Sedler

1957	in Bremerhaven geboren;
1978–1985	Architekturstudium an der Universität Gesamthochschule Kassel, Diplom bei Johannes Gsteu und Constantino Dardi;
1981–1982	Gaststudium an der Universität Rom bei Carlo Aymonino und Francesco Cellini;
1981	Mitarbeit im Büro Dardi/Rom;
1985/86	Mitarbeit im Büro Haus-Rucker-Co/Düsseldorf;
1986–1989	Mitarbeit im Büro Rittmannsperger, Kleebank und Partner in Darmstadt;
seit 1989	mit Anke Mensing Architekturbüro OPUS – Objekt Planung und Städtebau in Darmstadt;
1989–1993	Deutscher Stahlbaupreis 1990 (Anerkennung), Deutscher Architekturpreis 1991 (Anerkennung), Premio Internazionale di Architettura Andrea Palladio 1993 (Nominierung) sowie weitere Auszeichnungen für die Umnutzung von Tabakscheunen zur Stadtbibliothek Viernheim;
1989–1997	Kunst-Objekte und Installationen in Darmstadt, Utrecht, Offenbach, Frankfurt;
1990–1993	Lehrtätigkeit an der TH Darmstadt, Assistent von Max Bächer;
1993	Joseph Maria Olbrich Plakette für die Umnutzung einer Turnhalle in Viernheim und den Ausstellungspavillon «Alltag in der Stadt» in Darmstadt; wichtige Realisierungen: Stadtbibliothek Viernheim 1993–1996; Mehrzweckhalle Viernheim 1991–1992; Gemeindeverwaltung, Bank und Wohnungen in Seeheim-Jugenheim 1994–1996

Biographies

Anke Mensing

1963	born in Amsterdam;
1982–1987	«Architectonische Vormgeving» studies at Gerrit Rietveld Academy Amsterdam;
1986	collaboration in the office Haus-Rucker-Co/Düsseldorf and Peter Wilson/London;
1987	collaboration with OPERA three dimensional design/Den Bosch;
1988/89	stipendium at «Stichting Fonds vor Beeldende Kunsten, Vormgeving en Bouwkunst»;
1988	collaboration in the office Eisele and Fritz/Darmstadt;
since 1989	with Andreas Sedler architectural office OPUS – Objekt Planung und Städtebau in Darmstadt;
1989–1997	art objects and installations in Darmstadt, Utrecht, Offenbach, Frankfurt;
1993	Joseph Maria Olbrich placquard for the reutilization of a gymnasium in Viernheim and the exhibition pavilion «Alltag in der Stadt» in Darmstadt;
1994	«Kunstaanmoedigingsprijs Amstelveen voor Architetuur» (nomination);
1997–1998	guest professor at the State Academy for Fine Arts in Stuttgart, architectural faculty; important realizations: municipal library Viernheim 1993–1996; multi-purpose hall Viernheim 1991–1992; town administration, bank and apartments in Seeheim-Jugenheim 1994–1996

Andreas Sedler

1957	born in Bremerhaven;
1978–1985	architectural studies at Kassel University, degree with Johannes Gsteu and Constantino Dardi;
1981–1982	guest student at Rome University with Carlo Aymonino and Francesco Cellini;
1981	collaboration in the office Dardi/Rom;
1985/86	collaboration in the office Haus-Rucker-Co/Düsseldorf;
1986–1989	collaboration in the office Rittmannsperger, Kleebank und Partner in Darmstadt;
since 1989	with Anke Mensing architectural office OPUS – Objekt Planung und Städtebau in Darmstadt;
1989–1993	German steel construction award 1990 (recognition), German architectural award 1991 (recognition), Premio Internazionale di Architettura Andrea Palladio 1993 (nomination) as well as other awards for the reutilization of tobacco barns into the municipal library Viernheim;
1989–1997	art objects and installations in Darmstadt, Utrecht, Offenbach, Frankfurt;
1990–1993	teacher at TH Darmstadt, assistant to Max Bächer;
1993	Joseph Maria Olbrich plaquard for the reutilization of a gymnasium and the exhibition pavilion «Alltag in der Stadt» in Darmstadt; important realizations: municipal library Viernheim 1993–1996; multi-purpose hall Viernheim 1991–1992; town administration, bank and apartments in Seeheim-Jugenheim 1994–1996

Mitarbeiter seit 1994 / Collaborators since 1994

Jochen Backes, Frank Bösselmann, Felicitas Casser, Karen Ehlers, Christian Follert, Corinna Ganssloser, Heike Heinzelmann, Andrea Julius, Volker Kilian, Fabian von Köppen, Uwe Kühn, Felix Nowak, Raimund Maschita, Gert Maruhn, Tom Nieper, Jurek Pryzbilski, Dirk Reinhard, Silvia Resch, Martin Rudolf, Jan Schulz, Thomas Vogel, Richard Voss

Bibliographie (Auswahl) / Bibliography (selection)

W-IN-D World Interior Design 4/1988; MD 12/1989; Baumeister 2/1990; Bauwelt 26/1990; Bauwelt 28/1990; DBZ Deutsche Bauzeitschrift 6/1990; Domus 729/1991; Stahl und Form: Erneuerung in historischen Gebäuden, Düsseldorf 1991; BDA Hessen: 37 x Haus, Darmstadt 1993; Preis des Deutschen Stahlbaus, Berlin 1994; das bauzentrum 1/1994; W-IN-D World Interior Design 25/1994; Baumeister 2/1996; AIT 12/1996; Domus 795/1997; Baumeister 7/1997; DBZ Deutsche Bauzeitschrift 9/1997

Ausstellungen / Exhibitions

ruimte in de ruimte, Artis Den Bosch 1988; NL-NY, Parsons Gallery New York 1993; Premio Internazionale di Architettura Andrea Palladio, Vicenza 1993 (Wanderausstellung / traveling exhibition: Zaragoza, Berlin, Frankfurt); Kunstaanmoedigingsprijs voor Architectuur, Sandberg Instituut Amstelveen 1994

Auszeichnungen / Awards

Vorbildliche Bauten Hessen (Auszeichnung / award) 1989; Leon-Battista-Alberti-Plakette, Ziegeldächer in der Architektur (2. Preis / prize) 1989–1990; Deutscher Stahlbaupreis (Anerkennung / recognition) 1990; Deutscher Architekturpreis (Anerkennung / recognition) 1991; Premio Internazionale di Architettura Andrea Palladio (Nominierung / nomination) 1993; Joseph Maria Olbrich Plakette, BDA Hessen (zweifach / twice) 1993; Kunstaanmoedigingsprijs voor Architectuur (Nominierung / nomination) 1994; Joseph Maria Olbrich Plakette BDA Hessen 1998 für die Gemeindeverwaltung, Bank und Wohnungen in Seeheim-Jugenheim

Werkauswahl / Selected works

Stadtbibliothek / municipal library (1. BA/in Rittmannsperger, Kleebank u. Partner), Viernheim 1987–1989
Rathausforum / town hall forum (1. Preis / prize mit / with Gert Maruhn), Seeheim-Jugenheim 1989
Wand-Schrankwand / wall-cabinet wall, Installation Darmstadt 1989
1000 stoelen in de stad, Installation Utrecht 1990
Marktplatz / market square (4. Preis / prize), Esslingen 1990
Pavillon Alltag in der Stadt, Installation Darmstadt/Offenbach 1991
Veranstaltungshalle / events hall TSV, Viernheim 1991–1992
Wohn- und Bürohaus / apartment and office building, Viernheim 1992–1994
Wasserschloß (2. Preis / prize), Hofheim 1992
Stadtbibliothek / municipal library (2. BA), Viernheim 1993–1996
Design Horizonte, Lichtinstallation / Design Horizons, light installation Frankfurt 1993
Gemeindeverwaltung, Bank und Wohnungen / town administration, bank and apartments, Seeheim-Jugenheim 1994–1996
Denkmal für die ermordeten Juden in Europa / monument for the Jews killed in Europe, Berlin 1994
Stadtentwicklung / urban development Unterer Markt (1. Preis / prize), Würzburg 1994
Marktstände / market booths (2. Preis / prize), Würzburg 1994
Umbau / conversion Altes Rathaus, Seeheim-Jugenheim 1995–1997
Integrativer Kindergarten / integrated kindergarten (2. Preis / prize), Breuberg 1995
Arztpraxis / doctor's office, Seeheim-Jugenheim 1996
«Sweet dreams are made of this» (1. Preis / prize Architekten und Konditoren / architects and confectioners), Frankfurt 1997
Altenpflegeheim / senior citizens home (4. Preis / prize), Hettstedt 1997
Revitalisierung / revitalization Hallesche Höfe, Halle 1997–2000
Aufstockung Haus H / heightening House H, Griesheim 1997–1998

Carsten Roth

Carsten Roth
Rentzelstraße 10 b
D-20146 Hamburg

Biographie

1958	in Hamburg geboren;
1977–1980	Architekturstudium und Vordiplom an der TU Braunschweig;
1984–1985	Architekturstudium und Magister architecturae an der Akademie der bildenden Künste in Wien, Meisterschule für Architektur bei Gustav Peichl;
1985/86	Fulbright-Stipendiat, Virginia Polytechnic Institute and State University in Blacksburg und Alexandria/USA;
1986	Instructional Fee Scholarship;
1986	Graduate Teaching Assistantship und Master of Architecture;
1987	Ausstellung «Meisterschule Gustav Peichl», Deutsches Architekturmuseum Frankfurt;
seit 1987	Architekturbüro in Hamburg;
1996/97	BDA Hamburg Architektur Preis 1996 und «Bauwerk des Jahres 1996» des AIV Architekten- und Ingenieurvereins e.V. Hamburg für ein Ateliergebäude in Hamburg;
1997	Vorträge und Seminare an den Architekturfakultäten in Alexandria, Blacksburg und Denver/USA;
1997	Einzelausstellung «Substanz und Licht», Galerie Peter Borchardt, Hamburg; wichtige Realisierungen: Fabrikumbau Universal Prints, Hamburg 1991–1994; Ateliergebäude, Hamburg 1992/1995–1996; Büro- und Ausstellungsgebäude, Siek 1994–1996; Laborgebäude, Hamburg 1994/1997–1998;

Biography

1958	born in Hamburg;
1977–1980	architectural studies and preliminary degree at TU Braunschweig;
1980–1985	architectural studies and Magister architecturae at the academy of fine arts in Vienna, master school for architecture with Gustav Peichl;
1985/86	Fulbright-scholarship, Virginia Polytechnic Institute and State University in Blacksburg und Alexandria/USA;
1986	Instructional Fee Scholarship;
1986	Graduate Teaching Assistantship and Master of Architecture;
1987	Exhibition «Meisterschule Gustav Peichl», German architectural museum Frankfurt;
since 1987	architectural office in Hamburg;
1996/97	BDA Hamburg architectural award 1996 and «Bauwerk des Jahres 1996» of the AIV architects and engineers club Hamburg for a studio building in Hamburg;
1997	one-man-show «Substanz und Licht», Peter Borchardt gallery, Hamburg; important realizations: factory conversion Universal Prints, Hamburg 1991–1994; studio building, Hamburg 1992–1996; office and exhibition building, Siek 1994–1996; laboratory building, Hamburg 1994–1998;

Mitarbeiter / Collaborators

Peter Karl Becher, Juan Hildago, Ole Kretschmer, Sabine Kock, Patrick Lee, Stefan Matthay, Bettina Mau, Rupert Maurus, Uta Meins, Jens Merkel, Moritz Müller, Folker Paulat, Jürgen Remke, Timothy Schulz, Gudrun Schwennsen, Martin Zuska

Bibliographie (Auswahl) / Bibliography (selection)

Eigene Texte / texts: Carsten Roth: Natural Light in Architectural Space, Thesis, Virginia Polytechnic Institute and State University, Blacksburg/USA 1986; «Über das natürliche Licht in Bauten von Carlo Scarpa» in: Franco Fonatti: Elemente des Bauens bei Carlo Scarpa, Wiener Akademiereihe Bd. 15, Vienna 1984; Deutsches Architektenblatt 8/1996
Projektpublikationen / project publications: Bauforum 104/1984; Architektur in Hamburg Jahrbuch 1995; Möbel Raum Design international 3/1995; Architektur Aktuell 12/1995; Detail 3/1996; Architektur Aktuell 10/1996; Architektur in Hamburg Jahrbuch 1996; Baumeister 2/1997; Domus 792/1997; DBZ Deutsche Bauzeitschrift 11/1997; Ursula Schneider: Fabriketagen – Leben in alten Industriebauten, Hamburg 1997; Berliner Zeitung 2.1.1998; Frankfurter Allgemeine Zeitung 19.2.1998; Architektur Aktuell 3/1998; Jahrbuch Architektur in Hamburg, Hamburg 1998

Ausstellungen / Exhibitions

Künstlichkeiten, Sünnhofgalerie Vienna 1985; Meisterschule Gustav Peichl, Deutches Architekturmuseum / German Architectural Museum Frankfurt 1987; Substanz und Licht (one-man-show), Galerie Peter Borchardt Hamburg 1997

Auszeichnungen / Awards

Akademiefreundepreis, Vienna 1984; Meisterschulpreis, Vienna 1985; Fulbright scholarship 1985; Instructional Fee Scholarship 1986; Tau Sigma Delta, National Honor Society for Architecture and Allied Arts 1986; Architectural Award BDA Hamburg 1991–1996, Hamburg 1996; Bauwerk des Jahres 1996, AIV Architekten- und Ingenieurverein e.V. Hamburg

Werkauswahl / Selected works

Fabrikumbau / factory conversion Universal Prints, Hamburg 1991–1994
Ateliergebäude / studio building, Hamburg 1992/1995–1996
Aufstockung / heightening Universal Prints (Studentenwohnungen / student housing), Hamburg 1994
Büro- und Ausstellungsgebäude / office and exhibition building, Siek 1994–1996
Villa mit privater Kunstgalerie / villa with private art gallery, Hamburg 1994
Laborgebäude / laboratory building, Hamburg 1994/1997–1998
Wohnbaustudie / housing study Wohnen+X, Berlin und seine Zeit e.V. 1996
Chorruine / choir ruin St. Nikolai (Gutachten / expert opinion), Hamburg 1997
Doppelhaus / row-house Thiede, Hamburg 1997–1998
Wohn- und Geschäftshaus / apartment and commercial building, Hamburg 1997
Druckerei und Servicecenter / Print shop and service center, Röbel 1997–1998
Gestaltungskonzept Architekturausstellung «Hamburg – Rotterdam», Hamburg 1997
Staatliche Jugendmusikschule (3. Preis / prize), Hamburg 1998
Rhodarium, Bremen 1998

Andreas Scheuring
Claudia Hannibal-Scheuring

Scheuring und Partner Architekten
Schaafenstraße 25
D-50676 Köln

Biographien

Claudia Hannibal-Scheuring
1961   in Aarau/Schweiz geboren;

1979–1987 Architekturstudium an der TU Braunschweig, Diplom bei Gerhard Auer;
seit 1989 Architekturbüro mit Andreas Scheuring in Köln, 1989–1995 in Partnerschaft mit Rüdiger Ruby, seit 1997 in Partnerschaft mit Martin Lohmann;
1992 Förderpreis des Landes Nordrhein-Westfalen;
1994 Architekturpreis «Vorbildliche Gewerbebauten» der Westhyp-Stiftung für ein Therapiezentrum in Bad Lippspringe;
1996 Architekturpreis «Zukunft Wohnen» des Bundesverbandes der deutschen Zementindustrie;
1995/97 Kölner Architekturpreis 1995 und Deutscher Architekturpreis 1997 (Anerkennung) für Wohnhaus Scheuring in Köln;
wichtige Realisierungen: Therapiezentrum, Bad Lippspringe 1990–1994; Wohnhaus Scheuring, Köln 1994–1995; Hochschulbibliothek, Zwickau 1994–1998; Fachhochschule Westküste Schleswig-Holstein, Heide 1994–1999

Andreas Scheuring
1959 in Darmstadt geboren;
1978–1980 Architekturstudium an der TH Darmstadt;
1980–1987 Architekturstudium an der TU Braunschweig, Diplom bei Gerhard Auer;
1987–1989 Mitarbeit im Büro Schürmann in Köln;
seit 1989 Architekturbüro mit Claudia Hannibal-Scheuring in Köln, 1989–1995 in Partnerschaft mit Rüdiger Ruby, seit 1997 in Partnerschaft mit Martin Lohmann;
1992 Förderpreis des Landes Nordrhein-Westfalen;
1992–1996 Lehrtätigkeit an der Bergischen Universität Wuppertal, Lehrauftrag «Grundlagen des Entwerfens» bei Eckhard Gerber;
1994 Architekturpreis «Vorbildliche Gewerbebauten» der Westhyp-Stiftung für ein Therapiezentrum in Bad Lippspringe;
1996 Architekturpreis «Zukunft Wohnen» des Bundesverbandes der deutschen Zementindustrie;
1995/97 Kölner Architekturpreis 1995 und Deutscher Architekturpreis 1997 (Anerkennung) für Wohnhaus Scheuring in Köln;
wichtige Realisierungen: Therapiezentrum, Bad Lippspringe 1990–1994; Wohnhaus Scheuring, Köln 1994–1995; Hochschulbibliothek, Zwickau 1994–1998; Fachhochschule Westküste Schleswig-Holstein, Heide 1994–1999

Biographies

Claudia Hannibal-Scheuring
1961 born in Aarau/Switzerland;
1979–1987 architectural studies at TU Braunschweig, degree with Gerhard Auer;
since 1989 architectural office with Andreas Scheuring in Cologne, 1989–1995 partnership with Rüdiger Ruby, since 1997 partnership with Martin Lohmann;
1992 sponsoring award of Northern Rhine-Westfalia;
1994 architectural award «Archetype Industrial Buildings» of Westhyp-Foundation for a therapy center in Bad Lippspringe;
1996 architectural award «Future Living» of the German Federal Cement Industry Association;
1995/97 Cologne architectural award 1995 and German architectural award 1997 (recognition) for the Scheuring apartment house in Cologne;
important realizations: therapy center, Bad Lippspringe 1990–1994; Scheuring apartment house, Cologne 1994–1995; university library, Zwickau 1994–1998; university for applied science Westküste Schleswig-Holstein, Heide 1994–1999

Andreas Scheuring
1959 born in Darmstadt;
1978–1980 architectural studies at TH Darmstadt;
1980–1987 architectural studies at TU Braunschweig, degree with Gerhard Auer;
1987–1989 collaboration in the office Schürmann in Cologne;
since 1989 architectural office with Claudia Hannibal-Scheuring in Cologne, 1989–1995 partnership with Rüdiger Ruby, since 1997 partnership with Martin Lohmann;
1992 sponsoring award of Northern Rhine-Westfalia;
1992–1996 teacher at Bergische Universität Wuppertal, teaching assignment «Grundlagen des Entwerfens» with Eckhard Gerber;
1994 architectural award «Vorbildliche Gewerbebauten» of Westhyp-foundation for a therapy center in Bad Lippspringe;
1996 architectural award «Zukunft Wohnen» of the federal association of the German concrete industry;
1995/97 Cologne architectural award 1995 and German architectural award 1997 (recognition) for Scheuring House in Cologne;
important realizations: therapy center, Bad Lippspringe 1990–1994; Scheuring House, Cologne 1994–1995; university library, Zwickau 1994–1998; university for applied sciences Westküste Schleswig-Holstein, Heide 1994–1999

Partner / Partners

Rüdiger Ruby (bis 1995), Martin Lohmann (seit 1997)

Mitarbeiter seit 1991 (Auswahl) / Collaborators since 1991 (selection)

Uli Baierlipp, Elke Beccard, Guido Bornkast, Frank Hausmann, Jan Hertel, HeKung Lee, Mark Ley, Hans-Günther Lübben, Uwe Mehring, Patrick Ostrup, Ursula Pasch, Alexander Pier, Christina Strunk, Georg Taxhet, Norbert Theißinger, Fritz Vennemann, Karen Li Willius

Bibliographie (Auswahl) / Bibliography (selection)

Eigene Texte / texts: Deutsches Architektenblatt 3/1995
Projektpublikationen / project publications: Glas 3/1996; Glasforum 4/1996; db Deutsche Bauzeitung 8/1996; db Deutsche Bauzeitung 1/1997; Detail 3/1998; Werk, Bauen und Wohnen 5/1998

Ausstellungen / Exhibitions

Bauten und Projekte, Ministerium für Bauen und Wohnen des Landes Nordrhein-Westfalen / Ministry for Building and Housing of Northern Rhine-Westfalia, Düsseldorf 1994

Auszeichnungen / Awards

Förderpreis des Landes Nordrhein-Westfalen 1992; Architekturpreis Vorbildliche Gewerbebauten, Westhyp-Stiftung 1994; Kölner Architekturpreis 1995; Architekturpreis Zukunft Wohnen, Bundesverband der deutschen Zementindustrie 1996; Deutscher Architekturpreis (Anerkennung / recognition) 1997

Werkauswahl / Selected works

(*mit / with G.A.Schütz, Bad Neuenahr)
Peter Jörres Gymnasium / high school (1. Preis / prize), Bad Neuenahr* 1989–1998
Therapiezentrum / therapy center (1. Preis / prize), Bad Lippspringe 1990–1994
Technologiezentrum / technological center (2. Preis / prize), Hagen 1991
Bürogebäude Kortmann / office building (2. Preis / prize), Nordkirchen 1992
Kindergarten, Hahnstätten* 1993–1994
Zentrum / center Neustadt (1. Preis / prize), Hoyerswerda 1993
Alfred Delp Schule / school, Hargesheim* 1994–1997
Wohnhaus / apartment building Scheuring, Köln 1994–1995
Are Gymnasium / high school, Bad Neuenahr* 1994–1995
Hochschulbibliothek / university library (1. Preis / prize), Zwickau 1994–1998
Fachhochschule / university for applied science Westküste (1. Preis / prize), Heide 1994–1999
Fachhochschule / university for applied science (2. Preis / prize), Rheinbach 1995
Wohnhaus / apartment building Sass, Eckernförde 1995–1997
Innerstädtisches Einkaufszentrum / inner city shopping center (2. Preis / prize), Bautzen 1996–2000
Stadtentwicklung / urban development Gothaer Platz (3. Preis / prize), Erfurt 1997
Zentrum für Energie und Technik / center for energy and technology (4. Preis / prize), Rendsburg 1997
Altenpflegeheim / senior citizens home (2. Preis / prize), Hettstedt 1997
Unikliniken / university hospital (2. Preis / prize), Dresden 1997

Hartwig N. Schneider

Hartwig N. Schneider
Birkenwaldstraße 54
D-70191 Stuttgart

Biographie

1957 in Stuttgart geboren;
1977–1984 Architekturstudium an der Universität Stuttgart, Diplom bei Peter C. von Seidlein;
1980/81 Stipendiat des DAAD am Illinois Institute of Technology Chicago/USA;

1979–1984 Praktika bei Architekten in Stuttgart, Chicago und Frankfurt;
1985 Mitarbeit im Büro Peter C. von Seidlein in München;
1985 Preis der Freunde der Universität Stuttgart;
1986/87 Mitarbeit im Büro Norman Foster in London und Nancy;
1987–1989 freie Mitarbeit im Büro Heinle, Wischer und Partner/Stuttgart;
seit 1990 Architekturbüro in Stuttgart;
1991–1994 Lehrtätigkeit an der Universität Stuttgart, Lehrauftrag «Integrierte Lehre» bei Peter C. von Seidlein am Institut für Baukonstruktion und Entwerfen;
1996/97 Hugo Häring Preis und weitere Auszeichnungen für einen Holzleichtbau in Winnenden;
1998 Bauherrenpreis des BDA für einen Wohnungsbau in Ludwigsburg;
1998 Ruf an die TU Berlin, Lehrstuhl für Gebäudetechnik und Entwerfen; wichtige Realisierungen: Kindergarten, Winnenden 1992–1995; Sozialer Wohnungsbau, Ludwigsburg 1993–1997

Biography

1957 born in Stuttgart;
1977–1984 architectural studies at Stuttgart university, degree with Peter C. von Seidlein;
1980/81 stipendium of the DAAD at Illinois Institute of Technology Chicago/USA;
1979–1984 practical semesters with architects in Stuttgart, Chicago and Frankfurt;
1985 collaboration in the office Peter C. von Seidlein in Munich;
1985 friends of Stuttgart university award;
1986/87 collaboration in the office Norman Foster in London and Nancy;
1987–1989 freelance work in the office Heinle, Wischer und Partner/Stuttgart;
since 1990 architectural office in Stuttgart;
1991–1994 teacher at Stuttgart university, teaching assignment «Integrierte Lehre» with Peter C. von Seidlein at the Institute for building construction and design;
1996/97 Hugo Häring award and other awards for a lightweight wood construction in Winnenden;
1998 clients award of the BDA for an apartment building in Ludwigsburg;
1998 chair position TU Berlin, chair for building technology and design; important realizations: kindergarten, Winnenden 1992–1995; social housing, Ludwigsburg 1993–1997

Partner / Partners
Gabriele Mayer (seit 1992)

Mitarbeiter seit 1990 / Collaborators since 1990

John Barnbrook, Thilo Baur, Bernd Bess, Christoph Birkel, Martin Ebert, Annette Fisely, Andreas Gabriel, Petra Gekeler, Elke Gill, Olaf Gipser, Ulrike Hatau, Ursula Heinemann, Christopher Kellner, Mathias Ludwig, Franz X. Lutz, Oliver Ost, Michael Palmen, Ingo Pelchen

Bibliographie (Auswahl) / Bibliography (selection)

Eigene Texte / texts: Centrum Jahrbuch Architektur und Stadt 1996
Projektpublikationen: Arch+ 118/1993; das bauzentrum 1/1996; Architektur + Wettbewerbe (Kindergärten / kindergartens) AW 165/1996; Detail 1/1997; Bauwelt 15/1997; Centrum Jahrbuch Architektur und Stadt 1997–1998; Architektur + Wettbewerbe (Schulen / schools) AW 172/1997; Konvention-Innovation-Vision, Deubau Kongreß 1998; Bauwelt 6/1998; Tendenz Nachhaltig, Info-Börse Wohnungsbau, Deubau Kongreß 1998; Architektur Aktuell 5/1998

Ausstellungen / Exhibitions

Beispielhaftes Bauen in Baden-Württemberg 1996, Auszeichnung Guter Bauten in Baden-Württemberg 1996, BDA-Preis Baden-Württemberg 1997, Holzbaupreis Baden-Württemberg 1997, Hohe Qualität – Tragbare Kosten im Wohnungsbau 1998

Auszeichnungen / Awards

Preis der Freunde der Universität Stuttgart 1985; Auszeichnung Beispielhaftes Bauen, Architektenkammer Baden-Württemberg 1996; Auszeichnung Guter Bauten, BDA Baden-Württemberg 1996; Holzbaupreis Baden-Württemberg 1997; Hugo-Häring-Preis, BDA Baden-Württemberg 1997; Bauherrenpreis des BDA, Hohe Qualität und tragbare Kosten im Wohnungsbau 1998

Werkauswahl / Selected works

Institutsgebäude und Bibliothek / institute and library building (1. Preis / prize mit / with M. Webler), Universität / university Frankfurt 1988–1995
Büromöbel-Fabrik / office furniture factory Völkle (1. Preis / prize mit / with HWP GmbH Stuttgart), Loßburg 1989
Gärtnerei-Betriebshof / garden center yard, Ludwigsburg 1989–1991
Montage-Halle / assembly hall Fortuna-Werke (1. Preis / prize), Stuttgart 1990
Entwicklungszentrum / development center Mercedes-Benz (2. Preis / prize mit / with P. C. von Seidlein), Stuttgart 1991
Kindergarten (1. Preis / prize), Winnenden 1992–1995
Dresdner Bank (mit / with HWP GmbH Stuttgart), Magdeburg 1992
Sozialer Wohnungsbau / social housing (1. Preis / prize, mit / with P. C. von Seidlein), Ludwigsburg 1993–1997

Energieversorgung / energy provider Oberfranken (1. Preis / prize), Bayreuth 1994
Gymnasium mit Sporthalle / high school with gymnasium (1. Preis / prize), Vaihingen 1995
Landes- und Universitätsbibliothek / state and university library, Dresden 1996
Hauptbahnhof / main station Stuttgart 21 (Ankauf / purchase mit / with G. Mayer, J. Frowein, E. Schmutz), Stuttgart 1997
Aufstockung Haus S / heightening House S, Stuttgart 1997–1998
Grundschule / primary school (1. Preis / prize), Calw-Altburg 1997
Wohnanlage / housing complex Wachtelweg, Ludwigsburg 1998–1999
Technikum Prototypenbau Bertrandt AG (1. Preis / prize), Ehningen 1998

Ingrid Spengler
Frido Wiescholek

Spengler Wiescholek Architekten
Max-Brauer-Allee 34
D-22765 Hamburg

Biographien

Ingrid Spengler
1951 in Karlsruhe geboren;
1970–1978 Architekturstudium an der Universität Karlsruhe, Diplom bei Immanuel Kroeker;

1976   Förderpreis des Deutschen Stahlbaus;
1977   Ausstellung «art net» London;
1978–1980   Büropartnerschaft mit Otfried Weis in Karlsruhe;
1978–1980   Lehrtätigkeit an der Universität Karlsruhe, Assistentin bei Gunnar Martinsson,
            Fachgebiet Freiraumplanung;
seit 1979/80 eigene Projekte und Architekturbüro in Hamburg;
1982   BDA Preis Karlsruhe und 1987 Weinbrenner-Medaille mit Otfried Weis für ein
            Doppelhaus in Karlsruhe;
seit 1989   Zusammenarbeit mit Frido Wiescholek;
1992/94/97 «Bauwerk des Jahres» des AIV Architekten- und Ingenieurvereins e.V. Hamburg
            für eine Wohnhauserweiterung, eine Stadtvilla und Sozialen Wohnungsbau in
            Hamburg;
1993   Internationaler Workshop «Stadtvisionen» Hamburg;
seit 1994   Architekturbüro Spengler Wiescholek in Hamburg;
            wichtige Realisierungen: Haus Kruse, Hamburg 1989–1990; Stadtvilla am
            Alsterufer, Hamburg 1990–1993; Sozialer Wohnungsbau Farmsen, Hamburg
            1993–1996; Sozialer Wohnungsbau Bahrenfeld, Hamburg 1993–1996;
            Wohn- und Atelierhaus Ottensen, Hamburg 1995–1997; Typenhaus (Wunschhaus
            des Stern) 1996–1998

Frido Wiescholek
1961   in Opole/Polen geboren;
1976   Umsiedlung nach Hamburg;
1982–1983   Oberschule für Seefahrt-Technik in Hamburg;
1984–1989   Architekturstudium und Diplom an der FH Hamburg;
1988   Förderpreis des Deutschen Stahlbaus;
1989   Architekturstudium an der TU Berlin;
seit 1989   Zusammenarbeit mit Ingrid Spengler;
1992/94/97 «Bauwerk des Jahres» des AIV Architekten- und Ingenieurvereins e.V. Hamburg
            für eine Wohnhauserweiterung, eine Stadtvilla und Sozialen Wohnungsbau in
            Hamburg;
1993   Internationaler Workshop «Stadtvisionen» Hamburg;
seit 1994   Architekturbüro Spengler Wiescholek in Hamburg;
            wichtige Realisierungen: Haus Kruse, Hamburg 1989–1990; Stadtvilla am
            Alsterufer, Hamburg 1990–1993; Sozialer Wohnungsbau Farmsen, Hamburg
            1993–1996; Sozialer Wohnungsbau Bahrenfeld, Hamburg 1993–1996; Wohn- und
            Atelierhaus Ottensen, Hamburg 1995–1997; Typenhaus (Wunschhaus des Stern)
            1996–1998

Biographies

Ingrid Spengler
1951   born in Karlsruhe;
1970–1978   architectural studies at Karlsruhe University, degree with Immanuel Kroeker;
1976   sponsor award of the German steel industry;
1977   exhibition «art net» London;
1978–1980   office partnership with Otfried Weis in Karlsruhe;
1978–1980   teacher at Karlsruhe University, assistant to Gunnar Martinsson, faculty outdoor
            planning;
since 1979/80 individual projects and architectural office in Hamburg;
1982   BDA award Karlsruhe and 1987 Weinbrenner-medal with Otfried Weis for a
            double-house in Karlsruhe;
since 1989 collaboration with Frido Wiescholek;
1992/94/97 «Bauwerk des Jahres» of the AIV architects and engineers club Hamburg for an
            apartment house extension, an urban villa and social housing in Hamburg;
1993   international workshop «Stadtvisionen» Hamburg;
since 1994 architectural office Spengler Wiescholek in Hamburg;
            important realizations: Haus Kruse, Hamburg 1989–1990; urban villa at the banks
            of the Alster river, Hamburg 1990–1993; social housing Farmsen, Hamburg
            1993–1996; social housing Bahrenfeld, Hamburg 1993–1996; apartment and
            studio building Ottensen, Hamburg 1995–1997; prefabricated type house (dream
            house of Stern magazine) 1996–1998

Frido Wiescholek
1961   born in Opole/Poland;
1976   emigration to Hamburg;
1982–1983   high school for naval technology in Hamburg;
1984–1989   architectural studies and degree at FH Hamburg;
1988   sponsor award of the German steel industry;
1989   architectural studies at TU Berlin;
since 1989 collaboration with Ingrid Spengler;
1992/94/97 «Bauwerk des Jahres» of AIV architects and engineers club Hamburg for an
            apartment building extension, an urban villa and social housing in Hamburg;
1993   international workshop «Stadtvisionen» Hamburg;
since 1994 architectural office Spengler Wiescholek in Hamburg;
            important realizations: Kruse House, Hamburg 1989–1990; urban villa at the
            banks of the Alster river, Hamburg 1990–1993; social housing Farmsen, Hamburg
            1993–1996; social housing Bahrenfeld, Hamburg 1993–1996; apartment and
            studio building Ottensen, Hamburg 1995–1997; prefabricated type house
            (dreamhouse of Stern magazine) 1996–1998

Mitarbeiter seit 1997 / Collaborators since 1997

Sven Ahrens, Florian Busch, Julia Carstens, Karin Damrau, Sven Dunker, Stefanie Föcking, Ingo Hartfil, Oliver Kaps, Petra Koch, Fabian v. Köppen, Nicolai Koretzki, Carsten Kruizenga, Sven Liebrecht, Barbara Lücke, Martin Marschner, Andreas Martini, Silke Meier-Tuchtenhagen, Christine Recke, Ute Schnoor, Till Speetzen, Uda Visser, Joo Voß, Caroline Wegener, Margit Wiegand

Bibliographie (Auswahl) / Bibliography (selection)

Werk, Bauen+Wohnen 4/1984; Abitare 240/1985; Die Kunst 3/1985; Werk, Bauen+Wohnen 4/1990; Leonardo 1/1991; Leonardo 4/1991; Stadtentwicklungsbehörde Hamburg: Stadtvisionen, Hamburg 1993; Architektur in Hamburg Jahrbuch 1994; Jahrbuch 1995; Jahrbuch 1996; Stern 45/1996; Architektur in Hamburg Jahrbuch 1997; BDA Hamburg: Wohnen in der Stadt, Hamburg 1997; Stern 17/1997; Stern 46/1997

Ausstellungen / Exhibitions

art net, London 1977; Stadtentwicklungsforum Hamburg 1993; BDA Hamburg Architektur Preis 1991–1996, Hamburg 1996; Das Wunschhaus der Deutschen, Bundesweite Wanderausstellung auf Initiative des Stern 1996/1997; Wohnen in der Stadt, Hamburger Architektursommer 1997

Auszeichnungen / Awards

Förderpreis des Deutschen Stahlbaus 1976; BDA Preis Karlsruhe 1982; Weinbrenner-Medaille, Karlsruhe 1987; Förderpreis des Deutschen Stahlbaus 1988; Bauwerk des Jahres 1992, AIV Architekten- und Ingenieurverein Hamburg; Bauwerk des Jahres 1994, AIV Hamburg; BDA Preis 1991–1996 (Anerkennung / recognition) Hamburg 1996; Bauwerk des Jahres 1997, AIV Hamburg

Werkauswahl / Selected works

Haus / house Kruse Volksdorf, Hamburg 1989–1990
Stadtvilla am Alsterufer / urban villa at the Alster river bank (1. Preis / prize), Hamburg 1990–1993
Sozialer Wohnungsbau / social housing Farmsen (2. Preis / prize), Hamburg 1992–1996
Sportlerhaus / sportsman's house Neu Allermöhe West, Hamburg 1993–1997
Sozialer Wohnungsbau / social housing Bahrenfeld, Hamburg 1993–1996
Wohnungsbau / apartment building Neu Allermöhe West, Hamburg 1994–1997
Umbau Verwaltungsgebäude / conversion administrative building Volksdorf, Hamburg 1994–1996
Wohnbebauung / housing development Fontenay Villen, Hamburg 1994–1997
Wohn- und Atelierhaus / apartment and studio building Ottensen, Hamburg 1995–1997
Wohn- und Geschäftshaus / apartment and commercial building Eppendorf, Hamburg 1995–1997
Aufstockung Haus Brodersen / heightening Brodersen House, Wedel 1996–1998
Bürgerhaus / citizen's center Neu Allermöhe West, Hamburg 1996–1998
Wohnbebauung / housing development Iseplatz Eppendorf (1. Preis / prize), Hamburg 1996–1998
Umbau Haus Moritz / conversion Moritz House Schenefeld, Hamburg 1996–1998
Erweiterung Haus Zuschke / extension Zuschke House Blankenese, Hamburg 1997–1998
Wohnen und Arbeiten im Straßenbahndepot / living and working in the tram depot Eppendorf, Hamburg 1997
Typenhaus / prefabricated type house (Aktion Wunschhaus des Stern / dreamhouse of Stern magazine, 3. Preis / prize) Rissen, Hamburg 1996–1998
Messe / fair Düsseldorf «Nowea 2004», Düsseldorf 1997/98
Terminal 3, Flughafen / airport Stuttgart 1997/98

Zvonko Turkali

1986   collaboration in the office Richard Meier and Partners/New York;
1986–1988   architectural studies at Harvard University, Graduate School of Design, Cambridge/USA;
1988   Master in Architecture;
since 1988   architectural office in Frankfurt/M;
1988–1992   teacher at RWTH Aachen, scientific assistant to Vladimir Nikolic at the chair for building construction III;
since 1993   member of the urban counsel of Frankfurt/M;
since 1995   board member of BDA Frankfurt;
1996–1998   guest professor at Kassel University, experimental building construction and design;
since 1998   professor at Hannover University, institute for design and construction; important realizations: community center Guntersblum 1991–1995; office building, Frankfurt 1992–1995; Bromig apartment building, Frankfurt 1994–1996; Kulturmobil 1994–1995; office building, Hanau 1995–1996

Mitarbeiter seit 1988 / Collaborators since 1988

Jakob von Allwörden, Birgit Cornelsen, Jason Danziger, Matthias Feuer, Klaus Fudickar, Athanasias Georginas, Peter Germann, Jacqueline Gies, Bettina Grabs, Jan Heiken, Jochen Herter, Gundula Kappen, Viola Kruth, Philip von Magnis, Achim Nowock, Peter Schäfer, Stefan Scheiding, Frank Schmitz, Georg Seegräber, Roland Summ, Martin Unger, Stefanie Unger, Andreas Wolf

Bibliographie (Auswahl) / Bibliography (selection)

Frankfurter Allgemeine Zeitung 12.8.1989; Wettbewerb Niedrigentropie-Kindertagesstätten, Galerie Aedes Katalog Juli 1992; Arch+ 119–120/1993; Bauwelt 26/1995; DAM Jahrbuch 1995; Bauwelt 9/1996; Gerd de Bruyn: Zeitgenössische Architektur in Deutschland 1970–1995, Berlin, Basel, Boston 1997; Design Report 7–8/1996; Frankfurter Rundschau 20.7.1996; DAM Jahrbuch 1996; Neue Zürcher Zeitung 9.12.1996; Berliner Zeitung 2.1.1998

Ausstellungen / Exhibitions

Bauen heute, Architektur der Gegenwart in der Bundesrepublik Deutschland, Deutsches Architekturmuseum Frankfurt 1985; Mit der Umwelt umgehen lernen, Niedrigentropie-Kindertagesstätten, Galerie Aedes Berlin 1992; Frankfurter Architekturen, Archiv Deutsches Architekturmuseum Frankfurt 1997

Auszeichnungen / Awards

Vorbildliche Bauten im Land Hessen, Architektenkammer Hessen, Auszeichnung und Besondere Anerkennung 1996

Werkauswahl / Selected works

Ballsporthalle / gymnasium (1. Preis / prize Balser mit / with Seifert und Turkali), Frankfurt 1984–1988
Turnhalle / gymnasium Bonames (Spieler, Märker, Turkali), Frankfurt 1988–1993
Sportanlage / sports complex Eintracht Frankfurt (Spieler, Märker, Turkali), Frankfurt 1989
Bürogebäude / office building MAN Roland (3. Preis / prize), Offenbach 1989
Umbau Frankfurter Kunstverein / conversion Frankfurt Art Association (Spieler, Turkali), Frankfurt 1990–1993
Überbauung / superstructure Terminal Mitte / (5. Preis / prize), Flughafen / airport Frankfurt 1990
Erweiterung Bürgerhaus / extension citizens' center (1. Preis / prize mit / with H. Bechler), Guntersblum 1991–1995
Kindertagesstätte / day care center Sossenheim (1. Preis / prize), Frankfurt 1992
Bürogebäude / office building Brockmann, Frankfurt 1992–1995
Turnhalle / gymnasium Heinrich von Gagern Schule / school, Frankfurt 1993
Aufstockung Wohnhaus Bromig / heightening Bromig apartment house, Frankfurt 1994–1996
Kulturmobil des Hessischen Kultusministeriums / cultural mobile of the Hessian Cultural Ministry (1. Preis / prize), 1994–1995
Bürogebäude im Gewerbegebiet / office building in the industrial center, Hanau 1995–1996
Polizeipräsidium / police headquaters (Ankauf / purchase), Frankfurt 1995
Erweiterung Thüringer Innenministerium / extension Interior Ministry of Thuringia (2. Preis / prize), Erfurt 1996
Umbau eines Speichers zur Ausstellungshalle / conversion of a storage barn into an exhibition hall (3. Preis / prize), Würzburg 1996
Stadtentwicklung / urban development Friedberger Warte (2. Preis / prize), Frankfurt 1997
ICE-Bahnhof / station (5. Preis / prize), Limburg 1997
Sport- und Veranstaltungshalle / sports and events hall (2. Preis / prize), Linz/Österreich / Austria 1997
Umbau und Erweiterung Hauptstelle Kasseler Bank (1.Preis / prize), Kassel 1998

Turkali Architekten
Hanauer Landstaße 48 a
D-60314 Frankfurt

Biographie

1958   in Vrdnik/ehem. Jugoslawien;
1978–1983   Architekturstudium und Diplom an der FH Frankfurt;
1983   Internationale Sommerakademie Salzburg, Raimund Abraham/New York;
1983–1985   Architekturstudium an der Staatlichen Hochschule für Bildende Künste (Städelschule) Frankfurt/M ;
1986   Mitarbeit im Büro Richard Meier and Partners/New York;
1986–1988   Architekturstudium an der Harvard University, Graduate School of Design, Cambridge/USA;
1988   Master in Architecture;
seit 1988   Architekturbüro in Frankfurt/M;
1988–1992   Lehrtätigkeit an der RWTH Aachen, wissenschaftlicher Assistent von Vladimir Nikolic am Lehrstuhl für Baukonstruktion III;
seit 1993   Mitglied des Städtebaubeirats der Stadt Frankfurt/M;
seit 1995   Vorstandsmitglied des BDA Frankfurt;
1996–1998   Gastprofessur an der Universität Gesamthochschule Kassel, Experimentelle Baukonstruktion und Entwerfen;
seit 1998   Professor an der Universität Hannover, Institut für Entwerfen und Konstruieren; wichtige Realisierungen: Bürgerhaus Guntersblum 1991–1995; Bürogebäude, Frankfurt 1992–1995; Wohnhaus Bromig, Frankfurt 1994–1996; Kulturmobil 1994–1995; Bürogebäude, Hanau 1995–1996

Biography

1958   born in Vrdnik/form. Yugoslavia;
1978–1983   architectural studies and degree at FH Frankfurt;
1983   international summer academy Salzburg, Raimund Abraham/New York;
1983–1985   architectural studies at Städelschule Frankfurt/M;

Bildnachweis / Illustration Credits

Archivision: 138.
Claßen, Martin: 112, 113.
Cobanli, Can: 32, 39, 41.
Eicken, Thomas: 94 oben/top, 97.
Frahm, Klaus: 100, 102, 103, 104, 105, 106, 107, 108, 109.
Freytag, Andreas: 126, 129 (Modell/model).
Hawlik, Markus: 46.
Heidenreich, Stefan: 150 oben/top.
Heinrich, Michael: 78, 80, 81, 83, 84, 85, 86, 87, 88, 89.
Huthmacher, Werner: 44, 48, 49, 50, 51, 52 oben/top, 53.
Kandzia, Christian: 122, 123, 124, 125 oben/top, 130, 131 oben/top.
Kröger/Dorfmüller: 132, 137 oben/top, 137 unten links/bottom left.
Lecher, Jürgen: 142, 147, 149.
Leistner, Dieter: 90, 93, 94 unten/bottom, 95.
Meyer und Kunz: 144, 145, 148 unten/bottom.
Müller, Stefan: 20, 23, 24, 25, 26, 27, 28, 29, 31.
Müller-Naumann, Stefan: 34, 35, 43.
Ott, Thomas: 98.
Roth, Lukas: 68, 76, 110, 114, 115, 116, 117, 119, 131 Mitte/middle, 131 unten/bottom.
Seitz, Peter: 96 unten/bottom.

Alle übrigen Bilddokumente stammen aus den Archiven der Architekten.
All other illustrations are taken from the architects' archives.